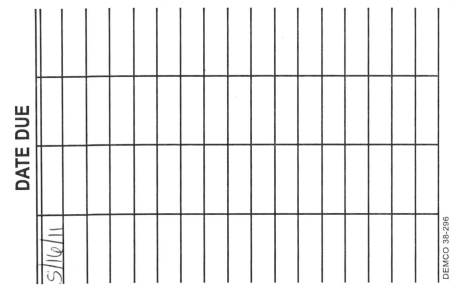

MULTICULTURAL
Comics

Cognitive Approaches to Literature and Culture Series

Edited by Frederick Luis Aldama, Arturo J. Aldama, and Patrick Colm Hogan

Cognitive Approaches to Literature and Culture includes monographs and edited volumes that incorporate cutting-edge research in cognitive science, neuroscience, psychology, linguistics, narrative theory, and related fields, exploring how this research bears on and illuminates cultural phenomena such as, but not limited to, literature, film, drama, music, dance, visual art, digital media, and comics. The volumes published in this series represent both specialized scholarship and interdisciplinary investigations that are deeply sensitive to cultural specifics and grounded in a cross-cultural understanding of shared emotive and cognitive principles.

MULTICULTURAL
Comics

FROM *ZAP* TO *BLUE BEETLE*

EDITED BY
FREDERICK
LUIS ALDAMA

FOREWORD BY
DEREK PARKER ROYAL

UNIVERSITY OF TEXAS PRESS   AUSTIN

Requests for permission to reproduce material from this work should be sent to:
   Permissions
   University of Texas Press
   P.O. Box 7819
   Austin, TX 78713-7819
   www.utexas.edu/utpress/about/bpermission.html

♾ The paper used in this book meets the minimum requirements of ANSI/NISO
Z39.48-1992 (R1997) (Permanence of Paper).

LIBRARY OF CONGRESS CATALOGING-IN-PUBLICATION DATA

Multicultural comics : from Zap to Blue Beetle / edited by Frederick Luis Aldama ;
foreword by Derek Parker Royal. — 1st ed.
      p.   cm. — (Cognitive approaches to literature and culture series)
   Includes bibliographical references and index.
   ISBN 978-0-292-72281-1 (cloth : alk. paper)
   1. Comic books, strips, etc.—History and criticism.   2. Multiculturalism in literature.
I. Aldama, Frederick Luis, 1969–
   PN6714.M85   2010
   741.5'355—dc22

                                                                        2010008795

For all those authors and artists of multicultural comic books working hard at their craft to create resplendent storyworlds for our delectation

Much overdue gratitude to friend and mentor Herbie Lindenberger, and with special thanks to Martha Cutter and Terence DeToy

CONTENTS

FOREWORD; OR READING WITHIN THE GUTTER

DEREK PARKER ROYAL

A LTHOUGH NOT SOLELY an image-based medium, comics get most of their power through their visuals, the ways in which authors construct the representations we see on the page or computer screen. Such art should not be taken lightly, for as history literally illustrates, the attitudes and prejudices of a culture can be greatly shaped by its caricatures, cartoons, and other forms of manipulated iconography. This is especially the case when it comes to the representations of minority populations, groups and individuals who live on—or who have been relegated to—the fringes of a society and whose place has historically been dictated by a more dominant culture. This is what Will Eisner, one of the pioneers in American comics, alludes to in *Graphic Storytelling and Visual Narrative* (1996) when he discusses the inescapable uses of stereotypes in graphic narrative. Comics, by necessity, employ stereotypes as a kind of shorthand to communicate quickly and succinctly. This being the case, it is up to the comic's artist to tell her or his story as effectively as possible without slipping into the trap, even inadvertently, of inaccurate and even harmful representations. To paraphrase Stan Lee, with great visual power must also come great responsibility.

The cultural potential underlying comics is all too apparent, and recent events around the world have underscored the stakes involved. Witness, for example, the violent outcry in 2005 over the Muhammad caricatures that appeared in the Danish newspaper *Jyllands-Posten*, the official charges of racism leveled against

Hergé's *Tintin in the Congo* made in both the United Kingdom and Belgium during 2007, or the more recent controversy surrounding Sean Delonas's cartooned allusions to President Barack Obama in the *New York Post*. Because they utilize picture texts to guide our understanding of narrative, comics can have a more direct effect than that dictated by prose, eliciting a reaction that takes relatively little time to process. And given its reliance on symbols and iconography, comic art speaks in a language that is accessible to a wide audience, transcending many of the national, cultural, and linguistic boundaries imposed by other media and giving it a reach that is as democratic as it is immediate. Comics artists who represent marginalized communities, or "the Other," do so under potentially liberating, yet nonetheless volatile, contexts.

Frederick Aldama understands this dilemma. He has spent much of his career exploring the crossroads of narrative and ethnicity, and he has also cast his gaze upon the manifestations of race in our popular culture. In works such as *Brown on Brown* (2005) and *Spilling the Beans in Chicanolandia* (2006), Aldama has looked at how visual media such as film and graphic narrative have represented the marginalized subject. His appreciation of comics is especially evident in the more recent *Your Brain on Latino Comics* (2009), a text exploring the kinds of visual dynamics involved in ethnoracial narrative. His present volume, *Multicultural Comics: From* Zap *to* Blue Beetle, furthers that understanding and does so by bringing together diverse voices within comics studies. This edited collection is a welcome addition to the ever-growing scholarship on comic books, graphic novels, and graphic narrative in all of its forms. The various essays that follow encompass a wide variety of readings from many different perspectives. Indeed, one of the book's greatest strengths is its willingness to enlarge our understanding of "multicultural" (a term that is usually linked to U.S.-based culture) and expand its scope beyond the confines of comics produced in or related to American ethnicity. Not only does Aldama's collection serve as a useful introduction to the topics of race, ethnicity, gender, and nation within graphic narrative—a field of study with a thin history—but it also stands as a valuable resource in two other fields: the study of comics in general, and criticism surrounding multicultural narrative as a whole, regardless of the medium employed.

Unlike contributors to several other recent scholarly studies of graphic narrative, the authors of this volume do not limit themselves to "literary," or nongeneric, comics—that is, the kind of comics that have come to define "the graphic novel" for so many readers. Standing alongside studies of Adrian Tomine, Robert Crumb, and Jessica Abel you will find discussions of Marv Wolfman and Gene Colan's *The Tomb of Dracula,* Grant Morrison's work for DC Comics, and the recent manifestations of Batwoman. What is more, several contributors focus on comics that fly under the radar of most studies. The essays on Anishinaabe-related comics, DJ Spooky's visual remix of classic film, and the role of graphic novels in India not only contest our conventional understanding of graphic narrative, but give Aldama's collection a truly democratic feel.

The politics of multicultural representations within comics is a rich field of inquiry, one that is just waiting to be tapped. In the pages that follow, Frederick Aldama and his compatriots demonstrate how a medium long regarded as incidental and disposable can take on some of our culture's most challenging questions. If, as Will Eisner believed, stereotypes are an unavoidable necessity of comic art, then the essays in this collection help us to revisualize those "gutter" spaces that lie outside of our more privileged cultural frames.

MULTICULTURAL
Comics

MULTICULTURAL COMICS TODAY

A Brief Introduction

FREDERICK LUIS ALDAMA

A LL WALKS OF LIFE are on display in today's alternative and mainstream comic book worlds.[1] I do not just mean those politically astute anthropomorphic lions that strut through a U.S.-invaded, bombed-out Iraq, as seen in Brian K. Vaughan and Niko Henrichon's *Pride of Baghdad* (2006).[2] Off the cuff, I think of: the dyspeptic Asian American Ben Tanaka in Adrian Tomine's *Shortcomings* (2007); the bipolar Latino Omar Guerrero in Wilfred Santiago's *In My Darkest Hour* (2004); the angsty Latino suburbanite teen Miguel in Gilbert Hernandez's *Sloth* (2006); former Gotham City police detective and lesbian Latina Renee Montoya as love interest of Kate Kane (Batwoman) in Geoff Johns and Grant Morrison's maxi-series 52 (issues 1–52, 2006–2007); the Japanese émigré superhero Sunfire, out of the closet as a lesbian in Judd Winick's *Exiles* (issue 11, 2001); and Asian American Dupli-Kate, her brother Multi-Paul, and well-heeled black Black Samson in Robert Kirkman's *Invincible* (issues 2 and 6, 2003).

With author-artists at the helm like Los Bros. Hernandez, Santiago, Kirkman, and Winick, to name a few, we see a multiplicity of shades, colors, and sexual orientations expressed in comic book storyworlds.[3] Today, for instance when Winick receives fan mail critical of superheroes like Sunfire or the introduction of Green Lantern's assistant Terry Berg as queer (Green Lantern, vol. 3, issue 137, 2001), he has to ask, "Which social agenda are you complaining about? Is it the gay people? or the black people or the Asian people? After a while, it doesn't look like a social agenda. This is the world we live in" (Gustines, "Straight (and Not) Out of the Comics," 25).

Of course, the world we live in offers an infinite array of possible experiences and identities for a given author-artist to aesthetically reframe and transform into comic book storyworlds. And this is exactly what author-artists do. They take from the real world *and* fictional worlds: author-artists of color talk about real, biographical experiences living at the margins of a xenophobic society informing their comics as much as they talk of the influence of fiction, film, and art. In the creation of *Rocketo* (2006), for instance, Latino Frank Espinosa's fictional world is as much an allegory of the Cuban émigré experience as it is an engagement and radical revision of Homer's *Odyssey*. (See Aldama's *Your Brain on Latino Comics*.)

This isn't too surprising, given that author-artists of color have the capacity to imagine and feel outside of themselves. While categories used by academics and the media like Latino, Asian American, or African American, and so on, might be useful at first to make these author-artists' work visible, at the end of the day, they want not only to have their work judged by the standard of the great comic book author-artists, but also not to have their talent and imagination squeezed into only one identity-politics box. As Espinosa declares, "If all we do is just talk about one experience in our lives, we will remain trapped" (*Your Brain on Latino Comics*, 165). These categories ultimately force the massive creative range of author-artists of color, as Gilbert Hernandez tells Derek Parker Royal in an interview, "back into a kind of ghetto" ("Palomar and Beyond," 227). Why shouldn't Latinos or Asian Americans or African Americans or Native Americans be writing, as Espinosa asks, "the new *Lord of the Rings*, the new *Star Wars*, the new *Harry Potter*?" (*Your Brain on Latino Comics*, 165).

There are many other author-artists of color who share this sentiment—and act upon it. For instance, while Roberta Gregory has created a biographical comic book vignette "California Girl" (collected in *Roadstrips: A Graphic Journey across America*) that touches on experiences growing up Mexican and American in the 1950s—Mexicans could only swim on certain days at her public pool—her eponymous protagonist "Bitchy Bitch" of her trademark comic book has nothing to do with this experience; in fact, she's about as white, racist, and bigoted as they get. And we can say the same of native Hawaiian R. Kikuo Johnson's non-ethnic-identifiable protagonist in *Night Fisher* (2005). In both we see author-artists of color place a large distance between their own biographical experience and the characters and storyworld they create.

Any and all comic book author-artists should be free to create any type of storyworld populated by any type of character. There has been a tradition, however, of gatekeeping race- and ethnic-identified experiences and characters. This said, steps have been made toward widening the scope of comic book representations. In the United States, in the wake of civil rights activism, we see a first big growth spurt in the late 1960s and early 1970s, when characters of color began to see the light of day. Behemoths like DC and Marvel, as well as the little guys publishing "underground comix," or others, were offering more than the typical chiseled white-guy comic book fare.

I will leave it to Leonard Rifas in his essay "Race and Comix" in this collection to provide the context and specific detail for this shift in the underground comix world. As far as DC and Marvel go, we do see the making of a handful of African American, Latino, Asian American, and Native American superheroes. Several highlights from the late 1960s and the 1970s include: Stan Lee and Gene Colan's inventing in 1969 of the Harlem street thug Sam "Snap" Wilson as the Falcon (*Captain America*, vol. 1, issue 117). In 1972, Archie Goodwin and John Romita Sr. brought to life the Shaft-blaxploitation-styled superhero Carl Lucas in the series *Luke Cage, Hero for Hire*. A year later Marvel featured the African American day-walker vampire Blade as a supporting character in *Tomb of Dracula* (issue 10); this was followed by Blade holding his own in a fifty-six-page solo story in *Marvel Preview* (issue 3). (See Elizabeth Nixon's "'It ain't John Shaft': Marvel Gets Multicultural in *The Tomb of Dracula*" in this volume.) In 1977, comic book readers came across one of the arguably more complex superheroes of the day: using his athletic prowess to get out of the ghetto, Jefferson Pierce is a high-school teacher by day and the bioelectric-charged Black Lightning by night (*Black Lightning*, vol. 1, issue 1).

The 1980s and 1990s saw other notable superheroes of color arrive on the scene, including: Steve Englehart and Joe Staton's creating of a team of immortals called the Chosen, as part of their series *Millennium*, who are recruited to "advance the human race" (issues 1, p.4, 1988). The team includes, among others, an Australian aboriginal woman, Betty Clawman; a Maoist from mainland China, Xiang Po; an Inuit, Tom Kalmaku; an Afro-Caribbean Brit, Celia Windward; and Gregorio de la Vega, born and raised Peruvian. In 1997 Christopher Priest (writer) and ChrisCross (artist) created the African American pro-basketball player Coltrane "Trane" Walker as the superhero Xerø, who performs a sort of white minstrelsy (blond-haired wig and whiteface mask) to sleuth out and foil espionage operations that threaten the nation.

While in this period we see African–American–identified superheroes picking up the relative lion's share of representation, there were several notable Asians, Asian Americans, and Native Americans, including the Japanese-identified Sunfire (*X-Men*, vol. 1, issue 64, 1970). There has been a tradition of Native

Americans appearing as sidekicks, the easily disposable, and the preternaturally ecological in comics. In mainstream comics, we had, for example, superheroes like Cheyenne William Talltrees, who dons the ceremonial garb of Red Wolf appearing in *Avengers* (vol. 1, issue 80, 1970), the Apache James Proudstar as Warpath (*New Mutants*, vol. 1, issue 16, 1984), and his elder brother John Proudstar as Thunderbird, with his super senses, strength, speed, and stamina (*Giant-Size X-Men*, issue 1, 1975).

There have also been some notable Latino superheroes. Marvel introduced Bonita Juarez as Firebird in 1981; DC introduced Paco Ramone as Vibe in 1984, as well as Rafael Sandoval as El Diablo in 1989. In 1993 Latino author-artist Ivan Velez Jr. filled out with rich complexity a team of queer and straight Latino superheroes (Dominican, Puerto Rican, Afro-Hispanic, among others) in the Milestone series *Blood Syndicate*. Velez not only represented characters of color, but did so in ways that point out that there is not one type of Latino or one type of African American in the United States. (See Aldama's *Your Brain on Latino Comics*. For a detailed discussion focused on gender in another Milestone series, *Icon*, see Jennifer Ryan's essay "Black Female Authorship and the African American Graphic Novel: Historical Responsibility in *Icon: A Hero's Welcome*.") And Velez also worked hard to bring "color" into Marvel's *Ghost Rider* (vol. 3, issue 1, 70–93), where, for instance, he gave the Ghost Rider not only a backstory that included his living in the Bronx and having an Afro-Caribbean Latina as his wife, but also a supporting cast made up of characters of color. (For more on this, see my interview with Ivan Velez Jr. in *Your Brain on Latino Comics*.)

Mainstream comic books in the twenty-first century put several interesting superheroes of color on the map. In 2001 we see a certain self-reflexive playfulness with race and representation in Peter Milligan and Mike Allred's revamped *X-Force* (beginning in vol. 1, issue 115, and collected as *X-Force: New Beginning*). Here, Axel Cluney, or "Zeitgeist," speaking tongue in cheek, tells African American superhero team member, Tike Alicar, or "Anarchist": "Hell, I'm a black mutant. In this country, that's like being black with a little black added" (vol. 1, issue 116, 2001). In this same issue, when Anarchist hears that another black superhero might be joining the team, he worries that he'll lose his spot on the team as the token minority. In issue 117 Milligan and Allred introduce, along with others of a younger generation of multicultural mutants, the green-eyed, mixed Irish and Latina superhero Saint Anna, who was, we are informed, conceived when an Argentinean priest crossed the line with an orphaned Irish girl in a mission. Saint Anna's mutant superpowers: to transform herself into gaseous form, move objects with her mind, and heal the "sick and sad."

In 2004 Robert Morales and Reginald Hudlin introduced Isaiah Bradley as an African American Captain America who is survived by his son, Josiah X, in *Truth: Red, White, and Black.* This same year, Cuban American editor-in-chief Joe Quesada of Marvel brought to life the voodun-practicing multicultural team called "The Santerians" in *Daredevil: Father* (issue 1). The team leader, Nestor Rodriguez, or NeRo, is by day a multibillion-dollar entrepreneur with a successful hip-hop label and cologne line for men, and by night he is Eleggua, with superpowers such as being able to scramble thought and communication. Just as NeRo, as Eleggua, derives his power from his Yoruban-Caribbean deity namesake, so, too, do the others on the team derive powers from the deities Ogun, Chango, Oshun, and Oya.[4] In 2006 Keith Giffen, John Rogers, and Cully Hamner introduced an El Paso Tejano, Jaime Reyes, as the new Blue Beetle. This same year Tamora Pierce and Timothy Liebe brought to life a new-generation White Tiger as the book-smart Latina Angela del Toro; unlike her uncle, the original White Tiger created by Bill Mantlo and George Pérez in 1975 (*Deadly Hands of Kung-Fu,* issue 19), del Toro is not the brown sidekick to an Anglo superhero like Spider-Man or Daredevil. She's the protagonist of her own six-issue series. In issue 3 ("Earth to Rita," 2008) of DC's series *Trinity,* Kurt Busiek (author) introduced a story that gravitates around the Latina superhero character Tarot. Tarot reads, well, Tarot cards and the future they portend, allowing her to help out down-on-their-luck members of her Latino community: "Hey, Tarot-chica, Gracias! I asked for a raise like you said—it worked" (issue 3, 23). Not all is morally on the up and up, however. In switching back and forth between her interior thoughts and her actions, Busiek gives her a shade of complexity. She's coerced into reading cards for street thugs as well.

While few and far between, sidekick or central protagonist superheroes of color have appeared. Of course, it's much harder for DC and Marvel than independents to introduce new superheroes generally: their worlds are more rigidly determined and circumscribed. So when brown or black or any other color superheroes appear, they are often reincarnations of existing characters in the DC and Marvel worlds. And, there is the pressure of market demographics: even today, those who read comic books still remain mostly white guys.

Once they're created, there's a revolving door for superheroes of color—some never return and others experience sporadic returns. There have been, for instance, multiple resurrections of black superheroes such as Blade, Black Panther, and Storm (the latter two even tie the knot in issue 18 of Reginald Hudlin's 2006 *Black Panther*). Blade, launched in 1973 and making further appearances in the 1970s and 1990s, reappeared again in 2006 only to disappear a year later, and after having her own four-issue miniseries in 1996, Storm took over as the leader of an X-Men team in 2001 (*X-Treme X-Men*) and was given a backstory makeover in another miniseries in 2005, *Ororo: Before the Storm* (issues 1–4).[5] And DC's 1987 creation of the African-identified female eponymous superhero Vixen (she lives in the present but is firmly anchored in the heritage of her past, deriving her superpower from a fox talisman ["Tantu Totem"] passed down by her ancestors) only finally starred in her own book (the series in which she was to appear was canceled before the first issue was even released) in a 2008 five-issue limited series, *Vixen: Return of the Lion*. In 2004 Marvel introduced the mixed Mexican/Puerto Rican American superhero Araña as the star of *Amazing Fantasy* (vol. 2, issue 1), then gave Araña her own title *(Araña: The Heart of the Spider)* in 2005 with a twelve-issue run; while the issues were collected and published in three manga-sized pocket volumes, Araña never again battled another "Sisterhood of the WASP" foe.[6] However, she did appear in Ms. Marvel for a while as well as in the alternate future of Spider-Girl.

THIS IS NOT TO SAY that racial and ethnic experiences and identities do not appear more lastingly in comic books today. They do, but mostly in the world of the alternative comic books self-published or issued by publishers like Seattle's Fantagraphics, Montreal's Drawn & Quarterly, Berkeley's Image Comics—even DC's more daring imprint, Vertigo. Here, too, we see author-artists exploring a range of storytelling styles and modes: from the superhero, crime-noir, sci-fi, and Western genres to the realm of erotica. Given that the sky's the limit in terms of the use of genres and the inventing of themes, characters, and storyworlds, I highlight here only a few to give readers a sense of the range of multicultural comic books out there.

Genre Mixtures

Author-artists can use all manner of formulaic storytelling vehicles to contain stories of race- and/or ethnic-identified characters. These include not only the superhero formula, but those of the crime-noir detective story, the gothic, the romance, and the Western, to name a few. Often, author-artists intermix these different storytelling forms to skew reader expectations and break up the monotony that following a genre rigidly can bring; intermixing of genres in a given comic book story can introduce variations in plot tempo and allow for a greater flexibility in character development. Rafael Navarro, in his *Sonambulo* series, infuses the gothic/horror into a dominant crime-noir story to follow the sleuthing adventures of Latino detective Sonambulo. Sonambulo has been walking in the land of the dead for decades before returning to the land of the living as a *luchador*-mask-wearing detective who solves crimes during his sleepless nights wandering L.A. By infusing the goth-horror into the noir genre, Navarro can plausibly introduce a range of living-dead villains to engage his readers.

We see this cross-pollination of genres in other multicultural comics such as *Scalped*. Here, Jason Aaron (author) and R. M. Guéra (artist) blend the crime-noir with the Western to present a story that blurs the boundary between right and wrong. Within this hybrid storytelling form Aaron and Guéra create a complex Native American protagonist, the Oglala Dashiel Bad Horse ("Dash"). He slips into neither the savage (noble or brute) stereotype nor that of an eco-warrior, both of which essentialize Native American identity. (For examples of contemporary comic books that essentialize Native American identity, see Rob Schmidt's 2001 comic book series, *Peace Party*, as well as Nunzio DeFillipis and Christina Weir's *Skinwalker*. For a detailed history of Native American representations, see Michael A. Sheyahshe's *Native Americans in Comic Books: A Critical Study*.) Even before opening to the story proper, the reader-viewer of *Scalped* is readied for this cross-pollinating of genres: Brian K. Vaughan's introduction identifies it as a "Western-slash-crime story" (1) that deals with all issues of "race, vice, class, family, and sex" (2).

Once the reader-viewer has opened to the story, Dash returning home to the Prairie Rose reservation after a fifteen-year absence, we see how Aaron's dialogue—including much code-switching between Oglala and English—and Guéra's bold lines, subdued colors, and frenetic mix of close-up, medium-, and long-shot panels, intensify our engagement with Dash and the characters who revolve around him. Moreover, as Dash uncovers the mystery behind the murder of an FBI agent on the reservation fifteen years in the past, the backstory fills in details relating to several important figures, including a lone Oglala cowboy who mostly keeps to himself; Dash's tribal-activist mother, to whom actions both good and bad are attributed; and the psychologically complex and corrupt Lincoln Red Crow—casino owner, sheriff, and Mafioso—who, as a child, was beat by Jesuit missionaries who wanted to "kill the Indian inside [him] in order to save the man!" The genre mixing gives Dash's detective work a sense of historical importance: revealing that the problems of drug and alcohol abuse, the internalized racism (Oglala versus Lakota, mixed-blood versus full-blood), and the capitalist greed that infect life on the reservation result from a time of "cowboys and Indians," when the ideology of Manifest Destiny, with its hierarchies of difference, smoothed over violent acts of genocide.

Coming-of-Age Story

This storytelling form allows author-artists of color to explore a wide range of early experiences inflected by race, culture, sexuality, class, and gender. Given that the stories take place while the characters are, well, coming of age, the types of racism, homophobia, sexism, and the like that they experience can be quite raw and eye-opening to reader-viewers. In *American Born Chinese* (2006) author-artist Gene Luen Yang intermixes chapters told in a third-person colloquial narrative voice that follow the adventures of the mythical Monkey King with chapters told in a first-person voice that texture the contemporary experiences of the Asian American character Jin Wang as he grows up in and around San Francisco. While author-artist Yang anchors his art in a traditional Chinese-style pictorial storytelling layout (four-square panel layout with wide margins of empty white space on each page), along with a soft muting of strong colors like red, he does so not to express how prescriptive Chinese cultural traditions constrain the experiences of his protagonist Jin Wang, but rather how they can ultimately, as we see with the final crossing over of the Monkey King story into that of Wang's, provide the foundation (cultural) for building and growing a strong Asian American identity in a sea of xenophobes. (For more on *American Born Chinese* see Jared Gardner's more detailed analysis in this collection.)

We see author-artist Ivan Velez Jr. employ the coming-of-age form in his *Tales of the Closet Vol. 1* (2005) to richly texture a variety of multiracial gay and lesbian teenager coming-out stories. Not only do these characters feel alienated from the adult world as teens with their own sets of issues, but they feel doubly and triply alienated as racially and sexually different. While Velez presents a certain affirmation of gay teen coalition-building as Tony, Imelda, and a handful of other characters discover their common closeted experiences, the inclusion of a tragic gay-bashing scene near the story's end acts as brutal reminder of the suffering experienced by gay and lesbian youth of color living in a homophobic and racist society. And in *Skim* (2008), creators Mariko Tamaki (writer) and Jillian Tamaki (artist) use the diary form as the vehicle to tell the story of high school growing pains. The story follows several episodes in the life of protagonist Kimberly Keiko Cameron, or "Skim," as she comes to terms with teen suicide, friends made and lost, her crush on her high-school teacher Ms. Archer, and growing up with divorced parents. The author-artist team here, however, choose not to foreground race or ethnicity in Skim's day-by-day coming-of-age narrative. Indeed, the only time race and racism come up is when Skim and her classmate Hien are the only ones to be thrown out of a birthday party filled with girls interested only in country clubs and blue-eyed guys who look like the TV star "Don Johnson" (84). In her diary entry, Skim reflects on what happened to her and her friend Hien as they were shut out of the party: "We waited and waited for them to let us back in. After a little while Hien left. Hien's parents adopted her from Vietnam two years earlier and she never got invited to parties. Maybe she thought that's how people left parties in Canada. Asians first" (86). And, after waiting awhile and thinking about the party, Skim concludes, "The more I thought about it, the less I wanted back in. It was a boring party anyway" (87).

Autobiography

Just as the coming-of-age story can offer a slice-of-life picture of young characters, so too can the autobiographical form—but with one crucial difference: the latter is expected to correspond in some way to the life of the author-artist. Of course author-artists can play with this expectation—and they do. They can choose to anchor their story more tightly to the facts of their life, or more loosely. In the case of Canadian Mark Kalesniko, his biographical self finds expression in a hybrid man (body)/dog (head) protagonist, Alex. In *Alex* (2006), his anthropomorphic biographical persona pines over his first high-school love, Asian Canadian Lori Chio-Lin Chen. In his *Mail Order Bride* (2001), the autobiographical appears in the shape of the protagonist's marriage to an Asian character—just as Kalesniko is married to an Asian Canadian. The autobiographical is kept in sight, but very distantly so in both cases. Perhaps this is to give Kalesniko more flexibility to explore issues outside of his proximate experience: life as a dog or the feminist emancipation of an Asian mail order bride. This blurring of the autobiographical with the fictional allows for Kalesniko to give, as Lesley Paparone concludes, "a more heterogeneous understanding of Asian womanhood" ("Art and Identity," 217).

And we see in *One Hundred Demons* mixed Anglo-Filipino author-artist Lynda Barry deliberately playing with the autobiographical mode. She begins *Demons* with the protagonist asking: "Is it autobiography if parts of it are not true? Is it fiction if parts of it are?" (7). (See Melinda de Jesús's essay in this collection for a detailed discussion of the significance of destabilizing the autobiographical genre in Barry's work.)

In the case of Percy Carey (writer) and Ronald Wimberly (artist), there's a closer adherence to the details of Carey's life story. While the title of their comic book *Sentences: The Life of MF Grimm* (2007) might not tell the reader that this is an autobiography, the jacket cover blurb does establish such an author-equals-character reader contract: "Percy Carey tells his own personal tale about his rise, fall, and rise again through the ranks of the Hip-Hop industry." As we open to the first pages, readers are situated in time and space: January 12, 1994. Harlem, New York City. A first-person narrative voice begins: "This was how it went down" (2). The visuals that follow indicate a shift to an earlier time (flashback) and this same voice embodied in the shape of a child: "My story begins on the street. . . . Sesame Street, that is" (10). Jacket cover blurbs and the first couple of pages of verbal and visual narration firmly establish that we are to connect the biographical life of the author Percy Carey with that of the visual (black and white washed over with a sepia tint) and verbal (urban, rhythmically hip, and quick-paced) narrated life of the protagonist, "Percy Carey." Finally, this autobiographical slice of the U.S. racialized experience doubles as a morality tale. Carey ends *Sentences* with: "I want to show the youth that there's other options out there that don't involve guns and crime. You CAN make it in this business—and any business for that matter—without taking the route I took" (128).

While *Sentences* provides a big life-story arc, the autobiographical form doesn't have to follow this type of big sweep. U.S.-Iranian comic book author Dara Naraghi uses the autobiographical to provide slice-of-life vignettes in his *Lifelike* (2007). He explains that in writing the first story, "The Long Journey," about the Iran-Iraq war, he "borrows bits and pieces from a wide set of experiences—my own, as well as those of friends and family—and wraps them all up in a healthy dose of fiction" (4). Nor does the autobiographical comic book have to be focused microscopically on the subject's life story within family and community. As with Arab American author-artist Toufic El Rassi's *Arab in America* (2007), the comic book can be anchored in one's life story and reach outward toward the historical. The first series of panels establishes this outward reach into a grand historical event. It opens: "I remember sitting there in the computer lab at school," followed by a panel with a computer screen monitor and an e-mail dated "11 September" and with the message "Hey man you better shave" (1). As the story of El Rassi unfolds, the reader-viewer learns how his life is caught up in the recent history of the United States and the Middle East—the civil war that led his parents to flee Beirut in 1979, the Israeli invasion of Lebanon in 1982, the first Gulf War, the post-9/11 invasion of Iraq and Afghanistan, and a September 12, 2006, raid by U.S. Immigration and Customs Enforcement (ICE), which "showed up at my family's house at dawn and pulled everyone out of bed" (15), to highlight several events. By intermixing the life story with the historical (and even privileging the latter), El Rassi aims to use the autobiographical content—the experiences of being Arab in America—to teach readers about a not-so-black-and-white racism that permeates American society. (For other contemporary examples of a variety of uses by author-artists of the autobiographical genre, see the diverse array of stories collected in Diana Shultz's edited volume *AutobioGraphix*.)

Memoir

Often author-artists of color will also use autobiography's close kin, the memoir, to capture specific moments in their past as retrospectively and critically interwoven into the stories of family and community. Well-known memoirs include Art Spiegelman's anthropomorphic rendering of mice in his Jewish Holocaust–set *Maus* (1986), as well as Marjane Satrapi's more recently published *Persepolis: The Story of a Childhood* (2003), which tells the stories of Satrapi's family living in a repressive post–1979 Islamic Revolution Iran. The memoir has also been used by author-artists such as Miné Okubo, whose *Citizen 13660* (1983) tells the story of the author's experience as a Japanese American in the internment camps during World War II. That Okubo chose to tell the story using the visual and verbal mode of the comic book is especially important. Xiaojing Zhou considers that the Us versus Them propaganda that identified Japanese Americans as an enemy of the state was "spatially constructed" ("Spatial Construction of the 'Enemy Race,'" 52), and therefore Okubo's visuals of the spaces from the point of view of those actually imprisoned offer an important resistant image repertoire. Asian Canadian author-artist Ann Marie Fleming uses the memoir form to interweave events from her life with those of her great-grandfather. In *The Magical Life of Long Tack Sam* (2007) we see Fleming carefully interweave anecdotes, interviews with family and friends, diaries, letters, postcards, and other archival evidence to destabilize fixed ideas of Asian-ness. Fleming begins by telling and showing her readers that she was born in Okinawa, but that she was "a lot bigger than the other Japanese babies in the maternity ward. Maybe that's because my father was a tall Australian. My mother was from Hong Kong, and not very tall at all" (2). The memoir continues to tell the story of her great-grandfather to complicate fixed categories of identity—he was a Buddhist but became a Roman Catholic to marry an Austrian woman, for example—as well as to show how global historical twists and turns impacted the shaping of this complexly defined Asian family. (See also Rocío G. Davis's essay "Locating Family: Asian Canadian Historical Revisioning in Linda Ohama's *Obaachan's Garden* and Ann Marie Fleming's *The Magical Life of Long Tack Sam*.") Recently, in *American Widow*, Alissa Torres (author) and Sungyoon Choi (artist) use the memoir form to tell the story of Torres's post-9/11 trauma and isolation (depicted in a simple visual style using black and white with light blue coloring) at the loss of her Latino husband in the mass murder that took place that day at the World Trade Center.

Biography

Those who choose to texture the multiracial experience and identity also find the biographical mode appealing. Like autobiography and the memoir, biography can either focus on the particulars that make up the facts of a given subject's life or reach by varying degrees into the social, historical, and political context in which that subject lives. Author-artists can choose to remain tightly tethered to the facts of the life told or wander more freely. Andrew Helfer's ear for dialogue and Randy DuBurke's no-nonsense black-and-white six-panel page layouts create the hagiographic *Malcolm X: A Graphic Biography* (2006). Flashbacks (the comic book biography begins and ends with his assassination), sudden juxtapositions of comic book drawing with photographs, along with snippets of information from *The Autobiography of Malcolm X* (1965), weave together the story of an individual very much shaped by and a shaper of his times. The story moves through various social and historical moments: Jim Crow segregation, lynchings, the Ku Klux Klan, the freedom of the Harlem renaissance, the rise of the nation of Islam, and the politicizing of African Americans nationwide. Pedagogically inclined, *Malcolm X: A Graphic Biography* aims to teach its reader-viewers about how Malcolm X's "words and teaching" (4) influenced black politics in the United States. (See also Don Hillsman and Ryan Monihan's more colloquial and factually loose *By Any Means Necessary: The Life and Times of Malcolm X—An Unauthorized Biography in Comic Book Form.*) In a move away from the visual and verbal "realism" of Helfer and DuBurke's *Malcolm X*, author-artist Ho Che Anderson goes for a more visually and verbally stylized portrayal of Martin Luther King Jr. In *King: A Comics Biography of Martin Luther King, Jr.* (2005) Anderson follows closely his subject's life—from childhood through college and the civil rights era—but does so in a visual style that announces its artifice at every turn: from a more cartoon-iconic style to artful abstract collage to Cubist expressionism. In this same performative spirit, Anderson uses the device of the Greek chorus to interrupt the flow of the life story and to comment critically and often ironically on the events taking place. Furthermore, as Stanley Crouch aptly observes in the introduction to *King:* "There is a level of complexity and a superb capturing of the range of Afro-American features, which include the frequent varieties of lighter skins and the patches of facial freckles that do appear very often in fine art paintings of black people by black people. . . . But notice that Mr. Anderson achieves this in black and white alone, which is a high mark of skill" (11). Moreover, not only does Anderson's juxtaposition of a variety of visual techniques self-reflexively comment on the use of the visual and verbal media within the comic book, but the visuals' increasingly "totemic" structure and feel as the story winds to a close transport MLK visually into the mythical, or, as Crouch puts it, "the land of dreams and tragic finality" (11).

Historical Fiction

Several author-artists of multicultural comics choose as a springboard to their making of fictional narratives the historical event or figure. The anchor here is not the verifiable facts of life presented in the various life-story modes mentioned above, but fiction. In an interview I conducted with Derek McCulloch (author), who teamed up with Shepherd Hendrix (artist) to create *Stagger Lee* (2006), he discusses how the comic book medium was particularly suited to alternating between a "comparatively conventional fictional narrative and a pseudo-scholarly examination of the story's progression into folklore" (Aldama interview with McCulloch, August 21, 2008). The comic book captures the double narrative dynamic the moment it begins: "Maybe you know about Stagger Lee. There are songs about him. . . . The songs are part of a very old tradition, and as they passed from singer to singer each voice would inevitably sing its own point of view" (*Stagger Lee*, 7). Working with an already very slippery figure of legendary proportions, as with the many versions of Stagger Lee's life circulating out there (over five hundred different songs, all with different details of his life and slight variations on his name), McCulloch is careful to remind the reader-viewers: "This book is a mixture of fact and fiction [and should] not be confused with a work of history" (225). For McCulloch and Hendrix, the greater leaning toward the fictional allowed them the flexibility to "fudge timelines, conflate episodes, [and] sneak in small anachronisms" (225). So while the inclusion of the primary archival sources gestures toward the historical, the freedom to invent character and event, play with chronology, and use multiple narrators, and the use of a not-so-contrasting and defining brown ink and sepia wash, lend themselves well to the comic book retelling of the story of Stagger Lee as *legend* that outstrips the actual, biographical man. Along with the sepia inking "making logical sense for the story," it was a way to "make sure it didn't *look* like other comics," as McCulloch remarks (Aldama interview with McCulloch, August 21, 2008).[7]

There are many other examples of author-artists who have as their subject one or another multicultural issue in their comic book realization of historical fiction. I think also of Ben Katchor's *The Jew of New York* (serialized from 1992 through 1993 and published as a collection in 2000), which bases characters on historically verifiable figures—Major Ham is based on the late eighteenth/ nineteenth–century polymath and Jewish advocate Major Mordecai Noah—as well as inventing completely new imaginary characters to fictionalize the factually based movement to make New York the Jewish promised land. (See Jennifer Glaser's "An Imaginary Ararat: Jewish Bodies and Jewish Homelands in Ben Katchor's *The Jew of New York*.") And, more recently, Mat Johnson (writer) and Warren Pleece (artist) intermix fiction and history in their so-called "graphic mystery," *Incognegro* (2008), to tell the story of Zane Pinchback, who sleuths out lynchings in the Deep South. Zane is inspired by former executive secretary of the NAACP Walter White, whose light skin allowed him to pass in the Deep South, where he uncovered and made public the lynchings that were still taking place in the 1930s. Johnson and Pleece begin the story with a single-panel spread that depicts a gathering of people—some with children and others wielding bats and sticks—surrounding a man hanging by a rope from a tree. A narrative voice fills in the detail: "Between 1889 and 1918, 2,522 Negroes were murdered by lynch mobs in America. That we know of" (7). While the lynchings persisted through the 1930s, the media were not interested. The light-skinned African American protagonist, Zane Pinchback, writing under the byline "Incognegro," passes in order to publicize these lynchings. His investigation becomes especially personal when he discovers that his brother, accused of murdering a white woman, is a day away from being lynched. Clearly within the realm of the fictional, Johnson's invented characters, dialogue, and events, along with Pleece's black-and-white chiaroscuro pen-and-ink visuals, open eyes to this abhorrently violent period in American history.

The historical events used do not have to be set in the distant past. Ryan Inzana also blends the historical with the fictional in the contemporarily situated *Johnny Jihad: A Graphic Novel*. In prefatory remarks, Inzana discusses his inspiration: the U.S. funding of terrorist training camps in Afghanistan, and John Walker Lindh, from Marin County, California, who became a Taliban freedom fighter. They are followed by a prologuelike sequence where a first-person narration recounts, across a series of five stretch panels, Walker's dream of flying through the air and colliding with two large buildings (from the visual we recognize these as the Twin Towers). On the next page appears a date, "October 25th, 2001," followed by the words "Check, one, two . . ." and then by a close-up photograph of a tape recorder. Then the story begins as a full-page spread on the next page: "The how and why of me being here, in the middle of American bombing raids in Afghanistan, is complicated. It is only a little over a month since two planes smashed into the World Trade Center in New York. The world can change a lot in one month. The following story is my life, my sorry, short life, and how it all went wrong" (1–3). Inzana's preface, the prologue sequence, then the story proper situate the reader-viewer fully in the realm of a comic book that employs the historical fictional mode to recount the private psychological struggles of an individual as they blow up (literally) into various forms of destructive fundamentalism. We see this same blend of the contemporary historical moment and the fictional in Jaime "Jimmy" Portillo's *Gabriel* (2007). Rather than use the faux autobiographical mode to recount contemporary events, as seen in Inzana, however, Portillo uses the horror gothic mode. As the story of vampire protagonist Gabriel de la Cruz unfolds, we learn of the very real and current horror of the hundreds of raped, mutilated, and murdered Mexican women along the Juárez/El Paso border.

Realism

All comic books refer one way or another and with lesser or greater degrees of verisimilitude to reality—even when they are stories of, say, lions in a bombed-out Baghdad. If that were not the case, we wouldn't be able to understand them. In *'85* (2008) we have Danny Simmons (writer) along with Floyd Hughes (artist), who invent a world for their character Crow Shade that resembles a mid-1980s drug-filled, hip-hop- and subway art–obsessed New York, for instance.

And comic book authors and artists might choose to blend in their realism the recognizable everyday with the fantastical otherworldly. Farel Dalrymple's *Pop Gun War* (2003) follows a young African American protagonist, Sinclair, who discovers a pair of discarded wings and has encounters with giants, homeless men, and talking fish. G. Willow Wilson (author) and M. K. Perker (artist) intermix the fantastical with the everyday in *Cairo: A Graphic Novel* (2007). Here we follow the stories of everyday types—contraband smuggling Ashraf, Lebanese American expatriate Shaheed, Egyptian journalist Ali Jibreel, American tourist Kate, among others—as well as the character Shams, a "real, no-shit genie" (32), otherwise known as a "djinn," who "manipulates probability" (34). And there's Espinosa's *Rocketo: Journey to the Hidden Sea, Vol. 1,* where futuristic fantasy—in a world, set two thousand years after the earth is nearly obliterated, that is now populated by Mappers, like Rocketo, and hybrid species Dogmen and Fishmen—overlies a contemporary Cuban American experience of identifying with a lost homeland. Kova ("Cuba") is one of the few land masses still left on the planet, but it's impossible to find without a Mapper like Rocketo. Espinosa's brand of realism includes, then, a plot unfolding in a fantasy other world but alluding strongly to Homeric epics, a dialogue reminiscent of Bogart films, an expressionist visual form, and an allegorical subtext of a pre- and post-Castro Cuban experience. (See *Your Brain on Latino Comics.*)

Another example of a realism that tips over into the fantastical is Grady Klein's *The Lost Colony Book 1: The Snodgrass Conspiracy* (2006). Even before the story begins, the jacket cover flap describes it as taking place on "a mysterious island unknown to the rest of the world, in nineteenth-century America. Its citizens: a colorful and outrageous band of capitalists, inventors, hucksters, and freemen, who jealously guard the island's fantastic wealth from the prying fingers of the outside world, even as they attempt to conceal its captivating secrets from one another." This other world is at once removed from the reality of the mainland, populated with cartoonish figures (in their visual and psychological portrayal) like Snodgrass and Dr. Pepe Wong, and filled with anachronistic dialogue (faux outdated language intermixing with "dude"). At the same time, this other world refers to a historical moment: the United States's transition from an agrarian slavocracy to a full-blown mechanized and industrialized capitalist society.

And there is the cartoonish realism of satires like Ilan Stavans and Roberto Weil's *Mr. Spic Goes to Washington* (2008) and Aaron McGruder and Reginald Hudlin's *Birth of a Nation* (2004). Both are grounded in fantastically imagined situations. *Mr. Spic* opens: "The day America finally becomes brown starts like any other" (11). In *Birth of a Nation*, East St. Louis secedes from the United States. At the same time, both refer to a reality we do recognize. In *Mr. Spic* the L.A. Mayor turned Democratic Senator Samuel Patricio Inocencio Cárdenas (s.p.i.c.) has a photograph (literally) of Bush and Che Guevara on his office wall; in *Birth of a Nation*, while the characters consistently appear in a cartoon-ish iconographic style, they include a malapropistic Bush Jr., a lynching-thirsty Dick Cheney, and sell-outs Colin Powell and Condoleezza Rice. (For more on *Birth of a Nation* see Michael A. Chaney's "Drawing on History in Recent African American Graphic Novels," which considers this comic book a political commentary on a history of slavery and minstrelsy continuing to haunt America today.) Both use the reference to our everyday reality to educate their audiences. In *Mr. Spic*, for instance, Mr. Spic mentions that less than 1 percent of schoolteachers in Los Angeles are Mexican American and asserts that we don't need a wall between the United States and Mexico, given that "the two countries are forever intricately linked" (23).

We also see the fantasy brand of realism at play in multiculturally dimensioned mythic comic books such as *India Authentic Vol. 1: The Book of Shiva* (published in 2007 by the now defunct Virgin Comics). As Deepak Chopra (creator along with Saurav Mohapatra) writes in the introduction, while based on the "primal stories" of Hindu myths and their gods (Shiva, Indra, Ganesha, Uma, and Kali, for instance), the comic book stories are not about myths and a long-ago past: "They are actually about us. They chronicle our greatest aspirations, our darkest fears, our collective experience as a species" (1). And the vampire myth comes alive, not as set in some Transylvanian never-never land, but in a contemporary multicultural L.A. in *Life Sucks* (2008) by Jessica Abel (author-artist), Gabe Soria (author), and Warren Pleece (artist). At one point the protagonist Dave hitches a ride from soon-to-be love interest Chicana goth Rosa from Boyle Heights—who speaks Spanish only to her mom and very occasionally sprinkles her English with Spanish like "qué mentiroso" (111) and "puta madre" (153)—to get home in time to watch a repeat of the telenovela *El amor de los amores.* He wonders if she's surprised at this, since he's a "dorky gringo" (45). Once Rosa finds out Dave is a vampire, to soup up her gender-regulated life—"I should be getting a full-time job, getting pregnant . . ." (117)—she declares, "If you love me, you'll make me a vampire. Right here, right now" (166).

In his comic book anthology *Trickster Native American Tales*, Matt Dembicki also uses a brand of realism to offset reader expectations of Native Americans as somehow frozen in a mythological past. He mentions in an interview that while "it's impossible to capture the art of Native American oral storytelling visually," the comic book's unique combination of visual and verbal storytelling devices can grab immediately the "attention and imagination" of audiences both mainstream and Native American, young and adult, in ways that prose narratives and/or children's books (the typical means for conveying the trickster tales) can't; it also offers a compelling way to record and archive Native American "stories for future generations" (Aldama interview with Dembicki, September 3, 2008). Rather than follow the life of a single protagonist, Dembicki chooses to follow multiple characters because, as he states in an interview, the trickster animal reflects the geographic domain of the tribe: "the coyote is the southwest, the raven is the northwest, the raccoon is the northeast, for instance" (ibid.).

Finally, we have the mix of fantasy in terms of plot and character with either extremes of comic book realism (drawn-over photographs) or comic book iconicity (cartoonlike characters). The cover of the comic book spin-off of the television show *Heroes* (drawn by Alex Ross, 2007) uses a photographic realism to depict clearly and recognizably those television actors that play the various members of its multiracial cast of fantastical humans in a contemporary world. Steve Ross's satirical *Chesty Sanchez* (1995) uses a graphic style that is iconic to depict the adventures of Latina-*luchador* superhero Chesty and her sidekick Torpedo in a contemporary Mexico City.[8]

Erotica

Author-artists of color have also used the storytelling mode of erotica to create worlds—both otherworldly and more recognizably that of our own everyday.[9]

This form seems to allow for characters of color to experience radical gender bending and sexual freedom. We see this with Latino author-artist Gilbert Hernandez in his creating of the stories that make up *Birdland*. And along with Hernandez, there is the Asian American author-artist Sandra Chang, who introduces in her series *Sin Metal Sirens* (2002) the character Anodyne. Anodyne is Asian, supermuscled, and smart. As she travels across the galaxy to rescue kidnapped victims, she encounters adventures that reveal her polysexual ways. Nothing is off-limits in this techno-bondage otherworldly story. Chang's work extends and revitalizes the Japanese hentai manga tradition, as well as the sci-fi erotic worlds of Michael Manning (his 1995 *Spider Garden* and 1996 *Hydrophidian*, for instance) and the work of Roberto Raviola, aka Magnus *(Milady 3000)*. And author-artist Adam Warren ups the ante on the erotica when he invents his over-the-top characters such as the latex-wearing, bulging-muscled Asian character, Kozue Kaburagi as "Ninjette," the hyperliterate Asian toyboy, "Thugboy," and the African American feminist supervillain, Sistah Spooky.

THERE ARE MANY OTHER comic books about how race and ethnicity interweave into issues of gender roles and sexual desire that I haven't mentioned. There are many comic books that focus on multicultural issues in other countries—India, for instance—that I have not discussed. (Those in India, at least, are discussed at length in an essay by Suhaan Mehta in this collection.) But this overview provides a taste of what has shaped multicultural comic book author-artists working today and summarizes their innovations.

Some argue that comic books are a particularly good medium to overturn denigrating stereotypes. As Derek Parker Royal writes, "Because of [their] foundational reliance on character iconography, comics are well suited to dismantle those very assumptions that problematize ethnic representation, especially as they find form in visual language. They can do this by particularizing the general, thereby undermining any attempts at subjective erasure through universalization" ("Introduction," 9). And Gillian Whitlock considers the visual and verbal ingredients of comic books important in that they "free us to think and imagine differently in times of trauma and censorship" ("Autographics," 967).

Certainly, comic books do engage and elicit a response. Wilfred Santiago's *In My Darkest Hour* wants us to feel a deep sadness; Gilbert Hernandez's *Birdland* wants to arouse us; Carlos Saldaña *(Burrito)* and Steve Ross *(Chesty Sanchez)* want us to laugh—with irony; Hudlin and McGruder seek to raise social awareness. And while the characters that fill up the storyworlds of these multicultural comic books don't themselves, as Terry Kading soberly reminds us, "actually intervene in the *real world*" ("Drawn into 9/11," 227), they might indeed push people to act. In Iran a strip both moved Azeri Turks to protest and moved the Iranian government's Press Supervisory Board to shut down the newspaper that published the popular cartoonist Mana Neyestani's suggestively derogatory depiction of Turkish Azeri as cockroaches. And there is a fatwa on the Swedish cartoonist who lampooned the Prophet Muhammad; the caricature's reprint in two weekly Jordanian newspapers also led to jail sentences for two newsroom editors.

It is important to consider carefully the craft—the aesthetics of multicultural comics. The aesthetic is neither in the object nor in the subject. The aesthetic is a form of relationship between the subject and the object. What the artist-author of multicultural comic books does is create a blueprint: he or she imagines, then writes and draws (alone, or collectively with another artist, inker, etc.), little by little in sequential manner the blueprint that is going to be one way or another read-viewed and assimilated.

The process of writing and drawing implies, at each instant, myriad choices (one word instead of another, one image instead of another, one or another style of lettering, etc.); in thinking in images, as with lucid dreaming, the author-artist (or author-and-artist team, as the case may be) is deciding which gaps to leave and which gaps to fill in. The author-artist of multicultural comics is deciding which gaps the reader-viewer is going to fill in. Here, too, we need to keep in mind that the author-artists discussed in this collection work hard to become proficient in their comic book craft, constantly educating their senses to produce visual and verbal narrative blueprints that engage and help reader-viewers, in turn, to educate their own senses in new and novel ways.

Thus, when reading and writing about multicultural comics, we might keep centrally in mind several of the following questions that the essays collected in this volume directly and indirectly raise. If one is to determine that a given comic book is multicultural through and through, is it so because of a character, a style of writing or drawing, a plot? Is there a specific narrative type (form and content) that we as scholars, students, and readers generally associate with "multicultural" comic books? Is this comic book storytelling form something defined or circumscribed *only* by sociological or political issues and racialized content? And if so, at what point can these be understood by those outside the experience? The many different approaches presented in the thirteen essays that follow consider one way or another that multicultural comic books are a unique expression—a narrative fictional "idiolect"—within a world of experiences and a world of comic books.

MULTICULTURAL COMICS: FROM ZAP TO BLUE BEETLE brings together scholarship that uses a range of approaches and methods to enrich our understanding of how multicultural comic books created by a variety of author-artists work. Whether focused more on character analysis, history, or formal verbal and visual features, each essay attends to how one or more author-artists—mainstream, underground, or independent—engage, move, and open the eyes of their reader-viewers in ways that complicate issues of race, ethnicity, caste, gender, and sexuality.

I divide the book into two main sections. The first section, "History, Concepts, and Methods," brings together essays that focus primarily but not exclusively on how author-artists resist, complicate, and occasionally capitulate to simple scripts of race, ethnicity, gender, and sexuality. The second section, "A Multicultural Comic Book Toolbox," collects essays that focus more (albeit not exclusively) on developing and deploying sets of tools for analyzing and evaluating the visual and verbal elements used by author-artists to cue, trigger, and move reader-viewers to engage with complex schemas of race and ethnicity.

Leonard Rifas's essay "Race and Comix" begins the section "History, Concepts, and Methods." Rifas offers a glimpse into an important moment in comic book history, the rise of the underground comix scene. While dominated by white comic book creators, this was by no means a racially monolithic moment in the history of the comic book. There were author-artists who slipped into the racial exoticism that characterized a late-1960s counterculture (in the name of peace, love, and equality, middle-class Anglos donning African dashikis, Indian feathered headbands, and Mexican serapes), and there were other comic book author-artists who resisted. Of the latter, Rifas discusses the self-reflexive parody and critique of race essentialism and exoticism in R. Crumb's "Whiteman" (issue 1 of his series *Zap*) as well as Gilbert Shelton's "The Indian That Came to Dinner" (*Feds 'n' Heads*). Rifas also reminds us that, while few and far between, there were black comix practitioners, including Larry Fuller and Richard "Grass" Green. However, as Rifas cautions, whether white or black, even the most multiculturally self-aware of underground comix author-artists could create characters who in their appearance and action conform to preexisting racial stereotypes. For Rifas, finally, it is not so much that one has to be black, brown, or whatever color to make interesting multicultural comix, but rather that the author-artist must detail character, events, and settings in ways that highlight a given racialized character's "unique humanity."

In "'Authentic' Latinas/os and Queer Characters in Mainstream and Alternative Comics," an analysis that explores a more contemporary comic book scene, Jonathan Risner further questions and complicates the notion of authorship: does one have to be Latino to create a comic book that expresses well a Latino experience and identity? To answer this, Risner contrasts representations of Latino-ness in Los Bros. Hernandez's series *Las Locas* with DC's new *Blue Beetle* series as well as DC's recent introduction of a queer Latina Batwoman.

Like Rifas, Risner upsets race-essentialist nativist paradigms that straitjacket the imagination of author-artists generally. So, for Risner, it is not only the obvious author-artists like Los Bros. Hernandez who infuse vitality into their Latino comic book worlds, but all those who create well and responsibly.

This sense of an author-artist taking seriously the crafting of storyworlds also centrally informs Margaret Noori's analysis in her essay "Native American Narratives from Early Art to Graphic Novels: How We See Stories / Ezhig'waabamaanaanig Aadizookaanag." Noori carefully outlines the three creative streams—oral, written, and visual—comprising contemporary native comic book storytelling. She then focuses on a number of Anishinaabe-authored comic books to demonstrate how these author-artists' sense of responsibility to their craft and subject matter stands against simpleminded portrayals of Native Americans in U.S. popular culture. Rather than depict natives perennially in loincloth, for example, author-artists such as Chad Solomon and Christopher Meyer (*The Adventures of Rabbit and Bear Paws*) clothe their characters in season- and setting-appropriate wear; other author-artists switch language registers from English to Anishinaabemowin not only to vary the rhythm of their prose, but to preserve their language.

Other essays in this section focus on how author-artists complicate the racial, ethnic, gender, and sexuality representational map in their destabilizing of single-minded cultural and national identities. In "Liminality and Mestiza Consciousness in Lynda Barry's *One Hundred Demons*," Melinda L. de Jesús situates mixed-race author-artist Barry and her strategically "naïve" visual comic book style within a Filipina American feminist narrative fiction tradition. Barry's various in-between figurations—narrator, character, and author—provide a model for a more inclusive Filipina American identity. In "Black Nationalism, Bunraku, and Beyond: Articulating Black Heroism through Cultural Fusion and Comics," Rebecca Wanzo situates Kerry James Marshall's *Rythm Mastr* within a diasporic aesthetic that shakes up essentialist notions of African American–ness and Anglo American–ness. James Braxton Peterson's "Birth of a Nation: Representation, Nationhood, and Graphic Revolution in the Works of D. W. Griffith, DJ Spooky, and Aaron McGruder et al." explores how contemporary African American author-artists use a "Hip Hopographic" style and radically explosive content to revise and engage anew mainstream ur-texts such as the film *Birth of a Nation*.

While still focused largely on questions of representation, other essays in this section telescope to single-character analysis. Patrick Hamilton's "Lost in Translation: Jessica Abel's *La Perdida*, the Bildungsroman, and 'That "Mexican" Feel'" goes against the grain of *La Perdida*'s laudatory critical reception and instead reveals just how the U.S. Anglo/Mexican character, Carla Olivares, experiences little of the kinesis of consciousness expected of the bildungsroman genre. She begins her journey into Mexico objectifying Mexicans and reifying Mexican-ness—and ends her journey with the same ignorant worldview. The mature Carla (postjourney) as narrator is no wiser for the experience than the young Carla experiencing the journey. In "Same Difference: Graphic Alterity in the Work of Gene Luen Yang, Adrian Tomine, and Derek Kirk Kim," Jared Gardner chooses as his subject the stereotype in Asian American comic books. A bridge piece to the next section, Gardner's historical and formal analysis provides a background context to many of the allusions made in today's Asian American comic books that complicate and parody those pejorative model-minority and Asian-invasion stereotypes. Indeed, the move from comic strip—and single-panel cartoon gag especially—to the comic book, with its narrative time and space opening the possibility for readers to imagine between panels, allowed for the development of the more sophisticated use of character type in Asian American comics today; it allows for, in Gardner's words, the "embracing of the radical consequences of an alterity that disables stereotype and the easy read-ings of the hegemonic gaze."

THE SECOND SECTION, "A Multicultural Comic Book Toolbox," focuses on how author-artists create comic book worlds that trigger very different emotions in their reader-viewer. With "'It ain't John Shaft': Marvel Gets Multicul-tural in *The Tomb of Dracula*," Elizabeth Nixon focuses specifically on the device of second-person narration and direct address ("You") to tease out just how the reader-viewer is encouraged to cross over into the silent margins inhabited by the literally mute Indian character, Taj Nital. While characterization (mute-ness) and visuals (Taj Nital appears at the fringes of the panels) marginalize and silence, the strategic use of second-person narration and direct address force-fully pulls readers into Taj Nital's complex interiority. In this way the second-person narrative device encourages reader-viewers to step across borders of subjectivity. Following a like thread, Evan Thomas also attends to how narra-tive devices work to give voice and complexity to the otherwise unheard and invisible people. In his essay "Invisible Art, Invisible Planes, Invisible People," Thomas analyzes how the gutter and interpanel tensions in Grant Morrison and Philip Bond's *Vimanarama* open a space for the "subaltern" character Ali to speak. Suhaan Mehta's "Wondrous Capers: The Graphic Novel in India" focuses on the use of image-versus-word tensions, as well as certain text letter-ing and positions, in explaining how nonmainstream comic book author-artists Orijit Sen *(The River of Stories)*, Naseer Ahmed and Saurabh Singh *(Kashmir Pending)*, Amruta Patil *(Kari)*, and Sarnath Banerjee *(The Barn Owl's Wondrous Capers)* give voice to those at the caste and sexual fringes of Indian society and resist kowtowing to an "air-brushed" (the technique used in the mainstream Indian comics) Hindu nationalist line. And Nicholas Hetrick's "Chronology, Country, and Consciousness in Wilfred Santiago's *In My Darkest Hour*" focuses on the devices of layout, color scheme, and style to show how Santiago blurs the boundary between his Puerto Rican American character Omar's interiority (private) and the post-9/11 American psyche (public). It is the atypical use of exterior narrating devices (layout, color scheme, and style as opposed to word balloon, thought bubble, or narrator box) as focalization technique (subjective filter through which the narrator presents the story) that makes physically present this blurring of the boundary between the private and public, the real and unreal, in a post-9/11 American consciousness. Bringing "direct representation of subjective states out of the province of interiority (i.e., speech balloons)" allows Santiago "to affect, literally, the shape and feel of the storyworld."

The collection ends with "Finding Archives/Making Archives: Observations on Conducting Multicultural Comics Research"—an analytical and descriptive bibliography coauthored by Rebecca Wanzo and Jenny E. Robb. Wanzo and Robb point readers to important archival and scholarly resources for approaching multicultural comics. They remind us that, given the scarcity of resources available, much still needs to be done in developing approaches to multicultural comics.

NOTES

1. Not only do comic books touch on all aspects of our everyday life, but the scholarship on comic books is likewise expanding. In their introduction to a special issue on the graphic novel for MFS: *Modern Fiction Studies* (2006), Hilary Chute and Marianne DeKovan write, "In our current moment, in which an array of new literary and popular genres aim to further the conversation on the vital and multilayered work of narrative, graphic narrative has become part of an expanding literary field, absorbing and redirecting the ideological, formal, and creative energies of contemporary fiction" ("Introduction," 768).

2. In the fictionalizing of a true event—four lions escaping from the Baghdad zoo and shot dead by U.S. soldiers after the 2003 U.S. invasion of Iraq—*Pride of Baghdad* gives a number of the young lions like Noor a worldly sensibility. Noor tells an older lion, Safa: "No matter how they treat us, those who would hold us captive are always tyrants" (87).

3. While this collection focuses on multicultural comic books and not comic strips, it is worth noting that artist-authors such as Latino Gus Arriola (*Gordo*, which ran from 1945 to 1986) and African American Jackie Ormes (*Torchy Brown in "Dixie to Harlem,"* which ran from 1937 to 1938, and later *Patty-Jo 'n' Ginger*, which ran from 1945 to 1956)

opened doors to other author-artists who would come after. I think of those author-artists of multicultural comic strips such as African American Barbara Brandon-Croft (*Where I'm Coming From*), Latinos Hector Cantú and Carlos Castellanos (*Baldo*), South Asian "Desi" American Nimesh Patel (*Badmash*), and African American Aaron McGruder (*Boondocks*). Ormes's Patty-Jo and her big sister Ginger were strong and sassy (critical of, for instance, the McCarthy witch hunts) and a first in being examples of an upwardly mobile African American class. For more on Ormes, see Nancy Goldstein's *The First African American Woman Cartoonist*; for more on Arriola as well as Cantú and Castellanos see *Your Brain on Latino Comics*.

4. The same year that Joe Quesada introduced the Marvel world to The Santerians, a Filipino author/artist duo, the Luna Brothers, brought to life a multicultural team of superhero women in their series *Ultra* (2004). The team includes: Chicana Pearl Penalosa as Ultra, Italian American Olivia Arancina as Aphrodite, and Anglo-Texan Jen Pederson as Janu. While each has a set of superpower skills and works for the company Heroine Inc. to serve and protect the people of Spring City, they have everyday worries such as their public poll ratings, securing sponsors, and lining up dates.

5. I mention a history of multicultural superheroes created in the United States. Today, we can see the influence of these superheroes and others in superhero comic books published in Algeria, Tunisia, Syria, Egypt, Iran, India, and the United Arab Emirates. In Algeria, for example, there is author-artist Abd al-Karîm Qâdirî's "Super Dabza," who flies around on a burnoose (a family heirloom from an angelic ancestor to make pilgrimages to Mecca), as well as the author-artist known as "Slim" and his superhero, "Maachou." In Dubai, there's Naif al-Mutawa, who has created the series *The 99*. Each Muslim superhero personifies one of the ninety-nine virtues (wisdom, generosity, etc.) that collectively embody the divine, and they hail from all over the world: Noora, for instance, is from the United Arab Emirates and helps people see the truth in themselves. And AK Comics out of Cairo features larger than life Arab superheroes like a time-traveling pharaoh and an Arabian swordsman. In China there is the comic book series *Great Ten*, which follows the adventures of the Celestial Archer, Mother of Champions, who gives birth to twenty-five super-soldiers every three days.

6. I have mentioned various multicultural characters. However, as some scholars like M. Thomas Inge have pointed out, Marvel and DC have also used a nonacknowledged multiculturalism to infuse their white characters with substance and power. Peter Parker has powers as Spider-Man, but an Afro-Caribbean spider-trickster genealogy is not included in his narrative, for instance. See Inge's *Comics as Culture*.

7. In this interview I conducted with Derek McCulloch, he remarks on how comic books have become less a niche market; while this does not mean that he is able to make a living writing comic books, it does promise to open new doors for exploring all variety of experiences: "Comics are now being taken seriously as both entertainment and literature by a wider cross-section of society than I would have thought possible ten years ago. My hope is that this will result in comics creators taking seriously an ever-wider cross-section of subjects for their work."

8. In an interview, Steve Ross tells how he works within the medium of the comic

book to create iconic characters, adding, though, that he wanted to avoid creating Chesty as a caricature—a woman as stripper as seen in the 1990s avatars of Wonder Woman, Vampirella, and Catwoman. He acknowledges British, Japanese, and American comic book art influences on his pursuit of these goals; of the British he mentions how "the artists have developed a stylistic tradition that includes a lot of detail, densely packed panels, with heavy blacks and shading"; of the Japanese he mentions how the "artists have also created ways of filling in the backgrounds of their black-and-white comics, using everything from the familiar speed lines to pre-fab, stylized patterns and shading"; and of the U.S. art he mentions the "busy work of Harvey Kurtzman's early *Mad* comics" (Aldama interview with Ross, June 5, 2009).

9. In Mexico there has been a long history of the erotic in comic books. Adolfo Mariño's adult *historietas*, such as *Yolanda* and *Picante* (1953), as well as his very popular series (especially with women) *Lagrimas, Risas y Amor (Tears, Laughter, and Love)*, exemplify the tradition. Often, Mariño would use the comic book erotica form not just to turn on his readers, but to explore politics, censorship, and freedom of expression. For more on the erotica generally, see Tim Pilcher's *Erotic Comics;* Pilcher also discusses the eight-page Tijuana Bibles (late 1920s through the 1930s), which depicted cartoon characters like Mickey Mouse, Donald Duck, and Popeye, among others, enjoying rather indecent sexual acts with one another—and in all sorts of compromising positions.

HISTORY, CONCEPTS, and METHODS

1 RACE AND COMIX

LEONARD RIFAS

T HE UNCENSORED STORIES, colloquial dialogue, and caricatured drawings in old underground comix provide a rich and psychemucky vein of
evidence for reimagining what was going through young people's minds during
a pivotal period in American history.[1] Although racial issues were not a central
preoccupation of underground comix, those comix in which race plays a role
shine a lava light on how people were thinking during a confusing turning point
in American race relations, soon after the main legislative victories of the civil
rights movement. At the same time, examining the various images of racial difference that appeared in comix deepens our understanding of the comix themselves. These representations confirm that comix dedicated themselves to the
cause of absolute freedom of expression.

Representations of racial difference in comic books of *any* kind have only
recently begun to receive much serious academic attention. Compared to those
in some other kinds of comic books and cartoons, the images of race in underground comix of the late 1960s and early 1970s do not seem to have been particularly influential, damaging, or important. Nevertheless, the racial images in
underground comix invite closer attention.

The idea that comics *could* influence readers, cause damage, or have importance follows from the principle that media both "reflect and affect" the wider
society. They do, but not in a simple, mechanical way. Comics supply evidence
of widely shared assumptions and also teach particular ways of looking at things.
Dr. Fredric Wertham, an antiracist psychiatrist, made both of these arguments

in the 1950s. He submitted panels from mainstream American comic books as evidence of American racism in one of the court cases that eventually led to the *Brown v. Board of Education* decision in May 1954, which ordered the end of racial segregation in public schools. Wertham's best-known book, *Seduction of the Innocent* (published in April 1954), included an extensive section condemning American comic books for indelibly impressing on their young readers that there exist "natives, primitives, savages, 'ape men,' Negroes, Jews, Indians, Italians, Slavs, Chinese and Japanese, immigrants of every description, people with irregular features, swarthy skins, physical deformities, [or] Oriental features" who are inferior to tall, blond, regular-featured men, and are "suitable victims for slaughter" (101).

Examples can be found without difficulty in early American comic books that show white characters in dominant positions over nonwhite domestics, natives, or sidekicks. Cases in which a white character was dominated by a character who is not white were usually a temporary inversion of the natural order of things that the story shows being put right. Racism was built into the foundations of entire once-popular genres, especially jungle comics (in which white "jungle lords" sometimes punched the faces of African challengers to maintain order in their realms) and war comics (which regularly showed white Americans fighting barbaric Japanese, Korean, or Vietnamese enemies).

Typically, when some comics fan-scholars have raised the issue of racist images in comics, other fan-scholars have interpreted their observations as unwarranted insults against the individual cartoonists who created these images. In the arguments against looking for racist imagery in comics, "racism" exhibits a dual status as something outside the bounds of polite discussion (so that imputing the creation of a racist cartoon to a cartoonist becomes a vile slur), but also as a once-basic assumption of our society (so that any racism found on the page must merely be a "reflection" of the common sense of that period, for which the cartoonist bears no personal responsibility). Underground cartoonists took special pride in operating outside the bounds of polite discussion, but they did so as part of a larger counterculture with multiracial roots that was self-consciously indebted for part of its philosophies, religions, fashions, and music to Native Americans, Asians, and African Americans. This did not free white hippies from myths about noble savages, oriental wisdom, or authentic primitives, but it added to the wide cultural distance between comix artists and racial segregationists.

Scholars who study racial imagery in comix do not merely check for the presence of offensive stereotypes. Comix can use racist stereotypes in various ways with various effects. An antiracist analysis asks where these works stand in relation to struggles to end special privileges based on race and advance the well-being of all people. Taking a critical approach to comics' racial imagery does not imply that comix or comics ideally should be designed as works of do-gooder propaganda or that the content of adult comix should be censored to respect people's "sensitivities." Focusing on comix' racial imagery also does not imply that this approach can be expected to yield the most interesting or important insights into underground comix. I originally undertook this investigation to prepare to discuss underground comix in a college classroom. The first time I lectured about R. Crumb's work, I had observed that his use of old racist images angers and alienates some students. In setting out to explore how comix had represented race, I was not looking for incriminating images to use as evidence against my favorite cartoonists, but rather an explanation that I could offer to those who encounter in these images an obstacle to appreciating these cartoonists' achievements.

To move past moralizing questions about a cartoonist's intentions or individual responsibility (which ordinarily remain both unanswerable and irrelevant to practical antiracist work), it helps to refocus on the larger patterns of cooperation that allow these picture-stories to come into existence and be circulated. We can better understand differences between underground comix and mainstream comic books—including differences in how they represented race—by contrasting how they were created than by speculating about the attitudes of the people who made them.

Generally, mainstream comic books were created by teams of full-time professionals (a writer, a penciller, an inker, a letterer, and a colorist) working for commercial publishers in New York City who sought to maximize sales by releasing titles with continuing characters on a regular schedule for young readers. The mainstream comic book industry developed a self-censorship code, administered by the Comics Code Authority, to protect their businesses from controversy. With this code, mainstream comics publishers bound themselves to limit the graphic depiction of violence, nudity, and suggestiveness, and to never "ridicule or attack . . . any religious or racial group" (quoted in Nyberg, *Seal of Approval,* 173).

By contrast, underground cartoonists usually wrote, drew, and lettered their own pages single-handedly. Sometimes comix creators also served as their own editors, publishers, distributors, and even printers. Most pages were created by amateurs. The underground model's emphasis on freedom of individual expression encouraged a diversity of experiments and viewpoints, including diverse (but usually white) views about racial matters. Comix artists often tried to outdo each other in violating the hated Comics Code's restrictions, including in their stories, for example, recreational drug use, sexual molestation of children, intense disrespect for the police and the president of the United States, and blasphemy. Cartoonists used extreme racial stereotypes in their comix as further demonstrations of this freedom of expression.

Without the constraints of strong editors, an industrial self-censorship code, mainstream distributors or retailers, or organized political guidance, the alternative "system" that comix created cleared an unusually direct path from the fantasies of the individual cartoonist to the published page. The stoned imagination of the artist touched the stoned imagination of the reader.

Current debates over "racism" often seem to come down to a disagreement between those who understand racism primarily as something institutionalized by our social system and those who understand it primarily as something that exists only in the thoughts and actions of individuals. The idea that we live in a racist system seems painfully self-evident to many people. To many others, that idea seems nebulous or false or pernicious. Given the choice between organizing a large-scale coordinated action for institutional change or "dropping out," the comix generation generally opted for individual and communal do-it-yourself solutions. The comix' strongly individualistic, nonrevolutionary bent stood out in contrast to the other radical comics that were available in those years, such as the Maoist propaganda comics booklets imported from China, the educational comic books by Marxist Eduardo del Rio (aka Rius), imported from Mexico, and the cartoons that Emory Douglas was doing as Black Panther Party minister of culture for the party newspaper.

The ethnic and racial identities of the cartoonists, editors, publishers, distributors, and retailers who were responsible for creating and distributing the work, and of the readers who supported them, count as additional production-related factors influencing the ethnic and racial messages of the comix. For example, black cartoonists' strips for black newspapers created more sympathetic black characters than the ones that appeared in the mainstream papers. (In a similar way, underground cartoonists created more sympathetic—though not always "positive"—hippie characters than those that appeared in the daily newspapers.)

Only a few of the cartoonists who did comix were perceived as people of color, and so acknowledging the contributions these men made brings us quickly from generalizations about a "system" and a "movement" to a couple of specific names. Two black cartoonists involved with the comix movement were Larry Fuller in the San Francisco Bay Area and Richard "Grass" Green in the Midwest. In both cases, these were cartoonists who began cartooning with an interest in superheroes, and found in the comix (and, in Green's case, the prior comics fandom that comix grew out of) an opportunity to get their work in print. Once connected with this movement, they turned to creating more provocative and outrageous material.

With the aid of Jay Kennedy's exhaustive cataloguing of the content of underground and newave comix, it becomes possible to reconstruct in detail how underground cartoonists formed into cliques that repeatedly shared pages in the same comic books (which were typically organized as anthologies of short graphic stories), and to distinguish the core members of the comix movement from those on its fringes. Clearly, Larry Fuller participated in comix by carving out his own niche, as an artist, editor, and publisher. After seeing that his superhero comic for black kids (*Ebon*) could not succeed through a distribution system geared toward adult, white readers, he changed over to publishing sex comics. Fuller did not participate in the comix titles organized by others. Grass Green, by contrast, contributed to several anthology comix published by Denis Kitchen in Wisconsin, was published in Los Angeles, and contributed pages to many newave comix after the underground comix distribution channels collapsed.

I have found in my personal collection of underground comix 227 examples of comix stories in which race plays an important role or in which some characters are represented as racially different, most of them in the Nixon years (1968–1974), the period covered in this article. These are from 174 different books, by almost 100 cartoonists. The artists who appear four or more times in this list of examples are Guy Colwell (7 items), R. Crumb (39 items), Dave Geiser (4 items; a large proportion of Geiser's work dealt with race), Justin Green (7), Bill Griffith (6), Jaxon (8), Jay Lynch (7), Trina Robbins (6), Sharon Rudahl (5), Frank Stack (6), and S. Clay Wilson (4).

By far, the most frequently represented racial "Other" was black people (often referred to as "spades"). Identities only rarely encountered in comix included Arabs, Chinese, Japanese, Jews, Indians, Mexicans, Polynesians, Puerto Ricans, and Vietnamese.

The comix movement coalesced out of a shared excitement about the untapped possibilities of cartooning itself, rather than a desire to communicate a particular content. Even when temporarily engaged in an overtly "political" comic book project (for the Berkeley Ecology Center or Students for a Democratic Society, for example, or to support the Chicago Seven), the comix artists did not conform to any politically ordained "correct" line. Indeed, underground comic books typically mocked the New Left, including its concerns over racial stereotyping. For example, in Bobby London's "Why Bobby Seale Is Not Black" (published in *Merton of the Movement* by Last Gasp Eco-Funnies in 1972), London depicts as a humorless drunk the editor of an underground newspaper who tells him that his cartoon of Black Panther Bobby Seale is an insultingly counterrevolutionary racist stereotype. To take another example, Jaxon's "White Man's Burden" condemned ethnic pride movements of Native Americans, Chicanos,

1.1. *"Whiteman," in R. Crumb's* Zap, *issue 1*

and Asian Americans, which had followed the model of the Black Panther Party, as basically just more varieties of racism. The story was published in *Slow Death #6* (Last Gasp, 1974).

Consider the two books that might be said to have launched the movement, R. Crumb's *Zap #1* and Gilbert Shelton's *Feds 'n' Heads*. Both had stories highlighting the racial category of "whites." The first story in *Zap #1* was "Whiteman."

In this story, a conservative, repressed white man encounters minstrelized stereotypes of blacks who offer him a more primitive and fun way of living. The uptight Whiteman spurns their invitation, but the story, expressing the revolutionary optimism of the times, concludes that he'll come around "eventually." The story appears more concerned with psychologically integrating some repressed parts of Whiteman's personality, symbolized by the blackface characters, than with actual interracial relations. In the last story of Shelton's *Feds 'n' Heads*, "The Indian That Came to Dinner," a conventional, liberal white couple invites a very stereotyped (loincloth-and-feather-wearing, tomahawk-carrying, dog-eating) Indian to dinner to celebrate "national-bring-an-Indian-home-to-dinner week." The laconic Indian turns his hosts on to peyote, and this inspires them to go native, ridiculously replacing their clothes with loincloths made out of their towels.

These pathbreaking comix sparked an exceptionally innovative movement, but the accomplishments of the comix were nourished by comix artists' antiquarian love for the works of earlier generations of cartoonists. While reviving lost traditions of American cartooning, comix artists dredged back into circulation racist minstrel stereotypes from the nineteenth and early twentieth centuries. The meanings of and struggles over these old images, however, had been largely forgotten.

The revived stereotypes resembled the flood of images that Americans had used—in magazine cartoons, advertisements, postcards, animated films, and other media—to rationalize slavery, segregation, and imperialism by depicting nonwhite people as childlike, dependent, incapable, and grateful for white control. Taken a few at a time, those old cartoons may seem innocuous or benign. Cumulatively, they had a terrible power. Exaggerating differences between groups makes it easier for privileged groups to act in oppressive ways, and racial caricatures also attack the confidence members of subordinated groups have in themselves as individuals and in each other. After a long struggle, African Americans had largely succeeded in driving the images derived from the "minstrel" tradition from mainstream comics. The old stereotypes had a disturbing half-familiarity when comix resurrected them in the form of parodies, satires, and homages.

Cartoonists often defend the stereotypes in their work by saying that the art of cartooning fundamentally relies on simplification, generalization, distortion, and exaggeration. Caricatures become racist stereotypes, though, when instead of exaggerating an individual's particular features to bring out his or her unique humanity, the cartoonist suppresses the individuality of a person's appearance to bring the portrait into conformity with a preexisting racial stereotype. The clearest example of how this worked in underground comix may be Jay Lynch's character satirizing San Francisco State College's conservative president S. I. Hayakawa as the toothy Professor "Hiacowcow." Professor Hiacowcow looks more like an anti-Japanese cartoon stereotype of the 1940s than a caricature of Hayakawa's own facial features ("Nard 'n' Pat," *Bijou Funnies* #2, 1969). Also, Hiacowcow speaks heavily and implausibly Asian-accented English, although Hayakawa, the butt of this satire, was born and raised in Canada.

Not all comix artists relied on the broken traditions of ethnic caricature, though. Two comix artists, Barney Steel and Guy Colwell, illustrate some of the diversity of opinion that could be found in the comix. Both cartoonists depicted sex and solidarity between blacks and whites, yet Steel and Colwell were far from political comrades.

Barney Steel's *Armageddon* #2 presented a didactic, antiracist fable about a black gold miner and a white logger who each marry worthy partners across racial lines and then form a business partnership, followed immediately by a sex orgy that all four participants freely and explicitly agree to in advance. Steel's tale expressed an anarcho-capitalist-libertarian ideology, largely inspired by the author Ayn Rand.

Steel depicted white and black communities as equally racist, and his individualist "solution" was for people to forget race and drop out of society, returning to an economy based on gold and bartering. He hammered this message home with some of the most wooden dialogue ever seen in comics. Although published by Last Gasp, one of the centrally important comix publishers, Steel's *Armageddon* comics were widely regarded within underground cartoonist circles as bizarrely right-wing.

Guy Colwell, by contrast, was a cartoonist who had spent time in prison for draft resistance and who aligned himself with radical left politics. His *Inner City Romance #1* told the story of three ex-cons (two black and one white), newly released from prison and plunging back into a ghetto milieu of hard drugs and loose sex. Its sympathetic and unflinching portrayal of the black underclass caused many readers (and cartoonists) to initially assume that Colwell was black himself.

Of all the underground cartoonists, black or white, Colwell most successfully communicated the frustration and rage within the inner cities of that era. His story "Choices" in *Inner City Romance #1* presents a protagonist with a choice

1.2. *From Barney Steel's* Armageddon, *issue 2*

between a life of drugs and whores or gunning down the pimps and pushers in the cause of black power. In spite of this false dichotomy, Colwell succeeded better than Steel in drawing and writing convincing stories.

With the increasing use of psychedelics in the late 1960s and early 1970s, comix creators became interested in exploring rather than suppressing their own innermost thoughts. Robert Crumb, for example, let his art become a conduit for whatever was deep and unspoken, regardless of whether what came up made him appear to be a "good person" (*R. Crumb Coffee Table Art Book*, 109). It was in this context that he put on paper the racist imagery that he found "bubbling up" out of him. Later Crumb reflected that "using racist stereotypes, it's boiling over out of my brain, and I just have to draw it! Pour it on as thick as I can and not leave any of the paranoia out. Put it all in there. Hey, in my own defense, I am NOT a racist! Come on!" Crumb could confidently disassociate himself from "racists," while drawing so perfectly the racist stereotypes that he calls "deeply embedded in our culture and our collective subconscious," partly because he had spent his alienated teenage years in a blatantly racist, racially segregated community. In those days, if he expressed his opinion that Negroes were not inferior to white people, classmates would call him a "black tail-licker" (ibid.).

MERELY NOTING THE PRESENCE of images of racial difference fails to account for the ways that cartoonists use these images, which might be satiric, ironic, parodic, or even idiotic. An alternative to the visual search for suspect imagery can be found in listening for the "conversations" that a comic participates in, and how the imagery contributes to them. To illustrate in greater detail how different competing voices can leave their traces even in a single panel of a single comix story, consider Jay Kinney's "New Left Comics." In this story, Kinney satirized the contradictions present in Students for a Democratic Society, the main New Left group, in 1968. The strip portrayed a group that plots "the Revolution," only to see all their plans unravel (except for the bombing, which goes off as scheduled). The panel in which the black revolutionists withdraw from the plan first captured my attention for the diagrammatic clarity with which it illustrates how people invent "races."

It can be hard to shake the commonsense idea that people naturally belong to different races. There is no question that human differences are observable in eye color, hair color, skin color, head shape, blood type, and many other biological dimensions; however, clear-cut boundaries between races do not exist as biological facts. People "construct" racial groups by emphasizing certain features and then exaggerating the differences between people who do or do not have these features, and then minimizing differences *within* those contrasting groups. Many years of cartoon history lie behind Kinney's picture of three

1.3. *Jay Kinney's "New Left Comics," in* Bijou Funnies, *issue 1*

nearly identical black men and a single, higher, larger white man. When we look past the obvious visual stereotypes and listen more closely, though, additional voices become audible in this picture.

Kinney, a recent high school graduate in 1968, a supporter of SDS and of local efforts to integrate housing, remembers the political background of this story as having been the tensions that SNCC and the Black Panther Party had aroused when they "served notice on the white New Left that it should attend to educating its own people" (personal e-mail October 9, 2003). The suppression of black individuality in this panel's caricatures echoes the image of unity and strength that the BPP tried to project with its uniformed "armed police patrols." These patrols—dressed in berets and black leather jackets and brandishing guns—set out with the stated goals of reducing police harassment and raising consciousness. In criticizing this development, the novice cartoonist made a onetime use, which he regards as dubious in retrospect, of incorporating the exaggerated lips from the old minstrel stereotype.

Kinney recalls that these lips had been "inspired in part by Crumb's devil-may-care use of racial stereotypes" (personal e-mail, October 9, 2003). Kinney had found in Crumb's strip "Don't Gag on It, Goof on It" an artistic command: "mock and satirize hypocrisy, cant, self-congratulation, injustice, and so on, wherever you find it." The artist's satirical task became to lay bare and break the taboos of the mainstream and the counterculture, of the left and the right, of sexism, feminism, and racism. The artistic choices in this panel, then, identified the story as an underground comic.

In addition to nineteenth-century whites who darkened their faces with burnt cork and performed as blackface minstrels, the Black Panther armed police patrols, and R. Crumb, another unexpected voice might be echoing through this picture. During this period, the FBI was using forged cartoons (among other tricks) to weaken support for the BPP and to stir up anger between rival groups. In one case, FBI agents got their hands on a coloring book by the BPP artist Michael Teemer—full of pictures of militant blacks killing humanoid pigs—that BPP officials had rejected as inappropriate. The FBI changed the captions to make them more antiwhite and then distributed copies as a BPP publication. It seems possible that this government cartoon disinformation action may have had some influence on the ideas expressed in the Kinney comix story.

The use of cartoons by the government's COINTELPRO campaign against the Black Panther Party brings us to consider the various ways that cartoons can be used. Another unusual and hateful use of blatantly racist cartoons has been to create hostile working environments: to intimidate, harass, or demean fellow workers based on their perceived racial identity. As far as I know, no underground comix have ever been implicated in such cases. The ordinary use of underground comix has been as pleasure reading for adults. Some of them have also been suitable as stroke books.

The meanings of comic book stories do not reside neatly encapsulated inside their panels, but are generated by the encounters between the works and their readers. It would be practically impossible to reconstruct after several decades have intervened how the comix' first readers interpreted them. During those early years of the comix movement, reader responses rarely found their way into print, even in the form of reviews or articles about comix.

A critic can go after the most extreme images and risk wasting time by making a boundary-pushing cartoonist into a scapegoat for a broader social problem, or focus on more everyday kinds of insults, omissions, and distortions, and risk being seen as hypersensitive and "PC." We must ask who, if anyone, do cartoons hurt, how the cartoons hurt them, and what can be done to relieve their suffering. In recent years, the most frequent controversies over racist cartooning have been over material published in college newspapers.

Whether racism remains an important issue in the United States depends on whom you ask. The number of Americans held behind prison walls has skyrocketed from 200,000 in the late 1960s when the comix movement was approaching its brief heyday to more than 2,300,000 today. Thousands of these are African Americans, imprisoned at disproportionate rates for possessing marijuana, a drug that helped to inspire some of the best comix.

To the extent that the underground comix movement had an agenda, it fought for the end of censorship and the revitalization of comic books as an art form.

It was wildly successful in achieving those two goals. For a number of reasons comix did not take up the cause of racial justice, at least not in any sustained, large-scale way. The movement was so small, though, I'm tempted to imagine that if a single comix cartoonist/editor had shown up who was as determined, prolific, and ardent about racial equality as comix artist/editor Trina Robbins was about gender equality, it could have been enough to turn the course of comix history in a different direction. The distance that comix could have gone in that direction, though, was limited. In 1991, Crumb looked back on the collapse of the counterculture and the comix distribution network and remembered that "There was organized, systematic, repressive action taken against every aspect of that outburst against 'the system,' including alternative print media, by the powers, agencies, institutions of the 'corporate state.' . . . They didn't sit back and passively watch while Abbie Hoffman and Huey Newton strutted and fretted their hour upon the stage." This repression succeeded because "the 'folks back home' were fed up. They wanted a crack-down on all this liberal-humanism-permissiveness crap!" (Crumb, *Complete Crumb Comics Volume 7*, vii).

As for how to summarize the evidence comix supply about how young people of the Nixon years were thinking about racial issues, what widely shared assumptions they reveal, and what particular lessons they taught, the examples resist summarization. Although not reflecting a complete range of opinions and not created by a demographically representative sample of young people, the comix approximated a free marketplace of ideas. Some of the images published in comix will surely remain as obstacles to some people's appreciation of that movement. In relation to the struggle to end racism, underground comix' most valuable legacy may have been their reinvention of comics as a medium of self-expression. Their example eventually evolved into the "graphic novel," a form through which an increasingly diverse group of creators has been able to add their stories to our common body of knowledge as American continues to wrestle with questions concerning racial inequality and the dream of a fair and free society.

- -

NOTES

1. This essay is adapted from "Racial Imagery, Racism, Individualism, and Underground Comix," *ImageText: Interdisciplinary Comics Studies* 1, no. 1 (2004) <http://www .english.ufl.edu//imagetext/archives/v1_1/rifas/print.shtml>.

2 "AUTHENTIC" LATINAS/OS AND QUEER CHARACTERS IN MAINSTREAM AND ALTERNATIVE COMICS

JONATHAN RISNER

I N MAY OF 2006, DC Comics announced with fanfare that two well-established superheroes, Blue Beetle and Batwoman, would undergo a metamorphosis of identities and be recast as a Latino teenager and a lipstick lesbian, respectively. Doubtless a move to capture emerging niche markets, DC Comics' decision came on the heels of the most recent visual depictions of Latina/o and queer characters on popular television programs such as *Ugly Betty*, *Dog Whisperer*, and *The L Word*. In addition, in 2006 media coverage of immigrant marches and same-sex marriages in the United States compounded the visibility of Latinas/os and homosexuals beyond the pop culture sphere and provided a backdrop to DC Comics' announcement.

Blue Beetle and Batwoman hardly qualify as the first Latina/o and queer characters to grace the panels of a comic. For the past twenty-seven years in the underground title *Love and Rockets*, the story line of Jaime Hernandez's *Las Locas*, also known as *Hoppers 13*, has related the adventures of young Chicanas/os in the fictional town of Hoppers, or Huerta, California. *Las Locas* often revolves around the intermittent romance between Margarita Luisa "Maggie" Chascarrillo and Esperanza "Hopey" Leticia Glass and largely forgoes superhero crusades, even sometimes playfully parodying the genre. Anchored by a punk aesthetic, the queer and Latina/o content of *Las Locas* contrasts with that of *Blue Beetle* and Batwoman. Differences in production, authorship, characterization, themes, and aesthetics highlight the distinct portrayals of Latina/o and queer characters in the alternative (Fantagraphics) and mainstream (DC and Marvel) comics addressed here.

Comparative readings of *Las Locas, Blue Beetle,* and Batwoman allow one to ask questions about Latina/o and/or queer authenticity insofar as the comics are aligned with particular identities—*latinidad* and queer.[1] In other words, does a particular comic hew closer to a Latina/o or queer aesthetic and, if so, on what basis does one conceive an idealized Latina/o and/or queer aesthetic? Or, alternatively, should questions of authenticity simply remain irrelevant at the risk of essentialism? Reading *Las Locas* alongside *Blue Beetle* and Batwoman ultimately asks whether representations of Latinas/os and queer characters can coexist in a comic universe without notions or models of authenticity against which readers may measure a Latina/o and/or queer character—underground or mainstream, superhero or otherwise.

In this essay, I will limit my analysis to a handful of trade paperbacks and issues originally published during or before 2006. In the case of *Las Locas,* I will examine the content from the recent compilations of Hernandez's work that span the period from the early 1980s until 1996—*Maggie the Mechanic* (2007), *The Girl from H.O.P.P.E.R.S.* (2007), and *Perla la Loca* (2007)—concentrating mainly on *Maggie the Mechanic.* In the case of *Blue Beetle,* I will confine myself to the collection of the first six issues entitled *Shellshocked* (2006). Finally, my close reading of Batwoman will focus on her brief debut in issue #7 of 52. Inevitably, some of Hernandez's work escapes these titles, and Blue Beetle and Batwoman have developed since their respective premieres. Circumscribing my scope, however, allows for a closer examination and will, I hope, facilitate a reader's search if he or she should elect to consult the primary materials.

I begin with a survey of the Latina/o and queer content in the aforementioned titles, starting with the work of Jaime Hernandez, to whom I will refer by first name to avoid confusion with his brother, Gilbert. Comic critics and the occasional academic rightfully laud *Love and Rockets.* Douglas Wolk reserves a spot for the work of Los Bros. Hernandez, as Jaime and Gilbert are sometimes collectively called, in his *Reading Comics,* and José David Saldívar, writing in 1991, pegged the duo as "the most widely read Chicano writers in America" ("Postmodern Realism," 539). For the past twenty-seven years, Jaime and Gilbert, with occasional help from their younger brother, Mario, have drawn and written *Love and Rockets.* Jaime and Gilbert refrain from collaboration, instead opting for an auteur approach, developing their own story lines in the worlds of Huerta/Hoppers (Jaime) and Palomar (Gilbert), and beyond. A motley cast populates Jaime's work, from dinosaurs and pioneer riot grrrls to *luchadoras* and well-heeled elderly women with fetishes for young women dressed in children's clothes. (See *Perla la Loca.*)

Love and Rockets abounds in queer content, characters, and story lines, some of which approach the outlandish; the aforementioned elderly women's fetish being a prime example. While Jaime's occasional tangents develop characters that previously seemed minor, the relationship between Maggie and Hopey permits a window into the depiction of queer themes in his work. Hopey and Maggie possess fluid sexualities. One reads of Hopey's various flings usually with other women, although she gives birth to a child after a one-night escapade with a male bandmate on a drunken whim (*The Girl*, 247–248). Maggie contends with crushes and relationships with both men and women, but still reserves a special intimacy for Hopey. Jaime typically portrays Maggie and Hopey's relationship with ambiguity as if toying with a reader's possibly prurient curiosities, even embodying those curiosities in characters who speculate about the nature of Maggie and Hopey's relationship. For instance, Doyle and Ray, the latter of whom is Maggie's boyfriend prior to suffering a tragic death, contemplate Maggie's sexuality (*The Girl*, 149), and, at the opening of an installment of *Las Locas* in *Maggie the Mechanic*, Isabel Maria Ortiz Ruebens, who is a nun at the time, provides a page-long synopsis of Maggie's character enviously characterizing her relationship with Hopey:

> This is Maggie my friend. . . . She's only five foot tall, has a cute face and ass, is kind of naïve about things, and lives with her best friend Hopey, who is just as cute, a little rebellious, and is even shorter. They live in a small run-down apartment in a Mexican neighborhood, always without food, months behind on rent, and rumor has it they're lesbians. How perfect can you get? (*Maggie the Mechanic*, 113)

Jaime appears to frustrate the reader who may be curious about Maggie and Hopey's relationship, often forgoing any panel that could visually dispel or countenance rumors (i.e., through a sexual act). The absence of a visual depiction of sex between Maggie and Hopey may suggest self-censorship or cold feet on the part of Jaime. And yet, Jaime undermines such an idea and indeed portrays Maggie and Hopey's sexual intimacy, albeit sparingly (see image 2.1). In "Locas vs. Locos" in *The Girl from H.O.P.P.E.R.S.*, Maggie and Hopey make love after Maggie alludes to how the two "haven't j'gged for an awful long time" (65). Only years later does Jaime again show Hopey and Maggie making love.

Setting aside its queer content, Latina/o, or more specifically Chicana/o, elements saturate *Las Locas*, a conscious move on the artist's part. For Jaime, "Our Chicano culture is so rich and has so much to offer. . . . Whether [readers] understand it or not, the comics aim to communicate a vision of the Chicano community so readers can see what it's all really about" (Aldama, "Jaime

2.1. *From* The Girl from H.O.P.P.E.R.S. *In the top series of panels, Jaime Hernandez refrains from showing a sexually explicit act between Maggie and Hopey. Hernandez could appear to frustrate a reader's curiosity about the nature of Maggie and Hopey's relationship or be engaging in self-censorship. Later in the same story line, Hernandez takes a different tack.*

Hernandez," 124). Chicana/o characters abound in Jaime's stories, allowing for diversity among individuals. Jaime typically recounts the adventures of a group of Chicanas he calls Las Locas, who include Margarita Luisa Chascarrillo (Maggie), Esperanza Leticia Glass (Hopey), Isabel Maria Ortiz Ruebens (Izzy), and Beatríz Garcia (Penny), embodying different styles such as goth (Izzy) and punk (Maggie and Hopey). *Luchadoras* (female wrestlers) of the likes of Rena Titañon, Maggie's aunt, and a long cast of Chicanos as *luchadores* (male wrestlers), punks, and *cholos* (gang members) populate Barrio Huerta and beyond. Chicanas/os are not the sole ethnicity depicted; Asians, African Americans, and Anglo-Americans, among other groups, enter Jaime's universe.

Besides the mere presence of Chicanas/os, code-switching between Spanish and English deepens the Chicana/o dimension of Jaime's work, reflecting the Chicana/o barrio in which Jaime grew up. For Juan Bruce-Novoa, code-switching makes up a crucial facet of a Chicana/o aesthetic and identity. Bruce-Novoa argues:

> Language is the best example of the intercultural space [between Mexican and U.S. cultures]. . . . There are certain grammatical usages, words, and connotations, spellings which to a native speaker of Spanish or English, or to the true bilingual, appear to be mistakes, cases of code switch-

ing or interference in linguistic terms, but which to the Chicano native speaker are common usages, the living reality of an interlingual space. (*Chicano Poetry*, 12–13)

While English predominates, a Chicana/o interlingual space between two larger cultures—Mexican and U.S.—exists in the narration and dialogue in Jaime's work and comes through in code-switching. In *Maggie the Mechanic*, characters occasionally greet one another with "Órale," a term sometimes translated as "Wow!" or "Right on!" (22), and characters at times refer to one another with epithets such as "gabacha" (white girl) (234), "chuca" (Mexican American girl) (234), and "huera" (light-skinned girl) (234). Jaime lends a degree of realism to his portrayal of Chicana/o culture by leaving untranslated some of the Spanish, while at other times providing a glossary at the bottom of each page in which Spanish appears. In several instances, Hernandez encloses in brackets words appearing in dialogue bubbles to signal that they are spoken in Spanish.

Chicana/o characters and code-switching speak to deeper elements of a Chicana/o identity insofar as those elements are embedded in a community, Barrio Huerta. When Jaime does not recount Maggie's adventures in a foreign land, Barrio Huerta functions as a backdrop for the daily lives of all the characters. One sees communal spaces: sidewalks, beaches, athletic fields, and punk rock venues. Jaime, as touched upon above, models Barrio Huerta after the Chicana/o neighborhood in which he grew up. Through *Maggie the Mechanic*, one peers into a community or barrio and not merely into one character's life.

The commitment Jaime makes to portraying a Chicana/o community recalls Raúl Homero Villa's notions of community consciousness and *barriology* in *Barrio-Logos*, a historical and anthropological account of the cultural practices that emerged from Chicana/o barrios in the face of legal disenfranchisement of Mexican immigrants and Chicanos/as. Villa defines barriology as "a playful but serious promotion of the cultural knowledge and practices of the barrio" (7). Barriology is often performed in opposition to external barrioization, practices by the dominant white population to displace and spatially manage populations of Mexican immigrants and Chicanos/as, such as zoning laws. Though Jaime's stories do not necessarily respond directly to external barrioization, his work foregrounds a Chicana/o barrio in a humorous and sometimes critical manner. Jaime has commented, "I've made it my job to make everybody understand [Chicana/o culture] without watering it down and without trying to protect the reader's feelings" (Aldama, "Jaime Hernandez," 124). The artist thus prizes communicating a Chicana/o cultural knowledge that emerges from his personal experiences in Oxnard, California. Even if the focus lingers on Maggie and Hopey, Jaime's stories encompass an entire community, thus placing the majority of his stories squarely in the realm of barriology.

Huerta's punk rock clubs in Jaime's work broach the historical significance of punk in Southern California and merit special attention in a discussion about authenticity, sexuality, and Chicanas. For Jaime, the culture in Oxnard was "where punk and *cholo* culture came together" (Aldama, "Jaime Hernandez," 121). While the amalgam's *chola/o* ingredient does not necessarily inform a dynamic of fluid sexual identities among female characters in Jaime's work, punk does. Writing on the role of Chicanas in the vibrant Los Angeles punk scene in the late 1970s and early 1980s, Michelle Habell-Pallán writes how "women experienced the punk scene as a liberating space where the lines between gender and race were easily, if temporarily, blurred" (*Loca Motion*, 157). Such blurring holds true throughout Jaime's work, and a punk attitude empowers many female characters. At work and in their relationships with family and friends, Las Locas are strong female characters who often clash with patriarchal structures and defy gender expectations. Powerful *luchadoras* are a common sight in Jaime's work, and Maggie works at times as a mechanic, a vocation for which her male coworkers and girlfriends sometimes chide her. Authority is invariably represented as male, and perhaps best captured by Hopey's graffiti art aimed at sadistically spiting Officer Sado (*Maggie*, 153–154). Punk provides a space for the complex representation of gender and sexuality in light of Maggie and Hopey's relationship and activities. Both characters are avid punk fans who regularly attend shows, and, in Hopey's case, play in bands and tour.

Punk at least partially characterizes the production and aesthetics of Jaime Hernandez's work. First, insofar as a do-it-yourself production can be aligned with punk, Jaime, as does his brother, Gilbert, writes, draws, and inks his own comics. This production dynamic differs from the assembled team of artists and writers who produce *Blue Beetle* and Batwoman. The images in *Las Locas* are invariably black-and-white, recalling the zine culture that evolved around some punk subcultures. The black-and-white images differ, of course, with the glossy color finish one sees in most mainstream comics. If punk rock was a reaction to the pop music excesses of the 1970s (Reyes and Waldman, *Land of a Thousand Dances*, 135), *Love and Rockets'* stripped-down illustrations follow that same impulse as a departure from mainstream color comics at the time.

The black-and-white images may also speak to a Chicana/o aesthetic based upon the notion of *rasquachismo*. Tomás Ybarra-Fausto explains *rasquachismo* and links it with Teatro Campesino, an artistic endeavor crucial to the Chicana/o civil rights movement: "The Teatro Campesino was also the genesis of what is known as rasquachismo, an underclass sensibility rooted in everyday linguistic practices and in artistic works put together out of whatever was

2.4. *From* Shellshocked. *This perspective of Blue Beetle shows various accoutrements of his costume.*

to his predecessors. Moreover, dressing a Latino character as an insect can be linked with a history of Latina/o cultural production such as Oscar Zeta Acosta's *Revolt of the Cockroach People* and Lalo Alcaraz's comic strip *La Cucaracha*.[2]

Considering Blue Beetle's costume, his mask marks him as Latino. The character's main penciller, Cully Hamner, assigns a particular significance to Blue Beetle's mask. The final pages of *Shellshocked* contain several rough sketches of Blue Beetle with Hamner's notes explaining the design of Blue Beetle's costume. Above one sketch of Blue Beetle's head, Hamner writes, "Mask suggests a sort-of Mexican wrestler motif" (Giffen, Hamner, and Rogers, *Blue Beetle: Shellshocked*, 140). *Lucha libre*, otherwise known as professional wrestling in the United States, commands an immense audience in Mexico, as well as among Latinas/os in the United States. As Paul Allatson notes, the sport-spectacle is "screened regularly on Spanish language television in the USA" (*Key Terms*, 145). Blue Beetle's mask, like Jaime Reyes's last name, marks the character as Latino. Finally, although not visible, an additional transnational dimension of Blue Beetle appears in the form of the scarab that latches onto Jaime Reyes's spine. Although unverified by Blue Beetle's creator, the scarab seems at least partially inspired by Mexican director Guillermo del Toro's *Cronos* (1993), "a third-world vampire movie" in del Toro's words, in which a man-made scarab plays a prominent role in the plot. Blue Beetle, in turn, embodies an amalgam of Mexican and Latina/o pop cultural artifacts.

Elsewhere in *Shellshocked*, *latinidad* manifests itself in other ways. The names of characters—Paco, Bonita, Alina, and Esteban—point to a cast of Latinas/os. In fact, with the exception of border guards and some villains, the characters in *Shellshocked* are almost entirely Latina/o. Reminiscent of Jaime Hernandez's work, code-switching between English and Spanish also infuses the comic with a veneer of *latinidad*. Throughout *Shellshocked*, numerous characters intersperse Spanish phrases and slang in their conversations. Jaime's parents refer to him as "mi hijo" (*Shellshocked*, 14, 48), Paco calls Brenda "chica" (10), and Brenda calls Paco "Pendejo" (23). Such words perhaps do not constitute the widest register of English-Spanish code-switching, but the mixture of the two languages still figures into the narrative. Finally, the story's setting in El Paso gives the reader a window into a border milieu, not an uncommon setting for a Latina/o work of fiction, and permits an exploration of issues typically associated with the U.S.-Mexico border, a topic discussed below.

Although Jaime Reyes at first vacillates about assuming a superhero's identity, Blue Beetle is unabashedly a superhero comic. Blue Beetle rights wrongs,

2.5. From Shellshocked. *Violence unfolds at the El Paso–Ciudad Juárez border checkpoint (notice the "MEX" in the smaller panel on the left). One sees the ridiculous dialogue of the monster-villain and a comic aesthetic that differs from that of Jaime Hernandez. The near lack of gutters and the cluttered imposition of smaller panels on top of a larger one lend a quick pace to the reading and, along with the onomatopoeia, give the fight a frenetic pace.*

and disposes of bad guys, albeit oftentimes in the nicest of ways. The steady stream of action and the general lack of gutters between panels make for a fast-paced read. The lines are smooth, and characters appear much more expressive than in 52, but less so than in *Love and Rockets*. While some villains speak as if they stepped out of a medieval text—"Demon! King of Lies, Get thee behind me!" (*Shellshocked*, 110)—the dialogue is usually infused with humor and playfulness.

Blue Beetle's superhero status should not disqualify the comic from addressing complex issues and attending to a spectrum of topics relevant to *latinidad*. In just the first six issues of the series, the comic tackles Latina/o gangs, generational and assimilation issues within some Latina/o families, nativism among U.S. citizens, the trafficking of immigrants, and the militarization and politics of the El Paso–Ciudad Juárez border. Soon after he acquires his powers, the Posse, a gang of Latina/o youths who possess superhuman qualities, confronts Jaime. The Posse, with which Jaime/Blue Beetle later allies himself, is less a gang than a group organized to protect itself against the bounty hunters of La Dama, a figure whose economic ventures are at times less than ethical. In terms of generational relations, Jaime's conversations with his dad reflect the disparities in Spanish-English proficiencies that can exist within Latina/o families. While Jaime's dad speaks English, his command of the language does not equal that of his son. The trafficking of immigrants also figures into *Shellshocked* as one of La Dama's business ventures. While her character remains concealed from Jaime, he learns from the Posse that La Dama amassed a fortune and "Started financing coyotes, ran a border bank sending money back and forth for illegals, [and] built that up into real money" (*Shellshocked*, 105).

Shellshocked at times treats nativism and the militarization of the border in the same breath. After a one-year hiatus during which Blue Beetle fought a giant satellite only to be abandoned by his superhero comrades, he returns to Earth to reestablish his relationship with his family and friends, Paco and Brenda. Jaime's superhero capacities enable him to locate Paco at the El Paso–Ciudad Juárez border. Upon arriving in costume, Blue Beetle fights off La Dama's minions, who try to capture Paco and Damper, a member of the Posse, which Paco has also joined. Blue Beetle has little trouble disposing of La Dama's suited henchmen. Yet, as Homeland Security guards arrest La Dama's bounty hunters, one of the men comments to Blue Beetle: "We'll be out before they finish booking you. Your kind aren't as welcome as they used to be" (ibid., 67). Within the context of the comic, the remark speaks to the general populace's reception of superheroes as reckless. Yet, given the historical and political moment of the comic in 2006, such a remark echoes the sentiments of nativists resentful of Latinas/os, who, whether U.S. citizens or not, may be perceived as immigrant (read: not white).

Having amassed evidence from the three different comics, we can begin to investigate notions of authenticity as they relate to tropes, authors, and setting. All the comics include queer and Latina/o identifiers that are recognizable to readers. As Isabel Molina Guzmán comments, "Latinidad is a performative and performed dynamic set of popular signs associated with Latinos/as and Latino/a identity. Common signifiers of Latinidad are language, linguistic accents, religious symbols, tropical and spicy foods, and brown skin as a phenotypic marker of racial identity" ("Mediating *Frida*," 235). Likewise, with the notion of queerness, common themes and tropes such as a lipstick lesbian function so that one may recognize *what is* queer. With an index of queer and Latina/o identifiers, those who consider themselves members of queer or Latina/o communities may use such tropes to self-identify. These same identifiers likewise enable comic artists, novelists, and filmmakers, among others, both within and outside of queer and Latina/o communities, to produce expressions of queerness and/or *latinidad*, even placing a work in the mainstream for mass consumption.

Questioning the authenticity of a work based on authorship is tempting. The creative teams behind *Love and Rockets*, *Blue Beetle*, and Batwoman may or may not be Latina/o and/or queer. For instance, does the fact that Jaime Hernandez is married to a woman disqualify him from portraying lesbians? Does the ostensible absence of a Latina/o artist on the team behind *Blue Beetle: Shellshocked* disqualify them from producing representations of Latina/o characters? To put it more succinctly, who can traffic in Latina/o and queer tropes and stereotypes?

Pondering a comic's setting provides a more concrete perspective on the question of authenticity. Jaime Hernandez's work emerges from his personal experience in a Chicana/o barrio, which informs his depictions of Huerta. As readers, we trust in the realism of his depictions based on an autobiographical element. In the case of *Blue Beetle: Shellshocked*, the dynamic of place and author changes. In an interview, when asked if *Blue Beetle* will feature scenes from El Paso, Cully Hamner responds: "Yes! There are a few little things in there that I hope people in El Paso will notice, though I won't say what. On the other hand, I've never been to Texas, so I'm relying on internet [*sic*] research. Hopefully, I won't make any glaring mistakes. But yeah, keep your eyes open!" (Offenberger, "Who's That Bug?"). Hamner's connection to El Paso is tenuous at best, which undermines the realism of the depictions of El Paso, and perhaps begins to erode the plausibility of characters who populate the comic's landscape. But does this make Blue Beetle any less Latina/o than *Love and Rockets*? Or, should there be a separate category created for Latina/o comic characters drawn by non-Latina/o artists? Such a move would in turn create a separate category of Latina/o comics based on the author's identity.

How can readers, especially non-Latinas/os and/or non-queer consumers, evaluate queer and/or Latina/o content except against some other standard, such as other forms of cultural expression or even reality? In terms of cultural production, would this be the job of a canon of queer and Latina/o literature, film, television programs, and perhaps eventually comics? Authenticity may be best left as an open debate within communities of readers and scholars. To institutionalize criteria for Latina/o and/or queer figures in cultural production would effectively fix terms that, while problematic at times, provide a pluralistic space for diverse and evolving identities.[3] Arlene Dávila's *Latinos, Inc.*, a study of marketing to Latinas/os, evidences the real-world problems inherent in notions of authenticity and fixing a conception of *latinidad*. Dávila describes how companies attempt to market their product through figures who possess a "generic Latino 'look'" (110) that is essentially white and eventually elides any specificity to *latinidad*, in terms of ethnicity.

In the world of comics, to point to a single character and deem him or her the *real* Latina/o, or the *real* queer figure, undermines the openness of the terms Latina/o and queer. As new characters emerge from both underground and mainstream comics, figures such as Maggie and Hopey, Blue Beetle, and Batwoman compose a multiplicity of Latina/o and queer characters. To leave the task of representing a queer and/or Latina/o identity to one comic character, whether a Chicana punk or a mainstream superhero dressed in tights or an evening dress, as with Batwoman, is simply too much to ask. And yet, the emergence of Latina/o and queer characters must undergo some scrutiny that should itself be fluid and open without any fixed criteria. Anyone aware of the historical and still contemporary (mis)representation of homosexuals and Latinas/os in media such as television and Hollywood films understands the need to ascertain and contemplate ideas of authenticity; comics should be put to the same test.

NOTES

1. I am using the term *latinidad*, as conceived by Frances Aparicio and Susana Chávez-Silverman in *Tropicalizations*, to refer to a pluralistic and fluid conception of what constitutes Latina/o in terms of race, ethnicity, national origin, sexuality, gender, etc. *Latinidad* in this instance also alludes to conceptions of Latina/o emerging from Latinas/os themselves, and a more hegemonic strain in which "the images are superimposed onto both Latin American and U.S. Latino subjects by the dominant sector" (15).

2. Acosta's novel *Revolt of the Cockroach People* (1973) is a fictional account of the Chicano Moratorium that took place on August 29, 1970. The author's label "cockroach

people" refers to U.S. society's undesirables, among whom Acosta included Chicanos. Lalo Alcaraz's *La Cucaracha* appears in several publications, including the *LA Weekly*. He has published several compilations of his work, including *La Cucaracha*.

3. In *Queer Latinidad*, Juana María Rodríguez separately mines the terms queer and *latinidad* and underscores their critical and open nature. For Rodríguez, by wielding the term "queer," one attends to a "breaking down of categories, questioning definitions, and giving them new meaning, moving through spaces of understanding and dissension, working through the critical practice of 'refusing explication'" (24). "Queer" thus functions here as a critical tool that destabilizes fixed paradigms. *Latinidad* "contains within it the complexities and contradictions of immigrations, (post)(neo)colonialism, race, color, legal status, class, nation, language, and the politics of location" (10).

3

NATIVE AMERICAN NARRATIVES FROM EARLY ART TO GRAPHIC NOVELS

How We See Stories / Ezhi-g'waabamaanaanig Aadizookaanag

MARGARET NOORI

Mr. Bloomfield, gaa gegoo noongo aapji nd'anokiisii.
Mr. Bloomfield, I am not really doing anything today.
Ndo'zhitoon maanda "record" weshki-bmaadzijig ji-noondmowaad.
I am making this "record" for the young people to hear.

—ANDREW MEDLER, Anishinaabe storyteller,
to linguist Leonard Bloomfield, 1938

If my work as an artist has somehow helped to open doors between our peo-
ple and the nonnative community, then I am glad. I am even more deeply
pleased if it has helped to encourage the young people that have followed
our generation to express their pride in our heritage more openly, more joy-
fully than I would have ever dared to think possible.

—DAPHNE ODJIG, Anishinaabe artist, 2002

All these stories are based on the Seven Grandfathers. The Seven Grand-
fathers are virtues we all live by, such as Love, Wisdom, Respect, Humility,
Courage, Honesty and Truth. I really needed to create a book that shares
with the universal audience, a better understanding of what native people
are really about. Not just warriors or the side-kick that most non-aboriginal
artists and writers create when they are writing about Native people in pop
culture stories.

—CHAD SOLOMON, Anishinaabe graphic novelist, 2006

NATIVE AMERICANS TODAY are more than warriors and sidekicks, just as comic characters are more than superheroes and villains. The old dichotomies of understanding once dominant in America are being subtly revised by graphic storytellers. Blending ancient and modern ideas, writers, pencillers, inkers, and colorists offer lessons in history, philosophy, language, and culture. In 1938, when Anishinaabe storyteller Andrew Medler made a record of events for future generations, he offered images through narrative. Later in the same century, Daphne Odjig painted images to "open doors" for young people by helping them see the stories of their culture on canvas. And today, the tradition of telling stories through pictures continues in comics as Chad Solomon and others work to provide a more complex understanding of native people's identity and experience. By connecting oral, visual, and literary tradition, the creators of comic books contribute to the landscape of Native American literature in a way that should not be ignored.

To do justice to the details found in comics by and about Native Americans, the definition of "Native American literature" needs to be understood in the context of 1,681 sovereign nations now situated within the borders of the United States, in Canada, and in Central and South America.[1] There was a time when simply acknowledging these alter nations—their alternate epistemologies, and narrative structures grounded in oral traditions rather than writing—was enough. Most often, this was done en masse without any attempt to comprehend the full range of diversity and complexity in language and culture. Token texts were used primarily to situate the voice of the "Native" in America and in the colonial or contemporary literary canon. Often, the criticism focused on the comparison of Native versus non-Native ways of storytelling. As Robert Parker indicates in his 2003 book *The Invention of Native American Literature*, the time for introductory space-clearing has passed. We need to rethink the definition of Native American literature and consider new forms of methodology. One approach to redefining Native literature, but by no means the only approach, is to look more closely at subsets of this canon. Who was telling stories and preserving history in the 1700s, or the 1800s? Who were the translators? In what forms can narratives be constructed—aural, visual, textual? How can early images be connected to contemporary combinations of image and narrative?

To do this we must rely on geopolitical and linguistic identities. By mapping communities according to definitions that existed prior to missionaries and Manifest Destiny, readers can overcome some of the colonial limitations imposed by always seeing "Native American literature" as the merged and muted voice of all natives in the Americas. In fact, the term "native" would only strictly be applicable during the time of colonization, when foreigners were a group separate from the aboriginal people already living on the continents. One reason to use tribal and national identities as designations is to make clear that the defining characteristics of the literature are based on more than the preexisting presence of a group. Subsets based on language and indigenous cartography group such various mediums as fiction, art, and comics more effectively. Imagine, for instance, how difficult it would be to construct a syllabus for a one-semester course titled "Poetry, Drama, and Literature Foreign to the Americas through the Ages." Although it might be a wonderful introduction to viewing the world from a less colonial and industrial perspective, it would also be extremely difficult to select just a few texts to represent the narrative art of so many cultures and time periods. No doubt, students would be eager for additional courses grouped by gender, genre, nation, century, and so on. Tribe-specific literary courses most definitely do not replace the survey courses, just as national pride does not preclude one from being a fully participating global citizen, but drawing the lines differently sometimes can produce new results.

The storytellers, artists, and graphic novelists discussed throughout this particular essay live in Anishinaabeg Akiing/Anishinaabe Land. The very etymology of the term Anishinaabe, meaning "First Man,"[2] implies a localized relationship between land and humanity. Stories of origin cite the waters and rocks of the Great Lakes region in North America as the birthplace of the Anishinaabeg people. For this reason, some of the oldest tales have more in common with global indigenous literature than literature produced by immigrants and heirs to the fruits and failures of French, British, American, and Canadian nation-building. This history forces readers to consider the various periods of Anishinaabe literature. Precontact images and narratives belong to the Early period. Then, between the arrival of French-speaking Jesuits in the mid-1400s and the period of war and decline in the middle of the 1700s, there are several centuries when Niswi Shkode Bimaadzijig/the Three Fires Confederacy flourished in places now known as Ontario, Quebec, Manitoba, Saskatchewan, Alberta, Michigan, Wisconsin, Minnesota, and North Dakota. This era falls after the dawn of Anishinaabe literature and therefore could not correctly be considered Early. It also exists prior to the eras aptly designated as Colonial, Post-National, and Modern times in either the United States or Canada. The most accurate adjective is "confederate," considering the strength and dominance of the Three Fires Confederacy at the time. During this Confederate period, many sociolinguistic, aesthetic, and stylistic changes must have taken place. Detailing some of those changes is a topic for another day. However, it is important to note there was a time when polyglots traded furs for guns and spices, and most likely traded stories with people from far, far away. When oral tradition became crowded by and compared to Roman, Greek, and European literature, assimilation began and early oral narratives grew more distant. To forget this period is as erroneous as moving directly from Anne Bradstreet to Maya Angelou without mentioning any of the voices between them.

The Three Fires Confederacy, which still has an international presence today, consists of over two hundred individual Anishinaabe nations variously known as Odawa (or Ottawa), Ojibwe, Chippewa, Salteaux, and Potawatomi. The language used in all of these communities is one of twenty-seven Algonquian languages and is most frequently referred to by speakers as "Anishinaabemowin." Moving from the study of all Native American literature to the study of literature created by people who speak Anishinaabe allows further categorization based on Early, Confederate, Colonial, Post-National, and Modern periods.[3] Adding this historical context shows more clearly how stories from vastly different times are connected by language and culture. In fact, the task of retaining Anishinaabe identity and transferring Anishinaabe knowledge is one of the primary goals of stories told in images, text, or a combination of both. Rather than view Anishinaabe literature against the background of American and Canadian nation-building, we can view it as part of Anishinaabe Confederate deconstruction and reconstruction.

By selecting a specific location and language, readers are also asked to rethink the words "American" and "Native," which are, of course, American English terms for diverse groups of people. Sorting out the legal and vernacular naming conventions that are the product of colonization and assimilation is no small task and, in the case of many nations and language groups, has not yet been done for a modern reading audience. For instance, author Louise Erdrich is often cited as a member of the Turtle Mountain Band of "Chippewa" Indians. One of her books is titled *Books and Islands in "Ojibwe" Country*. Three other titles by Erdrich contain extensive glossaries of "Ojibwa" terms.[4] Basil Johnston was described by HarperCollins on his own book jacket as "one of the few speakers of the ancient Ojibway (Chippewa) language," casting him more as a part of a distant past than a leading educator whose visionary work will influence the distant future.[5] Understanding ethnic and linguistic descriptions as related to one another, and distinct from "Native American," is important.

Knowing the language was not written by many native speakers until the mid-1900s and that there is still not a common writing system is equally important for reading older texts, as well as modern comics. The oral tradition, rather than being romanticized as a signifier of illiteracy or preliteracy, can be recast as an alternate means of narrative transmission. In short, if centuries of Anishinaabe were able to develop and deploy a complex agglutinative structure made mostly of verbs to communicate images, ideas, and relationships across time, there must then be a way of interpreting them based on more than printed and published texts. Furthermore, the layered construction of the sound and meaning is perfectly suited to the comic format, where text, line, and color combine to communicate action and relationships.

To begin exploring connections between early visual work and modern

Anishinaabe literature, we must read narrative as more than literary production. Anishinaabe stories can be viewed from multiple angles, using the descriptive terminology of visual art and graphic novels. According to artist and critic Scott McCloud, comics are "juxtaposed pictorial and other images in deliberate sequence, intended to convey information and/or to produce an aesthetic response" (McCloud, *Understanding Comics: The Invisible Art*, 1993, 20). McCloud's own opus of sequential art in comic book format illustrates his point that "comics offer tremendous resources to all writers and artists" because sequential art has "range and versatility with all the potential imagery of film and painting plus the intimacy of the written word" (212). Not only are comics rich with potential in their own right, they are historically one of the original formats of native narrative.

While it is considered inappropriate to provide lengthy descriptions or reproductions of them, it is well known that the traditional method of instruction in the Anishinaabe Midewiwin Lodge is based on cartography, cosmological charts, and two-dimensional drawings.[6] The medium of these lessons could be sand, bark, or stone, and all were considered no more than a repository for mnemonic notes due to their ultimate impermanence.[7] These early images were clearly an important form of communication. Perhaps they were signifiers that functioned like street signs, brand logos, song lyrics, editorial cartoons, or haiku, but they were irrefutably meaningful images created by people who traveled by canoe, hunted, stood together with one another for various reasons, and had a need to depict creatures not found in nature.[8] There is precious little evidence of the exact shape and sound of precontact Anishinaabe narrative that has not been filtered or distorted by the process of collection and publication, often in the name of translation, interpretation, and preservation. These early visual records are no exception. David Treuer gives several examples of how narrative can be clouded by "wild and willful misinterpretation" in his book *Native American Fiction* (22).

Read as narratives, visual images are the right place to begin when seeking the ancestors of today's native comics. They are records of the oral stories in Anishinaabemowin that preceded Confederate and Colonial writing in Anishinaabemowin, French, and English. After a Post-National period of attempted genocide and assimilation, community members living and working as citizens on the reserve, and as foreigners in nearby urban communities, began including early narratives in their work in order to construct and strengthen national and individual identities. In the 1970s, Native Americans in the United States and Aboriginal people in Canada began looking to their individual tribal histories for Modern artistic and literary inspiration. Although they were sometimes accused of altering the stories, and sometimes accused of disrespecting them by putting them on the page, they were working to restore a connection to the past. In some cases they knew no more than any other modern reader or listener. In other instances, they had rare access to elders who had been waiting for the young to carry specific stories, especially those about how to live well, into the future. Eventually, we arrive at several branches of Modern Anishinaabe litera-ture, which can trace numerous lines of descent. One branch includes the well-known English-language prose and poetry of Louise Erdrich, Heid E. Erdrich, Gerald Vizenor, Gordon Henry, Basil Johnston, Jim Northrup, Kim Blaeser, Anne Dunn, David Treuer, and a growing list of others. Another branch con-sists of the visual legends painted by the artists and followers of the Woodland school. Yet another contains narratives found in strip comics, graphic novels, and comic books created by Anishinaabe artists and writers. It is the visual approach to narrative that is often overlooked.

Between early images, oral stories, and contemporary comics is native art, which in the Great Lakes area has become primarily known as the Woodland

3.1. Together, *1979 serigraph by Daphne Odjig*

style. Leading Woodland artist Norval Morrisseau explained his art by saying, "My paintings are icons, they are images which help focus on spiritual powers, generated by traditional belief and wisdom. It is our Ojibwa tradition to recall our history or obtain our history in an oral manner. It is important for our children and others to benefit through the process of continuing to recall and make history."⁹ Recalling history, making it visible in the modern world, was, and is, the ongoing task of the Woodland legend painters. Taking just two examples, one from the early years of this tradition and one from the present, readers can see the myriad potential narratives in the images. *Together*, a 1979 painting by Daphne Odjig, illustrates the relationship of two figures (Image 3.1).

A four-color serigraph on paper, the painting is fifty centimeters wide and fifty-nine centimeters high. In content and composition, Odjig's style is most closely related to Impressionism (drawing the viewer into the everyday world of the family and community, in this case, of Manitoulin Island and the surrounding Anishinaabeg Akiing) and Symbolism (inspired by dreams and visions). Most viewers will agree *Together* is the image of a song crossing generations. Sound is implied by the open mouths of both figures and the clear positioning of the hand on the drum. Color is balanced across both figures, giving them equal, but different, weight. At the center of the image is a *dewegan*, a drum, which translates literally to "the heart sound." The eyes of the elder are open, while the eyes of the youth are not. The pattern of the elder's blanket is more complex than the pattern of the child's. The large earthen bulge that connects them is possibly the earth, but some viewers have claimed it is the back of an animal or a pool of blood. The image tells the story of communication—perhaps one person to the other, or perhaps together across time. Like an oral story that varies slightly with repetition, the image is predictable and translatable, yet retains some elements that can be manipulated within certain boundaries to produce similar meaning; for example, the exact text of the song or gender of the singers.

A more recent example of legend painting is *Daanisag Shkaakaamikwe'an/ The Daughters of Mother Earth*, created in 2005 by Bibamikowi—Brian Corbiere (Image 3.2). Bibamikowi is a follower of the Woodland style, and this acrylic on canvas is sixty centimeters wide by fifty centimeters high. The color scheme of the painting is black, white, and "ozhaawskwaa," which is the single Anishinaabemowin word for the full range of all green to blue.¹⁰ Sometimes, the artist uses the image of four women descending into the bay to illustrate complex teachings of ecology and stewardship. At other times, he may speak of the four daughters of the cardinal directions bravely facing the world, not their crying mother. All viewers see the earth lying in the water, supporting a forest full of life, and can identify the feminine form of the island. There is an undeniable

3.2. Daanisag Shkaakaamikwe'an/The Daughters of
Mother Earth *by Bibamikowi—Brian Corbiere*

gravitas to the image. It communicates an old story that is relevant in the contemporary world, and best of all, unlike modern literature, it tells the tale without using the language of the colonizer. Finding ways outside of colonial tradition to read Anishinaabe history and narratives should be one of the primary
tasks of Anishinaabe literary criticism.

What happens, then, when a text is introduced in combination with the
image? How might the text-and-image allow for an alternate perspective on
Anishinaabe history? To answer these questions, consider the work of contemporary writers, artists, colorists, letterers, and editors who create comics that
reflect the history and reality of the Three Fires Confederacy, as it was in the
past and as it is experienced by members of Anishinaabe nations today.

One example is *The Adventures of Rabbit and Bear Paws* by Chad Solomon
and Christopher Meyer. As explained on the frontispiece of this comic, this
story begins when "the French have moved into the Great Lakes region and
along the St. Lawrence and Ohio River valleys. To the southeast, small growing pockets of English and European settlements have moved into the area as
well. The aboriginal communities remain at peace with all these new neigh-

bors but the growing tensions in the region are affecting that peace and disturbing that harmony. Wherever they go, our heroes, Rabbit and Bear Paws, are playing games with values that have sustained their people for life" (Solomon and Meyer, *Adventures*, 1). Rather than creating generalized "Indians" who fit romanticized stereotypes, the native/aboriginal authors saturate the pages with recognizable detail. Sugar camps include birch wigwams fringed with the skirts of cattails. Toboggans (later to be used for hauling) lean against walls. Birch *makaks* (boxes) with woodlands floral designs rest ready to use in several work areas. Not least of all, the men and women of this woodland neighborhood are dressed appropriately, meaning their legs are protected from underbrush and they wear the sensible layers of summer, not the loincloths and leather miniskirts of the colonial imagination.

Another notable feature in this comic is the recurrent diversion away from the main story, with numerous embedded narratives that provide specific cultural and political information. It is not the fact that multiple narratives exist that makes this an authentic Anishinaabe text; it is the fact that the content, discourse patterns, and political perspective are accurate. When the boys get in trouble, of course their father says, "this reminds me of a story," which he tells with the preface "boys there's nothing heroic about picking on those smaller than you . . . in fact, it's just the opposite. Your lack of respect worries me . . . for long ago . . ." (ibid., 9). The phrase "long ago" is immediately recognizable to fluent speakers of the language as the English translation of "*mewenzha*," the Anishinaabe version of "once upon a time." It is the discourse marker that often signals the difference between an *aadizokaan*, a fable or legend with moral content, and a *dibaajimowin*, a far less formal tale. The story the father tells is a re-creation story about the time Nanaboozho found himself afloat on a log in the midst of a flood, which is further evidence that these authors are blending early narrative, art, image, and ethnographic detail of one specific culture into the graphic novel. They are not posing the natives as non-natives expect to find them; they are building a world full of detail on all levels: in text, image, and action.

The two main characters, human brothers named Rabbit and Bear Paws, are not limited to the old familiar stories. There is a world of colonial chaos, which is an extremely important point. It is difficult for modern non-native readers to confront colonial history and its consequences without feeling a sense of personal embarrassment, even anger, or perhaps a desire to misinterpret events. Although the authors work to validate and honor the lives of Anishinaabe ancestors, they also make them laughable. Best of all, they do the same for the French and British. Penciled faces, slipping wigs, dissent in the ranks, and anonymous bravery allow readers a broader view of the forefathers and the process of exploration and colonization. One of the best lessons contained in this comic is the lesson that there were participants without any thought bubbles at all who served a story line beyond the scope of their own imagination.

It is easy to hold all players accountable in hindsight. It is harder to imagine the fear and confusion on both sides of the colonial equation. For instance, when the British arrive and attempt to solicit the help of Rabbit and Bear Paws in confronting the French, many mishaps occur, and the constant miscommunication actually becomes hilarious. Most of this arc unfolds on one page in four tiers. The sea and the shore are differentiated merely by color and one line. The British flag lies sinking on the surface. When their ship is sunk by accident, the British of course blame the French, which readers know to be a false accusation. Rabbit and Bear Paws suggest this fate has befallen the British because they neglected to acknowledge the mermen with offerings (Image 3.3).

What is amazing about the entire exchange is that each panel is filled with action. Every figure in every panel is busy, moving out of the way, moving out of the water, salvaging material goods, arguing, answering, or simply attempting to get dry. This is the way any speaker of Anishinaabemowin would describe the scene—a world of verbs, not nouns. Material possessions are lost or not visible, and five of the seven pronouns would be used conjugating a translation of the text on this page alone: *I* know, *you* see, *we* (not you—exclusive) have wasted time, *we* (including you—inclusive) must march, *they* are plotting (ibid., 19).

The dialogue is also an indication of editorial perspective. A quick analysis of the text shows that together Rabbit and Bear Paws account for 10 percent of the total words, eleven British soldiers account for 48 percent, and General Braddock alone accounts for 42 percent. The diminutively drawn, bewigged "leader" of the mission says the most and is inaccurate on at least two counts, with regard to how his ship sank and which way is west, which calls into question many of his other statements. Yet both of his errors are of a type that can be entirely obscured by history, as is the fact that the "natives" did offer him advice that he chose to ignore. Much more can be found in the pages of *Rabbit and Bear Paws* for those who read from alternative angles. If this is not some kind of postmodern decolonization, it is certainly a retaliatory dénouement of colonization written by those who have not yet been allowed to heavily edit the history books.

A Hero's Voice (artists Steven Premo and Paul Fricke and writer Cindy Goff) is another comic book that rewrites history. Commissioned by the Mille Lacs Band of Ojibwe, it is, the cover explains, "the story of real life heroes who pass on the most powerful gifts in the world" (Goff, Premo, and Fricke, *A Hero's Voice*, cover). Written by tribal elders, writers, and artists, the comic book was designed to help local children, native and non-native, get to know important figures not mentioned in the public schools. The story begins with an adolescent wearing a cape, jumping off a roof, trying to "fly" like his comic book hero,

3.3. Rabbit and Bear Paws

3.4. A Hero's Voice

"Zero-G." His *mishomis*/grandfather stops him and warns him about the danger of pretending to have inhuman powers and the foolishness of risking your life. In a few short frames, the comic bluntly confronts the leading problem for native youth today: suicide and lack of self-esteem.

As the twenty-four-page narrative unfolds, Georgie is visited by the spirits of local ancestors. With close-up shots from four directions, including above and behind, his grandfather Mishomis begins by saying, "This is serious, Georgie. It's important that these lessons be passed on." Then he asks, "Will you hear them or not?" (ibid., 6). The comic book format allows the story to be read from the perspectives of the protagonist, storyteller, and ghostly visitors. Georgie and Mishomis are not alone, and the viewer is drawn into the text as more than a passive listener. As the speech balloons carry the story along, a reader is given detail as if listening to an oral presentation. The only narrative outside of the dialogue is presented in borderless panels where Mishomis's head appears and his words explain some of the highly specific events related to each visitor. Readers are part of the cycle of generations hearing the story and are asked to consider it from all angles. Leaders from long ago are remembered and allowed to speak again. Georgie meets: Naygwanabe, a spiritual leader who also took the first census of the band in 1849 in order to ensure that all members received their annuities; Shawbashkung, the chief who negotiated and signed the Treaty of Peace and Friendship in 1855 to prevent war with the settlers; Noodinens, who was one of the tribe's most famous storytellers; and Waywinabe, also known as Arthur Gahbow, the tribal chairman in the 1970s who witnessed the Trail of Broken Treaties march in Washington, D.C., and later started the first modern school to teach Anishinaabemowin on the reservation.

Each of the leaders appears according to a pattern that could only be supported by a combination of visual and textual narrative. Georgie and Mishomis sit in full color, talking about the past, when a new character appears also in full color, but with each color 50 percent lighter than the colors used on other characters. Significant events of their lives are relived in four to six tiers, with speech balloons, accurate clothing, and background detail, and the ever-present borderless narrative of Mishomis. Dialogue is frequently in Anishinaabemowin, and the oratorical style of the leaders is preserved. Phrases that could be wrongly romanticized as evidence of Native Americans' love of nature are instead contextualized as powerful political metaphors. For instance, in one panel Naygwanabe stands facing east before bureaucrats in LaPointe, Wisconsin, asking where their agreement has gone.

"Perhaps it has sunk in the deep waters of the lake, or it may have evaporated in the heavens like the rising mist." In the next panel he stands facing west, members of his community stand behind him, and gun-toting cavalry soldiers pause on horseback in front of him. In this panel he finishes his inquiry by say-ing, "ganabaj gewaybasin, perhaps it has blown over our heads and gone over the setting sun" (ibid., 7). *Waaban*/east is the direction where all things begin in Anishinaabe cosmology; *Epangishimag*/west is the direction of death's jour-ney. In *Rabbit and Bear Paws*, the British general couldn't tell the difference between directions; in *A Hero's Voice*, the Anishinaabe leaders are keenly aware of directional signifiers. The Anishinaabe were not eager to move to the West, where America's Indian Wars were raging, where land and resources were being taken forcibly from communities, ending generations of renewable steward-ship. Naygwanabe uses intransitive inanimate verbs most often to describe the weather, to communicate the abject disillusionment and powerlessness of his people. The English of Naygwanabe closely mirrors Anishinaabemowin word choice and syntax (Image 3.4). The subject, style, and construction of the comic not only accurately address history, they show how history is relevant to the lives of Mille Lacs Band members today. Certainly, this history is important for non-native readers to know as well, but the fact that the comic was created for an Anishinaabe audience means that it is held to a standard outside that of the American narrative.

Sacred Circles: Shadows of the Past is another comic created by and about native people. Created by Brandon Mitchell, a Mi'kmaq from Listuguj, a com-munity located in southeastern Quebec, this series could not be technically considered geographically Anishinaabe. However, this Aboriginal Canadian group of twenty-nine nations speaks an Algonquian language, shares the same history of French, then British influence, and uses narrative traditions closer to Anishinaabe than to other Native nations in the United States. For this reason, it is important to look across national borders to see the full range of potential visual and literary connections.

The main characters in *Sacred Circles* are fourteen-year-old Jesse Mitchell, his twelve-year-old sister Tyra, and his best friend Chad, who all go along on a camping trip with Jesse and Tyra's parents. Jesse and Tyra's dad, Eric, is an archaeologist specializing in Aboriginal artifacts, while their mom, Jennifer Mitchell, is a research analyst and high-school teacher. As the story unfolds, Eric accidentally unleashes an ancient evil that entraps him and his wife, and it is up to the children to try to rescue them. In keeping with the tradition in the narrow genre of Anishinaabe comics, the story includes a reference to colonial history beginning in 1703, "a time when we used to have a sacred bond with the forest . . . before our world was discovered by 'civilized' man" (Mitchell, Bradshaw, and Beaulieu, *Sacred Circles*, issue 1, 1). Rather than focus on the evils caused by the colonial confrontation, this story line acknowledges the spectrum of good and evil within the community prior to contact. One man decides to use his knowledge to do evil, and although his fellow man offers him a chance to repent, he is eventually punished by nature when his spirit is trapped "until the end of time" (7). Prior to meeting his end, he engages in a battle across several asymmetrical panels of chaotic motion with inset close-ups of faces filled with fear. Narrative boxes are rough-edged and the color of bark, while word balloons, normally smooth-edged, become jagged and sharp. His foes are a black-and-purple water serpent, drawn with a head thirty times larger than his and eyes so unnaturally green that their color bleeds across several panels, and a bird with talons the size of his body. Like the serpent, the bird is drawn with feathers of variegated brown and white, but the white is drawn as light which shines beyond the borders of the panel. Both water snakes and thunderbirds can be found in the rock art of the Great Lakes and serve to connect this modern action-adventure tale with the narratives of the past.

In fact, as when the archaeologist and his wife make a discovery in the forest, ancient visual images play a role in the story: "a spooky tree in the middle of a clearing surrounded by four piles of rocks" and symbols carved into rocks, which he interprets as some kind of warning but admits he cannot fully translate (13). The next day, as they continue to seek "findings," the two adults inadvertently release the evil spirit from the tree. Unlike the 1990 Native American Graves Protection and Repatriation Act passed in the United States, the proposed parallel legislation concerning archaeological sites and objects was never enacted in Canada. It is a fairly sophisticated comic that can include an international legislative comparison as a subplot.

In the second installment of the story, the children set out to find their parents. The animals they encounter are as powerful as the serpent and the thunderbird, but far more tangible for those with the right perspective. As the kids wait for their order to arrive in a modern restaurant booth, the stranger who offered to buy dinner and the waitress taking their order appear as a bear and an eagle to young Tyra.

Animals are read in multiple ways, as the "Justice League" of the natural world and as superheroes able to shift shapes in order to help those in need. By considering the story in the context of early Anishinaabe narratives, we find that there are natural connections between the comic genre and oral, episodic narratives of adventure.

Other comics, including *The Mtigwaki Strips* by Lynn Johnston; numerous editorial cartoons, most notably *Baloney and Bannock* by Perry McLeod-Shabogesic; the health and healing comics produced by the Healthy Aboriginal Network; *The Illustrated History of the Chippewas of Nawash*; and many more, serve as examples that the tradition of combining visual and verbal narrative continues. Reading the visual and verbal together in cultural context is not a

3.5. Sacred Circles

new form of literary or artistic criticism. Reading words and images in tribal context is also not the only way, but it is the best way, to approach Native American literature. Demanding that critics of Native American literature demonstrate proficiency in at least one of the indigenous languages they study may be a bit new, but I hope not for long. In fact, I look forward to the day when work like this looks dated and has been done for each of the 1,681 sovereign nations in the United States, Canada, and Central and South America, so that they may understand themselves as connected in new ways to one another and to the nations that surround them . . . so that the young people may hear and understand more about the ways of their grandfathers than anyone ever dared to think was possible.

NOTES

1. There are 581 sovereign nations within the borders of the United States. For a full list of nations, consult the Tribal Directory of Federally Recognized Indian Tribes, maintained by the National Congress of American Indians at http://www.ncai.org/Tribal_Directory.3.0.html. There are 600 First Nations in Canada; for the full list visit the Assembly of First Nations website at http://www.afn.ca/article.asp?id=3. The estimate of 500 nations in Central and South America comes from an article by Alison Field for the Indigenous People's Network.

2. Anishinaabe is most often translated as the "First Man" by native speakers when telling creation stories. However, it is worth noting that the literal etymology would be closer to "Best Man," based on "nishin" (good) and "abe" (male). This is just one of many often-overlooked linguistic details that are an indication of the interesting idiomatic and metaphorical differences between cultures.

3. The terms Early (precontact), Confederate (1400–1750), Colonial (1750–1890), Post-National (1890–1970), and Modern (1970–present) align with my personal theories of Anishinaabe literature and are not intended to reflect the history of any other group.

4. Written originally for young adults, *The Birchbark House*, *The Game of Silence*, and *The Porcupine Year* are examples of Anishinaabe fiction compelling enough to hold the interest of adults as well as children. One of the features of these books is art by the author, which is an unusual addition to any piece of fiction published in America today. The series of books also uses Anishinaabemowin throughout and includes a complete glossary of terms at the back of each book to help readers learn the language.

5. This quote was taken from the jacket of the 1995 hardcover edition of *The Manitous* by Basil Johnston.

6. More information on some of the early Midewiwin teaching methods can be found in the works of Edward Benton-Banai and Michael Angel.

7. The belief that memory is the most powerful way to transfer narrative knowledge

comes from a speech given by Ms. Sidney Martin during the Annual Petroglyph Cleansing, Sanilac, Michigan, June 21, 2008.

8. For more about the petroglyphs of the Great Lakes region, see the work of Steven Mithen.

9. http://norvalmorrisseau.blogspot.com/2009/08/spiritual-paintings-of-norval_21.html

10. The word "ozhaawskwaa" is still used primarily to indicate green.

4

LIMINALITY AND MESTIZA CONSCIOUSNESS IN LYNDA BARRY'S *ONE HUNDRED DEMONS*

MELINDA L. DE JESÚS

WHILE MOST FILIPINO AMERICAN artists have yet to register on American culture's radar screen, one Pinay[1] has single-handedly redefined and influenced American popular culture for over twenty years. Hailed by the *Village Voice* as "one of the greatest cartoonists in the world," Lynda K. Barry, born in 1956, is best known for the syndicated alternative newspaper comic strip *Ernie Pook's Comeek* and its high-spirited "gifted child" Marlys Mullen (quoted in Hempel, "Laugh Lines," 1).[2] She is heralded for her contributions to alternative comics and "wimmen's comix," and recently garnered critical acclaim for her disturbing first novel, *Cruddy*. What many of her fans may not know, however, is that Barry's earliest work includes stories of her growing up as a working-class, mixed-race Filipina in Seattle in the 1960s. *One Hundred Demons*, a series of twenty-panel full-color strips, published semimonthly online from April 7, 2000, to January 15, 2001, signals her return to this more autobiographical, self-reflexive mode.[3] Barry recently published these comics in book form under the same title. This essay will outline Lynda Barry's important but overlooked contributions to the growing body of Filipina American feminist (*peminist*) writings and to contemporary Filipino American cultural production in general.[4]

One Hundred Demons is an exploration of events and memories that deeply affected the artist, namely, her childhood and its manifold tragedies, large and small. It deftly exhibits the hallmarks of Barry's powerful storytelling aesthetic: her deliberately "naïve" graphic style complements the brutally honest musings of its young narrator and the often harsh subjects of the strips themselves. Issues of identity and liminality emerge from this collection of comics, themes which have particular resonance for Filipino Americans. Most significant is the fact that these themes are explored from the standpoint of a mixed-race Filipina narrator, "Lynda." With her freckles, bright red hair, and white skin, Lynda is blessed with "a funny way of being Filipina" (e-mail to author, December 14, 2001). Caught between her physical appearance and her racial identity as a mixed-race Pinay, Lynda must negotiate the double-edged sword of her whiteness and its significance within U.S. racial formations. Below I delineate how Barry's cartoon explorations of Filipina American mestizaness juxtapose the binaries of liminality and mestiza consciousness in order to proffer alternative conceptions of being that contribute greatly to Filipina American visibility, agency, and decolonization. Before discussing these aspects in detail, however, I will contextualize Barry's work within contemporary cartoon history and criticism, as well as within Filipino American theorizing about identity formation and mestizaness.[5]

"New" and "Wimmen's" Comics

Lynda Barry, one of the very few syndicated American female cartoonists, is known for her signature storytelling and bold graphic style, what critic Bob Callahan deems her "brilliant narrative skills" ("Let It Bleed," 12–13). Her work is said to embody the spirit of "New Comics," as well as "wimmen's," or feminist, comics. New Comics, comic art oppositional to the corporate-produced and syndicated comic strips like *Spider-Man*, the *X-Men*, and *Garfield*, and created by independent artists like Art Spiegelman, Los Bros. Hernandez *(Love and Rockets)*, and Roberta Gregory *(Naughty Bits)*, have been described as antiheroic, nihilist, subversive, political, autobiographical, and postmodern (ibid., 6–14). Art Spiegelman insists on the term "commix" to emphasize the comixture of text and graphics in this art form and maintains that "commix" are twenty-first-century art, graphic literature, rather than just amusing cartoons about funny animals ("Commix," 61). Callahan, in his introduction to *The New Comics Anthology* (which includes work by Barry), maintains that New Comics signal the shift from "entertainment to new pop art form"; furthermore, he identifies the contributions of women artists like Barry to the genre as strong storytelling via autobiography and an overtly feminist stance ("Let It Bleed," 12–13). Moreover, Callahan asserts that the autobiographical writings in *The New Comics Anthology* best demonstrate comics as a "vital new branch of contemporary literature" (ibid., 12).[6]

Barry is also regarded as a vanguard "wimmen's" cartoonist since she helped to develop the genre's hallmark, the autobiographical comic. In the early 1970s American women cartoonists created their own artistic venues to counter the very misogynistic underground comics scene of the period (exemplified by R. Crumb's *Zap Comix*).[7] Beginning with the foundational feminist cartoon collectives Tits and Clits and Wimmen's Comix, wimmen's comics have been characterized by a specifically feminist and autobiographical tone.[8] Cartoonist Diane Noomin, creator of anxiety-wracked suburbanite Didi Glitz and editor of *Twisted Sisters: A Collection of Bad Girl Art* (which includes work by Barry), maintains that wimmen's comics manifest an "uncompromising vision reflecting a female perspective . . . frequently expressed in deeply felt, autobiographical narratives. Often the art graphically reflects inner turmoil" (*Twisted Sisters: A Collection,* 7). Indeed, in her introduction to Noomin's *Twisted Sisters 2: Drawing the Line,* Susie Bright contends that this is the most important aspect of wimmen's comics: "There is literally no place besides comix where you can find women speaking the truth and using their pictures to show you, in vivid detail, what it means to live your life outside of the stereotypes and delusions that we see on television, in shopping malls and at newsstands" (Bright, "Introduction," 7).

The world Lynda Barry creates in *One Hundred Demons* fits Bright's statement to a "T." Barry's centering of the Filipina American experience in an online mainstream magazine like *Salon.com* signals just one more way that Filipinas are making their voices heard. Indeed, claiming space and asserting voice are particularly important for American Pinays for several reasons. Compounding mainstream American culture's tiresome stereotyping of all Asian American women as passive, submissive, silent "lotus blossoms" or exotic-erotic "dragon ladies" is the parallel erasure of Filipinas from the construction "Asian American women" itself, which is most often understood to signify only women of Japanese or Chinese descent. Furthermore, all Filipino Americans continue to be marginalized within Asian America as well as Asian American cultural studies, and this marginalization complicates further the struggles of Filipinas to be acknowledged beyond the roles of mothers/daughters in cultural nationalist Filipino America. Contemporary Filipina American cultural productions testify to these complicated realities and must be regarded as tremendous acts of courage and defiance. Indeed, the significance of Barry's achievement—a comics assertion of Pinay presence—is rendered even more remarkable when we consider how American imperialism has resulted in the virtual erasure of Filipino America itself. Read in this light, *One Hundred Demons* is a powerful act of remembering that problematizes and resists the forces that have deemed Filipino America to be unrepresentable (see Oscar Campomanes's "The Empire's Forgetful and Forgotten Citizens"). I discuss this aspect in detail.

Comics as "Autobifictionalography"

Barry's centering Filipina American realities in American popular culture underscores her work's drawing upon distinctively eclectic and diverse narrative traditions: its linking wimmen's and New Comics to mainstream American feminist and U.S. Third World feminist writing. For example, American women writers have always focused on gender identity and conflict via mother/daughter stories; what U.S. Third World feminist writers have added to this genre is the delineation of how women of color must negotiate not only sexism in American society, but its simultaneous intertwinings with racism, classism, heterosexism, and imperialism. Barry, like many other Asian American women writers such as M. Evelina Galang, Maxine Hong Kingston, and Hisaye Yamamoto, retells and reworks childhood memories and folktales in order to discover her history and thus herself: retelling the stories of her mother and *lola* (grandmother), and analyzing her very different relationships with them, Barry constructs a hybrid new identity, consciously deciding which aspects she will claim and which she must discard.

The full-color graphics of *One Hundred Demons* are an integral part of this process of self-creation. Barry's exquisite storytelling power lies in the potent mixture of her narrative and drawings: her comics enable the reader literally to "see" Barry's world as she does and thus enter it even more fully.[9] Moreover, while Barry's narrative compels us to "read" further, the striking *visual* contrast of Lynda to her Pinoy extended family throughout *One Hundred Demons* signifies and reinforces the distances she, as a red-haired, fair-skinned mestiza Filipina in America, must travel in order to find herself and to find her way back to her family.[10]

Barry presents the concept of "autobifictionalography" in *One Hundred Demons* to describe her art, drawing the reader's attention to the rhetorical strategies of invention and elaboration that are inherent in all forms of self-representation: "Is it autobiography if parts of it are not true? Is it fiction if parts of it are?" (7). Reflecting further upon her own creative process, in the collection's introduction Barry features a "demon" who explains the genesis of the cartoons themselves:

She [Barry] was at the library when she first read about a painting exercise called "One Hundred Demons." The example she saw was a handscroll painted by a zen monk named Hakuin Ekaku in 16th century Japan. . . . She checked out some books, followed the instructions and the demons began to come. . . . They were not the demons she expected. . . . At first they freaked her, but then she started to love watching them come out of her paintbrush. (8–10, 12)

One Hundred Demons' genesis in a Zen painting exercise further underscores the exceptional hybridity that informs Barry's work. Indeed, the demons that emerge here highlight Barry's search for identity and belonging, the same themes dominating Filipino American writing from Carlos Bulosan and Ben Santos through Peter Bacho, Jessica Hagedorn, R. Zamora Linmark, M. Evelina Galang, and Brian Ascalon Roley. In this way, *One Hundred Demons* evokes and ponders the very same "demons" that haunt contemporary Filipino America.

Filipino American Identity Crisis: From Liminality to "Mestiza Consciousness"

The themes of lost identities and forgotten histories dominate Filipino American cultural studies. Many critics delineate how a heritage of dual colonizations (first by Spain and then by the United States), coupled with American cultural imperialism, has left an indelible mark on the Filipino American psyche. Epifanio San Juan Jr. writes that the "reality of U.S. colonial subjugation and its profoundly enduring effects" has created "the predicament and crisis of dislocation, fragmentation, uprooting, loss of traditions, exclusions and alienation" for Filipino Americans ("The Predicament of Filipinos in the United States," 206–207). According to Eric Gamalinda, Filipino Americans are alienated as a consequence of this amnesia, regarding "their own culture as inferior," further reinforcing "the Filipino's invisibility. It is no wonder that second- and third-generation Filipino Americans feel they are neither here nor there, perambulating between a culture that alienates them and a culture they know nothing about, or are ashamed of" ("Myth, Memory, Myopia," 3).

This history of "forgotten" colonization, and its ramifications for Filipino/American subjectivities, identify the construction of Filipino mestizoness. Mestizos are regarded as the literal embodiment of the perfect mixture of European and Asian heritages: "Light-skinned, big eyes with of course double folds, a not-too-Anglo, but not-too-flaring, perfectly *mestiza* nose" (See "Mourning the Blood," 9). Consequently, Filipino culture reifies mestiza looks, the physical manifestation of our colonization, which leads to our internal colonization: we devalue our flat noses and dark skin, and admonish one another to stay out of the sun, while our *lolas* and mothers threaten to put clothespins on our noses to make them less flat.

Within the United States, the signification of the mestiza is complex. Maria

P. Root writes that the mestizo "carries unjustified connotations of superiority in the Philippines and, ironically, the connotation of imposterhood or inauthenticity in this country. . . . Those Filipinos of immediate European heritage may be regarded as less authentic by some, yet enviable by others" ("Contemporary Mixed-Heritage Filipino Americans," 81, 83). These competing ideologies result in an identity crisis for mestizo Filipino Americans:

> Contemporary mixed-race Filipinos, particularly during adolescence and young adulthood, may be unable to untangle their feelings of alienation from the typical adult experience, marginality as a person of color in a society in which race matters, and difference as an ambiguous Filipino. (88)

There is something tragically ironic about Filipino America's reifying mestizo looks while at the same time alienating and marginalizing its mixed-race members. Filipino American literature often uses the mestizo to discuss aspects of identity formation and liminality: for example, Rio in Hagedorn's *Dogeaters*, Mina in Galang's short story "Rose Colored" from *Her Wild American Self*, and brothers Gabe and Tomas in Roley's *American Sons*.

I contend that Lynda Barry's exploration of this schizophrenic cultural response in *One Hundred Demons* results in her revisioning mestizaness itself: she shows how the Filipina mestiza's experience of liminality, while confusing and painful, is a necessary part of the process of "mestiza consciousness." Rafael's discussion of liminality situates the mestiza as object and symbol defined by what she is *not*, but Gloria Anzaldúa, in *Borderlands/La Frontera: The New Mestiza*, reconfigures the mestiza as agent and subject: "mestiza consciousness" enables her to create a new way of being and seeing that transcends the oppositional forces/narratives that would divide her:

> The new *mestiza* copes by developing a tolerance for contradictions, a tolerance for ambiguity. . . . She learns to juggle cultures. She has a plural personality, she operates in a pluralistic mode. . . . Not only does she sustain contradictions, she turns the ambivalence into something else. (79)

For example, a distinctive and significant aspect of *One Hundred Demons* is its exploring the complexities of whiteness and its significations for mestizaness in Filipino America: what does it mean to be a *white* mestiza in America, one who has the ability to try on different identities because she has the privilege of white skin?

Like Galang and Roley, Barry problematizes aspects of physical and cultural hybridity here by asking what makes one "mixed": can one claim Filipino-ness if she doesn't "look" Pinay? Moreover, Barry critiques our investment in whiteness itself by asking if erasure of the physical attributes of Pinay-ness truly ensures "becoming American"—and what that costs. In this way Barry's work resonates across the Filipino American canon, linking Bulosan's desire to "claim" America and Galang's "wild American self," while underscoring the contradictions inherent in the concept of "Filipino American" identity itself, which R. Zamora Linmark so aptly summarizes in "They Like You Because You Eat Dogs": "They like you because you're a copycat, want to be just like them / They like you because—give it a few more years—you'll be just like them / And when that time comes, will they like you more?" (Rolling the R's, 72).

These critiques are particularly well suited to the visual nature of comics: the interaction between text and graphic in One Hundred Demons continually alludes to racial representations through the contrast of Lynda's whiteness to the darker skin and hair of her very Pinoy-looking extended family members. Barry investigates white Filipina mestizaness by delineating its significance indirectly, never mentioning the term mestiza explicitly. Her refusal to "name" mestizaness here capitalizes on the graphic capacities of comics to critique the colorism endemic to U.S. racial formations, for Lynda's "whiteness" forces the readers of One Hundred Demons to acknowledge how colorism and racism are related and to think about significations of white skin privilege. Additionally, Barry's exploration of mestizaness as whiteness in One Hundred Demons is a strong assertion of her own Pinay-ness, for Filipino American readers will recognize this issue and its ramifications immediately.[11] The graphic and narrative tensions here allow Barry to focus on mestiza identity issues through the visual "discrepancies" between Lynda's appearance and who she really is, which, in turn, underscore Lynda's struggle to be "the hyphen in American-born" (Galang, Her Wild American Self, 86). Barry's comics thus resist internal colonization: these distinctly Filipina American explorations of identity formation include a strong critique of Filipino American culture's investment in cultural imperialism (valorizing whiteness), as well as the racial politics of the United States in general.

In sum, the identity struggles Barry presents in One Hundred Demons must be regarded as contributing to the process of Filipina American representation and decolonization, rather than as just humorous depictions of ethnic American adolescent angst. Gloria Anzaldúa writes:

> The struggle is inner: Chicano, indio, American Indian, mojado, Mexicano, immigrant Latino, Anglo in power, working class Anglo, Black, Asian—our psyches resemble the bordertowns and are populated by the same people. The struggle has always been inner and is played out

in the outer terrains. Awareness of our situation must come before inner changes, which in turn come before changes in society. Nothing happens in the "real" world unless it first happens in *the images in our heads*. (*Borderlands*, 86; emphasis added)

As if taking this for a cue, Lynda Barry, through *One Hundred Demons*, contributes to the struggle for liberation and consciousness by giving us new images of Filipina American selfhood. Tracing the dual and dueling significations of Filipina American mestizaness as both liminality and mestiza consciousness, Barry shows how they represent two sides of the same coin.

Reading Comics

The narrator of *One Hundred Demons*, Lynda, is presented as a lonely, sensitive, and nervous child with "emotional problems" (117). She is raised by her mother, a dark-haired mestiza beauty whom Barry describes as "unpredictable and quite violent," and her earthy grandma, with whom she has a very strong bond (91). Barry's drawings of the three women quickly and efficiently highlight Lynda's physical dissimilarities from her foremothers, who have much darker skin and hair. Lynda is doted on by her grandmother, from whom she learns much about Filipino culture; on the other hand, her mother, whose attention she craves, remains very distant.[12]

This sense of disconnection is emphasized by the fact that throughout the collection Lynda yearns to be popular but is often shunned by her peers. For example, in the cartoon "Head Lice/My Worst Boyfriend," Lynda describes herself as a weird "cootie girl," whose social ostracism leads to her inordinate interest in bugs (17). Only during a summer trip to the Philippines during fifth grade does she make friends easily with Pilar and "the Professor," who share her fascination for lice and are particularly intrigued by Lynda's red hair and white skin (18–19). This is the only mention of Lynda's interaction with other Filipino children in *One Hundred Demons*. Interestingly, the cartoon "Resilience" briefly describes Lynda's inability to connect with other Asian American girls. The drawings here emphasize her physical dissimilarities from these girls (again, this element is not commented upon), while the narrative describes her unsuccessful attempts to become part of the Asian clique:

It was a very hip, very stable in-crowd, very into fashion and student government and innocent dance parties. . . . I didn't fit in, I thought it was because of my bad teeth and clothes. I didn't know how see-through I was, how obviously desperate I was to be part of their good lives, to be one of the good people. (69)

One Hundred Demons includes a number of comics that explore Barry's racial identity and family history, including "The Aswang," "Head Lice/My Worst Boyfriend," "Dancing," "Girlness," "The Visitor," and "Common Scents," yet space considerations permit me discussion of only two comics that focus on aspects of mestizaness. "Common Scents" and "The Visitor" illustrate how a white mestiza like Lynda grows into awareness and understanding of racial difference and its connotations. I explore how Barry's delineation of Lynda's sense of alienation, both within her own family and socially, depicts American adolescent angst and the search for identity, but also highlights the process of racial formation in the United States and its effects upon Filipina/American mestiza identity.

"COMMON SCENTS"

The cartoon "Common Scents" gets its title from a pun on "common sense" and "common scents"—i.e., the fact that every human being smells. Through the seemingly simplistic viewpoint of a child fascinated by odors, Barry critiques how white mainstream culture discriminates against racial minorities: she shows how the assimilation process can induce shame in children of color by reinforcing negative associations with cultural practices that differ from white norms. Here, the practices deemed to be most offensive are those that signify ethnic/racial difference, such as the preparation and consuming of redolent ethnic foods. Thus the cartoonist presents a lighthearted but pointed reflection about the American consumer culture's successful marketing of products designed to mask "natural" odors by asking what it is we are trying to hide. Barry's exposé of assimilation via consumerism in this comic has particular significance for Filipino/Americans, given the intense cultural imperialism we live under both in the United States and the Philippines.

The cartoon begins with a young Lynda thinking of the homes on her street and how "No two houses ever smelled alike, even if the people used the same air freshener" (Figure 4.1). Barry then goes on to write that "the biggest mystery of all was my own house. I couldn't smell it at all. I didn't think it had a smell, which was strange considering all that went on there."

The graphic in this panel depicts Lynda's extended Filipino family and its smells: "9,000 cigarettes"; her aunt's "Jungle Gardenia" perfume; her uncle, wearing "Jade East" aftershave, announces, "N'ako [exclamation]! Ma bungo [It smells good]!"; while her grandma, hair smelling of "½ a can of Adorne hair spray," is cooking "fried smelt, garlic, onions" and urging her family to eat, "Ang

4.1. *From Lynda Barry, "Common Scents"*

sarap [So delicious]!"; while Lynda and her "dog that rolls on things" look on happily. Lynda's whiteness here is a strong contrast visually, but is not commented upon.

She continues, writing: "I probably had the strongest smelling house in the neighborhood except for the bleach people, but I had no idea what it smelled like until I heard a comment about it." The comic's major conflict is revealed in the graphic below: Lynda's white neighbor tells her, "My mom says *your people* fry weird food and save the grease and also that you boil pig's blood which is the reason for the smell" (emphasis added). The girl goes on to explain that "the smell" is the reason why she can't visit Lynda's home: "That's why I'm not 'sposta come over, 'cause the smell gets on my clothes and makes my mom sick." Lynda, "shocked . . . with the news about the smell of [her] house," learns the negative lesson that what her family does daily sickens others. Moreover, the girl's mother, "the most disinfecting, air freshener spraying person that ever lived," who "had those car freshener Christmas tree things hanging everywhere," was quite "free with her observations about the smell of others: 'Your Orientals have an array, with your Chinese smelling stronger than your Japanese and your Koreans falling somewhere in the middle *and don't get me started on your Fili-*

pinos'" (emphasis added). From this Lynda learns that Filipinos are the worst offenders of all the Asians in terms of odors.

Indeed, this woman also shares with Lynda her ideas about the odors of other people of color, teaching her about "the smells of Blacks, Mexicans, Italians . . . and the difference it made if they were wet or dry, fat or skinny," thus insinuating that whites do not smell at all.

Barry's comic implies that Lynda is made privy to her neighbor's racist "honesty" because Lynda appears to be white like her, although it's clear from her daughter's initial comments that these neighbors know who Lynda's "people" are. For the mestiza, this is the beginning of liminality: her appearing to be "white" encourages other whites to disparage racial minorities in her presence, for they assume a tacit agreement grounded in their common white skin privilege. Thus whiteness distances Lynda from colorism and racism but also from her family and culture.

Interestingly, Barry does not deal directly with Lynda's feelings after becoming privy to this information, but focuses the comic on Lynda's grandma's making sense of this interaction, and the commonsense advice she gives her granddaughter about how to regard such racist attitudes.

Lynda shares the air freshener lady's ideas with her grandmother, "a philosophical sort of person who always had an interesting take on things," Barry notes dryly. Outraged, Grandma responds first with exasperation: "Aie n'ako [exclamation]! White ladies smell bad too, naman [also]! She never wash her pookie [vagina]! Her kili-kili [armpit] always sweat-sweating! The old ones smell like e-hee [urine]! That lady is tung-ah [stupid]!" In the next panel, Grandma continues her critique: "You know, my darling, God has made every people! And every people makes ta-ee [feces]! And every ta-ee smells bad! Ask this lady does perfume come out of her pueet [anus]? N'ako, I don't think so, darling! It is not God's way. You tell her!" In the next panel Lynda notes, "The air freshener lady moved before I could communicate my grandmother's wisdom to her. It took the new people a year to chase her smell out." Thus, while Lynda learns that what smells "good" is relative to the smeller, the reader also assumes from this panel that Lynda's neighbors moved to avoid further contact with the smells from Lynda's home. Near the comic's end, Barry writes that she recalled this incident after reading about a woman who tried to hide the smell of her murdered husband's body with stick-on air fresheners. Of her former neighbor, Barry notes, "I don't think she had a body in her attic but there was *something* she was trying to spray away. She saw smelly devils everywhere."

In another panel Barry writes, "I've never heard a single person say they loved the smell of air freshener and yet there are so many people who fill their homes with it. When combined with natural but power-filled smells, the results can be traumatic" (Figure 4.2). The graphics here feature hilarious combinations like "cherry pop-up fried liver," "tropical passion aromatherapy cat box," and "piney woods pig's blood stew breakdown," demonstrating how covering up natural smells with artificial scents only creates worse odors. However, what these panels point to is Lynda's neighbor's obsession with eradicating odors and the "smelly demons" they symbolize (the cultures of people of color), as well as the lengths to which whites might go to distance themselves from those they define as racially "Other."

This series of panels ends with Lynda stating, "Our house smelled like grease and fish and cigs, like Jade East and pork and dogs, like all the wild food my grandma boiled and fried. And if they could get that into a spray can, I'd buy it." The narrator's rejecting the logic of air fresheners for the familiar smells of her childhood home is linked to the cartoon's final graphic: here Lynda's grandma offers her the notoriously bad-smelling but great-tasting durian fruit, extolling her grandchild to eat: "N'ako, Lynda! This duran [sic] fruits smells so badly but taste so goodly! You try it! God made it! My Golly! Eat! Eat!" Grandma teaches Lynda that smells can be deceiving: just because they are unfamiliar doesn't mean that something is "bad"; in this way, she connects Lynda to her Filipino heritage of "wild food" and pungent odors.

4.2. *From Lynda Barry, "Common Scents"*

Clearly Lynda's grandma's nurturance and attitude are crucial here in helping Lynda understand this incident from a space of power. Grandma refutes the racist ideology of her neighbor, striving to ensure that Lynda maintains positive connections to family and culture, and its cuisine; in this way she reaffirms Lynda's ties to her Filipino heritage. Nevertheless, Lynda has witnessed how whites regard Filipinos and other people of color and also how her whiteness earns her different treatment from her family members, and she is thus interpolated and inculcated into the United States' colorist and racist discourse.

Indeed, later in the collection, Barry shows how an older Lynda participates in her own alienation because she has internalized the negative stereotypes of people of color endemic in white American culture. Throughout *One Hundred Demons*, Lynda's grandma symbolizes heritage and nurturance. After her grandmother moves out, however, Lynda loses her maternal anchor and her connection to her roots; she has no one to guide her in thinking through her mestiza identity issues.

Gradually, Lynda's self-consciousness about her Filipina identity becomes equated with discomfort and shame, which leads to her desire to "pass" as white. Again, the reality of American cultural imperialism and its effect on Filipino/American cultures renders Lynda's rejection of her family's Filipino-ness as signifying much more than the typical representation of adolescent angst, where an unhappy protagonist deems her entire family "weird" and attempts to separate herself from them. As a white mestiza, then, Lynda finds her light skin and red hair to be mixed blessings: they allow her to pass into mainstream white culture at the same time they mark her as "different" from her own family.

"THE VISITOR"

This comic is the opposite of "Common Scents": it delineates how Lynda's internalizing "Otherness" and rejecting her Filipina identity ultimately hurt her. Lacking the wise counsel of her grandmother, Lynda enacts what has been enforced by her surroundings: it's easier and better to "pass" as white (what she appears to be), even if it means lying. Despite Lynda's best efforts, however, her mestiza identity cannot be repressed—which has heartbreaking repercussions.

The cartoon begins with a sixteen-year-old Lynda describing meeting Dean, a "bag boy" at the Lucky's Foods "in a bad part of town." Dean is from "a different part of town [she'd] never been to but he wasn't talking about it" (Figure 4.3). Clearly, Dean has class privilege but thrives on working amid possible danger. He tells Lynda about being in three holdups, and that the secret to surviving is "to stay cool." "The worst part about it was if a customer freaked out because she'd never been robbed before," he explains. Lynda is very attracted to him.

4.3. *From Lynda Barry, "The Visitor"*

Dean tells her "he had lived everywhere but . . . hadn't seen anything until he first got high." He becomes very interested in Lynda after she admits she has access to drugs. Dean tells Lynda she'd "be an incredible person to trip with," but she doesn't tell him her "drug-taking days are sort of over." He asks her to get some acid so they could get high in Chinatown and skid row: "Don't you think that would be so cool?" In the graphic, Lynda assents to his request while rolling her eyes. Thus, against her better judgment, she agrees, and Barry introduces the comic's sense of foreboding: "I was a person who freaked out easily. I was a person whose main quality was nervousness. I was also a person who wanted incredible experiences and an incredible boyfriend. Dropping acid in Chinatown. How bad could it be?"

Here, too, Barry portrays Dean's and Lynda's contrasts and commonalities: "Dean had moved so many times in his life and I'd lived in the same house forever but we had certain things in common. We experimented with identities. We went to strange parts of town. We both were looking for something, but what was it?" While Lynda is searching for romance and a place of belonging, Dean is looking for thrills by "slumming." His desire for danger and entertainment is based upon his privilege to move in and out of neighborhoods like Chinatown and skid row at will. Moreover, he assumes that Lynda shares his interest in "strange parts of town," but never imagines that she might actually *live* there. As they walk through Chinatown, Dean is impatient for the acid to kick in; he mentions to Lynda that "A guy at work says there's like a million chickens somewhere down here, all in bamboo cages," and is surprised that she knows where these chickens are located. Thus Barry develops the comic's central conflict: Dean assumes Lynda to be like him (white) and also assumes she craves the same kind of exotic, carnivalesque excitement that Chinatown and skid row signify to him.

In this same series of panels Dean tells a smitten Lynda, "You're like me. You like to explore insane places. I never met a girl who was so much like me," but the panel's narrative describes what Lynda withholds from him: "I didn't tell him I spent a lot of time in Chinatown when I was little, that my relatives hung out in a Filipino restaurant on the next block, that my uncle was cutting hair in the barbershop we just passed, and that my mother could be around the corner parking the car." Barry underscores how Lynda, by specifically failing to mention her family connection to Chinatown—indeed her own Pinay-ness—knowingly uses her whiteness (her ability to "pass") and her insider knowledge of Chinatown and drugs to maintain Dean's attention.

The acid kicks in as Dean and Lynda leave Chinatown. The graphics in the next five panels illustrate the surreal giddiness, then dislocation, fear, and para-

4.4. *From Lynda Barry, "The Visitor"*

noia, of their tripping (Figure 4.4). The Chinatown/skid row (Lynda's neighborhood) sequence of panels is presented as surreal and dangerous. This representation simultaneously underscores how the attraction to the exotic draws outsiders like Dean and reminds readers of Lynda's working-class mestiza Filipina roots.

Dean and Lynda, holding hands, finally find their way back to Chinatown and begin to come down from their high. One of the panels shows a shocked Lynda saying, "It's my mom!" and another illustrates Lynda's irate mother yelling obscenities (which Barry describes as "very intense swearing in Tagalog!") juxtaposed to Dean's confusion: he "tried to say it wasn't my mom, how could it be my mom, the lady wasn't even shouting in English," but Lynda runs away. "I could handle a lot of things on acid, but my mom's screaming head wasn't one of them." Barry develops quite skillfully the "return of the repressed" here: Lynda has tried to conceal her Filipina identity, but her own mother "outs" her just as she's getting closer to Dean. Thus Lynda's running away here signals her double shame: shame at Dean's finding out that she's not really white, and shame at denying her own mother and culture.

Only because she is forced to does Lynda come clean with Dean about who she really is: "I told Dean things about myself. About my mom. About China-

4.5. *From Lynda Barry, "The Visitor"*

town. About living in the 'insane places' he was only visiting. About falling in love with him. He nodded." But her honesty is too much for him: Dean, "crashing," decides acid does not agree with him; this can also be read as his rejection of all that they have just shared. Clearly Dean was more comfortable with the "fake" Lynda: what she symbolizes as a Filipina mestiza who can pass for white renders too close a reality he had been keeping at arm's length. Thus "The Visitor" ends bleakly: treating the whole incident like a "bad trip," Dean announces to Lynda that he's quitting working at Lucky's, and, as they wait for his bus to arrive, he tells her about a girl he's in love with. Lynda notes: "I sat on the bench for a long time afterwards. I was cool. Very cool. It wasn't like I had never been robbed before."

Lynda's numbed dialogue here indicates her feelings following Dean's rejecting her. On one level, from the teenager's melodramatic point of view, she has been robbed of her chance for romance with Dean. However, the cartoon clearly means to explore the loaded choices that Lynda makes to gain Dean's attention in the first place: passing for white and denying her Filipina identity and running away from her own mother indicate how Lynda undermines her own self-esteem—all for the attention of a boy who was only using her for entertainment. Barry thus shows how whiteness benefits Lynda while at the same time it cripples her: she can never be whole by denying her mestiza Filipina heritage. By capitulating to those who would ask that of her, Lynda is left abandoned at the bus stop.

"The Visitor" presents a very difficult lesson: how Lynda sets *herself* up for heartbreak by pretending to be something she is not, i.e., by denying her Pinayness. As in "Common Scents," Barry shows how our choices concerning racial identity affect us profoundly: for Lynda to believe the air freshener lady, to "slum" with Dean and run away from her mom, are choices predicated upon the idea that "white is right," and thus they maintain the psychic space of Filipina mestiza liminality, alienation, and dissatisfaction. Showing the negative consequences of these choices—in fact to demonstrate that Lynda even had a choice—is an act of "mestiza consciousness" on Barry's part as cartoonist. Her work continually underscores the reality of our agency to transcend the static space of mestiza liminality for the possibilities that mestiza consciousness, a new way of thinking and being, might offer.

Owning and Loving Our Demons

As I have outlined above, comics inherently depict a border-crossing between graphic and text, high art and popular culture; likewise, Lynda Barry's *One Hun-*

dred Demons is itself a hybrid anomaly linking together Filipino American culture, wimmen's and New Comics, and peminist critique. Charting new territories of representation, it asserts a Pinay presence in cyberspace and in the cartoon world, for Barry's comics reach far more mainstream readers than the creations of any other Filipino American artist today. Thus Barry's work helps us to recognize Filipino American heterogeneities in terms of form (comics) as well as content: by exploring white Filipina mestiza realities in *One Hundred Demons*, she dives right into the heart of the Filipino American identity crisis, problematizing the idea of who is "Filipina" and what makes one Pinay. In this way, *One Hundred Demons* cuts very close to home: it explores identities and childhood through a sometimes devastating lens. Indeed, her exploration of the mestiza borderlands forces us to see things we want to ignore—namely, the demons within our own communities. Thus Lynda's anxieties about being mestiza and Filipina mirror the community's anxiety in embracing and dealing with mixed-race realities and representations.

One Hundred Demons delves into the complexities of Filipino/American racialization. Exploring what Linda M. Pierce identifies as the "physical and metaphysical" struggle of being mestiza ("Just Not My Closet," 33), Barry helps Filipino Americans to understand that what we might assume to be individual/personal issues (like dissatisfaction with appearance, a sense of not fitting in) or debilitating family secrets (valorization of whiteness, fear of darkness) are really symptoms of our larger cultural and national dis-ease. This knowledge allows us to connect our individual experiences to larger systems of oppression and thus gain insight into why we must resist our inherited narratives of colonization and cultural imperialism. Lynda Barry's reworkings of childhood "demons" are whimsical, but must also be regarded as acts of survival by remembering and by resisting amnesia—acts of decolonization and healing.

The Filipino American history of disarticulated *racial grieving* finds its form in Barry's work; indeed, it is this tension between racial grieving (Filipino American identity crisis) and hope (mestiza consciousness) that gives Barry's vision its agency: testifying to the reality of pain and confusion caused by colonization and forgetting, her comics underscore our agency in the maintenance or dismantling of these systems.

One Hundred Demons refutes the idea of Filipina American "unrepresentability," because its form (aesthetic/artistic) and themes link mestiza consciousness to decolonization. It points out the real demons in Filipino America, encouraging us to own and confront them.

In the collection's final comic vignette, "Lost and Found," Barry describes her childhood narrative models and influences (the classified ads) and then ends with a direct address to her readers: "Lost. Somewhere around puberty.

Ability to make up stories. Happiness depends on it. Please write." Her request is followed by an invitation to "Paint your demon!" She also includes "Do It Yourself" instructions and photos of herself at work for inspiration. In this way she provides readers with a model and a method for our own decolonization and growth.

One Hundred Demons, then, is a portrait of the artist as a Pinay cartoonist that delineates how cartooning and remembering can transform Filipino/American liminality into mestiza consciousness. We would do well to follow Barry's lead.

NOTES

1. Tagalog slang for "Filipina woman"; however, this term is used interchangeably with "Filipina" by Filipina Americans (instead of "babae," which literally means "girl"). In an e-mail to me (March 18, 2003), Stockton, California, historian Dawn Mabalon traces the term's history as follows:

> [Y]ou really can't interchange "babae" and "Pinay." The origins of "Pinay" can be traced to the early migrations of Filipina/os to the United States.... [The term] has historically been used by Filipina/o Americans to denote Filipina/os either living in or born in the United States.... The term was/is in constant use in Filipina/o American communities from the 1920s to the present, and seemed to be particularly reclaimed and politicized by Filipina/o American activists and artists in the Fil Am movements of the 60s/70s.... [It] was also a source of class conflict between oldtimers and Filipino Americans and post-65, professional immigrants.... In more contemporary times, "Pinoy" and "Pinay" are used as slang by Filipina/os in the Philippines and the US to identify anyone of Filipina/o descent.... It's interesting how that term traveled from the United States back to the Philippines, and the controversies surrounding its usage in the 60s and 70s point to the ongoing issues surrounding class in Filipina/o American communities.... I LOVE the term "Pinay" because it's a term created by Filipina/o Americans early in the twentieth century as a way to differentiate their identities and experiences from Filipina/os in the Philippines, and it's a very positive and affirming term in my own experiences.

2. The character Marlys Mullen was originally conceived as Filipina, as the comic entitled "Fine Dining" shows (*dinuguan* and *bagoong* are particularly redolent Filipino foods) (Barry, *Greatest!,* 6). Barry decided not to develop this aspect further in *Ernie Pook's Comeek.*

3. Available at http://www.salon.com. I would like to thank Cathy Quinones for sending me the link to the *One Hundred Demons* site at Salon.com, and my mother, Eloisa D. de Jesús, for translating Barry's transliterated Tagalog. *Salamat po* to Karen Kuo and Karen Leong for their incisive comments on earlier drafts and support of this project.

4. "Peminist" describes Filipina/American feminist thought, with the "p" signifying specifically "Pinay/Pilipina." Some Filipina/American critics prefer the term "pinayism" or "Pinay Studies" to describe Filipina/American feminist theorizing; nevertheless, all of these terms describe Filipina/American struggles against racism, sexism, imperialism, and homophobia, and for decolonization, consciousness, and liberation. I prefer the term "peminist" over "feminist" because it signifies both an assertion of a specifically Filipina/American standpoint and a radical repudiation of hegemonic white feminism.

5. Since this article's initial publication, the study of multicultural comics has grown tremendously. Other readings of Barry's work include my article, "Of Monsters and Mothers: Filipina American Identity and Maternal Legacies in Lynda J. Barry's *One Hundred Demons*" (2004), and Theresa Tensuan's "Comic Visions and Revisions in the Work of Lynda Barry and Marjane Satrapi" (2006). Book-length examinations of multicultural comics include Frederick Aldama's *Your Brain on Latino Comics: From Gus Arriola to Los Bros Hernandez* (2009) and Michael Sheyahshe's *Native Americans in Comic Books: A Critical Study* (2008).

6. In fact, the online *Lambiek Comiclopedia* notes: "Barry has achieved, in some ways, the alternative comics dream. Her work reaches adults who might not read any other comics, adults who, because of work like Barry's, don't question that this art form can produce sophisticated reading matter."

7. Cartoonist Roberta Gregory, creator of the infamous character Bitchy Bitch, describes her harrowing experience in editing the violent, misogynistic work of Robert Crumb for Fantagraphics Books in her comic *Naughty Bits #1* (1991).

8. See the chapter entitled "Womyn's Comics" in Robbins, *From Girls to Grrlz*, for a comprehensive history of the genre.

9. McCloud writes: "The cartoon is a vacuum into which our identity and awareness are pulled . . . an empty shell that we inhabit which enables us to travel in another realm. We don't just observe the cartoon, we become it" (*Understanding Comics: The Invisible Art*, 1994, 36). He continues, "Storytellers in all media know that a sure indicator of audience involvement is the degree to which the audience identifies with a story's character. And since viewer-identification is a specialty of cartooning, cartoons have historically held an advantage in breaking into world popular culture" (42).

10. See McCloud, *Understanding Comics: The Invisible Art*, "Chapter 8: A Word about Color," for an incisive discussion of how color comics work.

11. Barry's inclusion of a transliterated childhood Tagalog without English translation forces the readers to negotiate her "Taglish" borderlands.

12. It is beyond the scope of this essay to delve into the complex relationships among the three generations of Filipinas in Lynda's family as presented in *One Hundred Demons*. Barry highlights the issues of maternal legacies and Filipina identity in two other cartoons, "Girlness" and "The Aswang." "Girlness" explores Lynda's and her mother's discord as rooted in the mother's devastating experiences during World War II, while "The Aswang" uses a Filipino folktale to explore three generations of grandmother/granddaughter bonding and maternal estrangement in Lynda's family.

5 BLACK NATIONALISM, BUNRAKU, AND BEYOND

Articulating Black Heroism through Cultural Fusion and Comics

REBECCA WANZO

> At a certain point, it's just not . . . psychologically pleasant to keep working
> from a white image.
>
> —KERRY JAMES MARSHALL, in
> Martin and Marshall, *Behind the Scenes*

O NE OF MY COLLEAGUES was out one day with her niece when they saw some Spider-Man decorations. Asked if she would be interested in decorating her room with Spider-Man paraphernalia, the little girl exclaimed, "Spider-Man is for boys!" A proper feminist, my friend was perturbed by this assertion, and she tried to tease out the logic behind the claim, only to become more alarmed when her niece said, "Girls aren't interested in Spider-Man unless he saves them!"

By the time we talked, my friend had recovered from the heart attack induced by her niece's retro-wilting-flower subjectivity. We agreed nostalgically that the problem is that contemporary girls do not have what influenced us in the late 1970s and early 1980s. We have a generation of girls who are inundated with the pleasures of Princess accoutrements, and models of strength such as the superpowered kindergartners the Powerpuff Girls still frame power within the pleasures of girly-girl accessories and tiny, unimposing bodies. However, I must acknowledge that my role model as a child was problematic in her own ways. She was also a princess—an Amazon princess—but she left the world of the princesses to fight evil created by the "man's world." I clearly remember singing in the universal, atonal way of vocally ungifted children: "Wonder WOH-MAAAN! WON-der WOH-MAAAAAN!" Humming the bass beats of the television show theme song, I would begin my daily twirling exercises—spinning my body until I felt the giddy combination of light-headed energy and nausea. I was a wild-haired brown child, with a crown of aluminum foil in my hair, mumbling under my breath, twirling with a slightly off-center momentum, ripping something off to reveal the shirt and short ensemble of Wonder Woman underoos. I was often alone except for the unseen and voiceless victims and villains who peppered my imaginary world: *Wait you Nazis, I am Wonder Woman and I will stop you!* My valiant claims were only interrupted by the change in wardrobe from T-shirt to underoos.

I begin my contribution to this volume with a personal narrative because of how important the affective dimension of revision has been to a number of cultural productions that make racial or ethnic minorities the center of creation. Creators like artist Kerry James Marshall, whom I will discuss in this essay, often mine beloved texts for inspiration. This inspiration is not only shaped by the pleasure they received from the consumption but the unfulfilled desire to see stories or representations that feature people like themselves. Multicultural superhero comics are often quite explicitly marked by this reflexivity. Multicultural superhero comic revisions entail the rich texturing of locale and the cultural context within which the superhero narrative unfolds; an aesthetic attention to the rendering of the racial or ethnic minority body; and a self-consciousness about the process of identification with cultural icons. The superhero comics that may have most systematically demonstrated a revision aesthetic were produced by Milestone, a short-lived comics imprint run by African American creators. Their Superman-like hero, Icon, was a black conservative from outer space whose sidekick was a teenage single mother who inspired him to help the community. The superhero group, Blood Syndicate, was an amalgamation of street gangs who became superheroes in the wake of an industrial "accident" in a predominantly black neighborhood. The scientist-turned-superhero, Hardware, was cheated out of his intellectual property by a white businessman. These three models flip the script of archetypal kinds of superhero stories, placing the narratives in the context of black history and the challenges facing the black inner city.

These thoughtful representations were not available to me when I was young. And I was not a comic book reader until adulthood; thus I was unfamiliar with early black superheroes such as Luke Cage, Black Panther, or even Nubia, the black Wonder Woman who appeared in a few issues in the 1970s. Wonder Woman was nonetheless both productive and challenging for my self-image. I was no Lynda Carter, with alabaster skin and long, flowing hair, but the romance of power and agency remained with me. In putting on the underoos, I could imagine a validated outlet for my strong personality. While heroes represent to adults what they stand for, researchers have suggested that heroes help children define their place in society and construct ideal roles for themselves to play.[1] However, even as Wonder Woman represented a particular ideal of women being able to have and demonstrate their power, I was also quite physically dissimilar from my hero. Adopting Wonder Woman was one of my first clearly remembered acts of seeing myself in a cultural representation that was clearly not meant to address anyone who looked like me or had my history. However, identification is a complex process that cannot be easily described as a function of people's attachment to those most like them, and superheroes may illustrate the vagaries of identificatory practices better than many cultural productions. No real person can have the attributes of the superhero, and they offer the fantasy that with a cape, mask, or pair of underoos, the wearer can transform herself into another person. Comic book superheroes have traditionally offered the fantasy of outsiders transforming into ideal citizens, making them ideal Rorschachs for people of color. People can identify with those like themselves and with idealized versions of themselves. Superheroes have given the world both representations.

Nevertheless, for many people of color in the United States, the experience of consuming comic book heroism in print, television, and film has involved reconciling themselves to representing the antithesis of heroic ideals. Even in a twenty-first-century casting of a new Wonder Woman, would anyone imagine that Hollywood producers would cast a black or Asian actress in that role? Comic creators have imagined people of color in these roles, but their presence is always short-lived. While identification with fictions involves imaginative leaps and textual poaching for all consumers, people of color often must negotiate a string of representations (hypermasculine men and emasculated women) that set them apart from heroism. Hence, a truly radical departure from traditional representations of superheroes requires sidestepping the exaggerated stereotypes of blacks in mainstream comics.

Another means of revision is the creating of the self-conscious comic book that foregrounds the hybrid nature of black identificatory practices that draw from multiple cultures. For example, African American cartoonist Aaron McGruder's popular comic strip *The Boondocks* (1996–2006) mixed black nationalist rhetoric with a Japanese manga and anime aesthetic. In providing radically different models of the body in black comics, artists began to create an iconography contrasting with the damaging history of the visual representation of black bodies.

In this essay I discuss an unusual comic book text that provides a wholly other comic book aesthetic—an exhibit by artist Kerry James Marshall and the performance piece derived from it, *Every Beat of My Heart*. Marshall first began this project with *Rythm Mastr*, an exhibit, blending African, African American, and traditional superhero narratives, for the Carnegie Museum International show in 1999. In 2008, he blended the comic book project with a community performance piece using the Japanese form of Bunraku puppetry at the Wexner Center in Columbus, Ohio. He makes an intervention into the absence of black bodies in superhero texts by presenting alternative body models for superhero narratives. His work illustrates the kind of cultural fusion informing some black comic artists' productions: a fusion that illustrates how the future of black comics is one that moves away from purely black nationalist, Afrocentric, or traditional superhero narratives and instead embraces the hybrid subjectivity of blacks in the African diaspora. His project is instructive, not only through what it offers as an alternative model, but by the absences in his vision of black heroic narratives.

Where Are Our Bodies?: Transforming Black Representations in Comics

> In the black community there's great resistance to extreme representations of blackness. Some people are unable to see the beauty in that. So I've been very conscious of the way I render my figures. I try to give them subtlety and grace and there's a delicacy in the way I handle the features, especially the lines and contours. Extreme blackness plus grace equals power. I see the figures as emblematic; I'm reducing the complex variations of tone to a rhetorical dimension: blackness. It's a kind of stereotyping but my figures are never laughable.
>
> —KERRY JAMES MARSHALL, in
> Marshall et al., *Kerry James Marshall*

Until the gains of the civil rights era affected mass media in the 1960s and 1970s, representations of African Americans in many comics were routinely racist, with few exceptions. Daily newspaper strips such as Will Eisner's *The Saint* featured a sidekick named Ebony White, whose features were a hybrid mix of human and primate and who served as comic relief. African American cartoonists such as Chester Commodore and Jackie Ormes produced progressive representations of African Americans in editorial cartoons or their strips for the black press, but the vast majority of visual representations depicted African Americans as comedic buffoons.[2] In 1966, the Black Panther appeared in an issue of the *Fantastic Four*, and that marks the beginning of a new era of black representations in comics. And yet, as Anna Beatrice Scott argues, representations of African Americans as human, as opposed to stereotype, have historically been difficult to find in comics, as African American superheroes have typically been portrayed as coons, magical negroes, or supermacho models of black nationalist masculinity. Part of the challenge is the medium itself. Caricature has been one of the most important aesthetic modes of comic production, but the phenotypic excesses of caricature produce challenges for creators of black characters, who recognize that blacks are always already stereotyped when their bodies are represented.

Artist Kerry James Marshall says he was ten when *The Black Panther* was introduced and that comics were one of the media that engaged him when he began drawing as a child (Marshall, "Thousand Words," 149). Marshall has routinely blended popular culture and a variety of cultures in his works throughout the years. He first emerged in the national art scene in the 1980s, working primarily as a painter, and then working more with video, collage, photography, woodcut, and installation in the 1990s. In 1999, he added the comic strip form to his adult repertoire, drawing on an early influence and continued interest in comics as a medium. *Rythm Mastr*, displayed in the 1999 Carnegie International Exhibition, was an original comic strip printed on newsprint. The disposable medium of newsprint featuring a genre often viewed as disposable—comics—was part of the artist's intervention into how people view the form. Marshall calls attention to the ways in which newsprint typically has no value after it is read, and the Carnegie allowed him to post his strip in the Treasure Room at the museum, a space traditionally allotted to items characterized as precious.[3] Marshall's strip blocked the display windows, and by privileging the strip, the artist questioned the intrinsic value assigned to objects generally.

Marshall's work thus makes a comment on the invisibility of comics as a genre, while he also critiques the invisibility of blacks and culturally specific stories in comics. Because African American superhero comics had not managed to have sustained runs in the comic book industry, Marshall produces his own version of the superhero comic, not only incorporating the traditions of superhero comics but combining them with aspects of African American history, African mythology and aesthetics, and Bunraku puppetry.[4] *Rythm Mastr* tells the story of a young African American couple, Farrell and his girlfriend Stasha, whose lives are irrevocably transformed when they cross paths with gang violence. Separated from Farrell during a gunfight, Stasha is shot and paralyzed, and the two of them take different paths to deal with the aftermath. In the tradition of the accidental superhero, Farrell stumbles upon an ancient Egyptian museum and encounters a superhero based upon an African mythos. Rythm Mastr uses drums to bring African statues to life. When he dies, Farrell takes up his mantle. Meanwhile, Stasha, in the tradition of the superhero who is physically damaged but uses his technological savvy to fight crime, develops a set of remote-control cars that can retaliate against the gangbangers. This narrative is a riff on the superhero narrative of friends or lovers who are divided by a violent incident and take different paths. Marshall also explains that the story is about a conflict between history and modernity, and he seems to be pushing people to critique the embrace of the modern at the expense of the lessons and tools of history, signified by the African influence.

This initial exhibit drew extensively on the aesthetic of the traditional comic book—Marshall produced highly detailed colored drawings on newsprint. When Kerry James Marshall transformed the project as an artist-in-residence at the Wexner Center in Columbus, Ohio, from 2007 to 2008, he transformed the aesthetic of the represented black body by rendering the characters in three different forms—the black-and-white strip, the Bunraku puppet, and the real teenagers who became part of the narrative. This strip featured stark black-and-white drawings that were still attentive to the pacing and details of the comic book format even as the faces of the characters were radically transformed. In the 1999 exhibit, the characters were rendered in shades of brown, with largely realistic constructions of the face. In the second exhibit, he utilized a version of what Terrie Sultan explains is his "signature image": "the highly stylized black persona, drawn as much as brushed in pure black paint, whose features are barely discernible, except for gleaming white eyes and teeth" ("This Is the Way We Live," 12). In *Every Beat of My Heart*, more features are discernible, but they are thin lines accenting the shape of the black mask. Marshall is always concerned with presenting blackness conceptually: "these streamlined, self-consciously iconic figures embodied Marshall's developing strategy for addressing the complicated, intertwined cultural and political rhetoric of racial representation" (ibid., 12–13). While African masks were evident in the original *Rythm Mastr* exhibit, they are the model for the predominant facial rendering in *Every Beat of My Heart*. The characters' faces are starkly black; the lines of the eyes, cheekbones, and faces are in white. By making the faces so thoroughly masked—a racially inflected riff on the superhero mask—the images draw away from the individual privileging of one face over another and focus on the complex narrative Marshall is telling with the strip.

By setting the strip in a declining inner city marred by violence even as part of the city offers prosperity to others, Marshall calls attention to urban decay. Many cities in the United States have been hit by failing industry and schools and the violence that entered to fill the void opened by fewer economic and educational opportunities. The artist paints the picture of the challenges facing the cities, while also calling attention to the damaging forces of commodity culture. Marshall interrupts the strip with advertisements for imaginary items, and with representations of women selling themselves in a city where so many people have forgotten their worth.

The African mask is also three-dimensional in the exhibit, as Marshall shapes Bunraku puppets in the style of African sculpture. Marshall traveled to Japan to study the making of Bunraku puppets. Bunraku is a form of Japanese puppet theater in which a number of visible puppeteers operate a single, large, beautifully constructed puppet. These puppets, by being fashioned in the style of African sculpture, have features that are large but subtle and unmoving. In contrast to the excesses of many renderings of cartoon and comic book expressions, the noble shape of the African features defies caricature. In a discussion of the way that he deals with blackness in his work, Marshall once commented that "extreme blackness plus grace equals power." He sees himself as making "emblematic" figures, "reducing complex variations of tone to a rhetorical dimension." While he acknowledges he does "a kind of stereotyping," it is also true that his "figures are never laughable" (Marshall et al., 90). The mass production of comics depends upon the stereotypical rendering of characters—the repeated representations of a character with minor changes, moving through scenes. Some comic genres, such as the editorial cartoon, depend upon the immediate recognition of the stereotypical referent to communicate identity and idea. By shaping the story through repeated representations of black figures that cannot be laughable, even as he sometimes tells jokes, through his script, that are amusing, Marshall removes the black body and face—consistent referents of derogatory jokes—from the logic of humor.

Even comics such as *The Black Panther*, which inaugurated a new era of superhero comics and were inflected with black nationalist discourse, have been hampered by stereotypical renderings of blacks. Hypermasculine embodiment of black men is hardly revolutionary; thus one of Marshall's interventions into the shape of the body is to use the puppet bodies whose long limbs are masked by costumes. Real bodies are also present in the performance—the teenagers operating the puppets who give the characters emotion and voice.

Young Visions: The Future of Comics?

This is my version of "No Child Left Behind."

—KERRY JAMES MARSHALL, in
Martin and Marshall, *Behind the Scenes*

If the African-influenced Bunraku puppets make an important intervention into reimagining how black phenotypes and bodies can be represented, Marshall's inclusion of real bodies in his comic book narrative also expands the idea of graphic storytelling. Superhero stories originating in comic books have long circulated outside of the page in television and film. Thus "comic-book" has become an often derogatory modifier for representations connoting the absence of complexity or characterization. While scholars and readers of comics know this universalizing of superhero comics as the antithesis of depth is inaccurate, this marker of comic books not only as "medium" but as a broader mode of representation and sensibility has circulated widely in U.S. culture. Thus to understand fully the broad range of possibilities of approaches to multicultural graphic storytelling in the United States, it is necessary to understand the "comic" as a set of narrative conventions and not only as a medium. The fusion of media, linked by these conventions, is more than likely an important part of the twenty-first-century future of comics. Marshall's fusion of real bodies into the narrative is one of his major interventions into African Americans' traditional relationship with the superhero comics genre.

In September 2007, Kerry James Marshall held auditions for local high school students in Columbus, Ohio, to participate in the *Every Beat of My Heart* performance. Almost two hundred students applied to participate, and of these applicants approximately twenty students were selected.[5] Marshall used a selection process that he described as "democratic"—students were placed into teams that competed in various challenges. The two winning teams were selected to participate. Students were not selected based on artistic or performance ability, but because of their effort on teams and a certain amount of luck. By eliminating educational hierarchies that give certain students access to activities if they have aptitude, Marshall was making an argument with the method he used to choose participants that mirrored one of the arguments in his text—it is necessary to engage with children who might not be given opportunities in cities. While he joked that this process was his version of "no child left behind," his narrative is also a commentary on how African American children are being left behind.

The set for the performance is in the gallery and across from the strip hanging on one wall. Various images of black history hang, as if flags, above the fictional city set. The performance begins with a parade of characters walking down the city street. The puppeteers are dressed in black. Black gauze hangs from backward-turned baseball caps, masking the puppeteers' features. The two faces we see are of the narrators. They explain that the story takes place "in a time of rapid renewal," but that people "hanging on at the margins" were not gaining riches. Instead, they were evidence of a "wretched asymmetry" in the city. It was the "lack of imagination . . . all around . . . that would guarantee that their situation would never really change." The narrators comment on people spending what they do not have, and failing to look at history for guidance. They conclude their introduction with a version of the traditional comic book introduction of a hero, explaining that in difficult times, a hero rises up among the people to save them. In this story, his name is the Rythm Mastr. The tale is set in a "city near enough" and "far, far away," and is a parable of what the future may hold for all of us. It is the "new Black Metropolis."

Three puppeteers each operate the main characters, Stasha and Farrell. The young couple talk with their friends in the street, and we discover that Stasha has a talent for robotics. As described in the aforementioned plot summary, the couple have a negative encounter with a gangbanger in a car, and then are caught in the crossfire of gang violence. Stasha is shot and becomes paralyzed. At the climax, Stasha rages at her condition, while Farrell encounters the Rythm Mastr, a mystical being who tells Farrell that he had been waiting for him for a long time. The performance ends with both of them beginning on their paths— Stasha begins working on a robotic means of retaliation, while Farrell is taught what rhythms of the drums will bring the African sculptures to life.

The presence of the puppeteers models a different kind of superhero identification. The students, predominantly African American, are in the superhero narrative and yet not. Their attire is about erasing their presence, but without their presence, the narrative could not have life. In choosing Bunraku and a form of audition that did not demand a previously developed skill set, Marshall transformed what is often an individualistic narrative—the superhero tale— into a collaborative project where individual identity is not privileged even as every person is necessary to the collective project.

Having real bodies present is one of the many ways that the overembodied nature of comics is challenged in Marshall's narrative. If one of my challenges as a child was that I clearly could not have the physical characteristics of Lynda Carter, Marshall circumvents the problem of direct identification with a body type by removing the heightened musculature of the superhero comics and by having many bodies participate in the presentation of the characters. While Marshall's creation of the comic strip is actually more individualistic than many mainstream comic productions—as he is the writer and penciller of the text— when he produces the live version of his project many people are involved, not only the teenagers but other collaborators who help construct the show.

Marshall aims to provide an introduction to the varied concepts and media that he hopes will impact not only the students' way of viewing the world but of participating in it. In the performance, the children are largely ventriloquists, performing Kerry's vision, with some subtle hints of their own voices. When speaking, the children can use their own narrative inflections; when moving the puppets, they imbue the puppets with the movements that might match the rhythm of the teenage amble. While they participate in a number of activities in rehearsals that teach them how to move and express themselves creatively, their own voices are not strongly present in Marshall's production.

That absence may have produced a generational tension. In the *Behind the*

Scenes video, Kevin Fish, the assistant director, comments that it is difficult to get the children to invest, that attempting to do so is like "pulling teeth." In contrast, Marshall suggests that he is very comfortable with the teenagers' lack of investment, believing that they may not know now the impact the experience may have on them later. The participants make a variety of comments highlighting a generational divide—that Marshall is a "typical adult" and that he "explains things a lot." And Marshall does have a great deal to explain, because he hopes the students will be interested in the content, art form, and process.

However, the audience could gain a glimpse of one of the most interesting generational tensions in a Q&A after a preview show. One of the students commented that while she enjoyed the show and the process, she wished that the images Marshall presented were not so "negative." Marshall later commented that he did not see what they found negative, although the student was—most likely unknowingly—speaking in a long tradition that criticizes negative representations of black culture. The student would prefer not to have a story about gangbangers overcoming the city, because that is not her experience of the inner city. In examining the strip, she may have been uncomfortable with the "hos" who function as a dysfunctional Greek chorus. Yet Marshall uses them to identify transitions in the narrative, as well as to emphasize that bodies can be bought and sold in the new Black Metropolis. A project that the students had a role in shaping aesthetically and ideologically might present commodity culture as offering some political possibilities.

The tension between the historical and the modern that shaped the project from *Rythm Mastr* to *Every Beat of My Heart* reflects a generational divide between Marshall and younger comics consumers and producers. This is most vividly illustrated by the character of Stasha, whose educational skill set is devalued in Marshall's script. In response to her disability, Stasha turns to her computer, and proactively decides to take action against her attackers. In contrast, Farrell stumbles upon the Rythm Mastr, and yet his heroism is foreordained. The fated special boy narrative has famously played out in any number of stories—such as the film *The Matrix* and the Harry Potter series. *The Matrix*, another text of cultural fusion deeply influenced by Asian culture and superhero comics, also expressed wariness of technology and told the story of human beings mentally enslaved by machines. The specialness of the white hero, Neo, was visually marked by the fact that he was surrounded by highly competent people of color and one woman whose direction, vision, and faith would make any one of them capable of being "The One" if they existed in narratives that privileged hard work and eschewed a superior white masculine destiny. I would like to think that the phenomenally successful story of Harry Potter would have been as successful if it had been the story of Hermione Potter, but the fantasy of the "special boy" is in so many narratives that it is unclear how many people question the gendered (and often racial) construction of the convention when they see it.

Thus, for all of Marshall's profound innovations in the treatment of blackness in the comics medium, the artist is still traditional in a particular kind of black nationalist formation that looks to Africa for inspiration and neglects the heroic possibilities of female characters. From the set to the critiques of commodity culture to the choice of hero, Marshall looks to the past in order to shape the future, and technology is a dangerous presence. Other revisions of representations of the black body might include cyborg or virtual bodies, and might take up the issues of Stasha's disability as a metaphor for the broader disabling of black culture that demands a framework that might enable black subjects to have more agency.

Nevertheless, Kerry James Marshall's use of Bunraku was an important step in illustrating how those interested in the black representation in comics can begin to imagine alternatives to the traditional, problematic forms of caricature. While some of Marshall's content looks to traditional touchstones for black heroic narrative, the solution is not to reject totally traditional models but fuse them with new ones. What if Stasha discovered a way to use technology to animate the African statues? What if the blend of technology and tradition was the means of rescuing the new Black Metropolis?

Marshall's project invites such reimaginings, if not through all of the content of the text, then through the creative process that integrates teenagers into the project. Introducing participants and audience to forms of comics beyond what they see in traditional comics or in Hollywood film, the project invites them to rethink the traditional comic frame. As a museum-worthy, theatrical, and even interpersonal means by which people think about conceptualizations of the hero, the comic book in general and the black superhero in particular can be a provoking means for rethinking our relationship to our spaces and our worlds. A key to reconceptualizing the superhero form, one we think we know, is bringing in other material that can cause us to revisit the genre and its content. *Every Beat of My Heart* blends the old and new in its mixture of traditional comics, African mythology and aesthetics, and Bunraku. It illustrates one of the many possibilities of fusion in new black comics that move beyond traditional stereotypes and look to new futures.

NOTES

1. See Douglas V. Porpora, "Personal Heroes, Religion, and Transcendental Metanarratives"; Anne Haas Dyson, "Cultural Constellations and Childhood Identities: On

Greek Gods, Cartoon Heroes, and the Social Lives of Schoolchildren"; Norma Pecora, "Superman/superboys/superman: The Comic Book Hero as a Socializing Agent."

2. For examples see Tim Jackson, "Pioneering Cartoonists of Color," as well as Nancy Goldstein's *Jackie Ormes: The First African American Woman Cartoonist.*

3. To see what the exhibition looked like, see the catalog for the exhibit: Carnegie Museum of Art, *Carnegie International 1999/2000*, 64–65.

4. One of the most important attempts to maintain a series of black superheroes was the Milestone line, a short-lived imprint of DC in the 1990s produced by African American creators. Comics such as *Icon, Blood Syndicate, Static,* and *Hardware* were set in the fictional town of Dakota and addressed issues such as teenage pregnancy, gang violence, and theft of black intellectual property. See Jeffrey Brown, *Black Superheroes, Milestone Comics, and Their Fans.*

5. I say "approximately" because more than twenty students were selected, but some students did not complete the project.

6 BIRTH OF A NATION

Representation, Nationhood, and Graphic Revolution in the Works of D. W. Griffith, DJ Spooky, and Aaron McGruder et al.

THIS ESSAY EXPLORES subtle intertextual relationships between D. W. Griffith's film *The Birth of a Nation* (1915), DJ Spooky's performative "remix" of the film, and the comic/graphic novel *Birth of a Nation*, written by Aaron McGruder and Reginald Hudlin and illustrated by Kyle Baker. Griffith's film, repeatedly hailed as a classic, influential contribution to the American film catalogue, chronicles the fear and hatred of a postbellum racist America. *The Birth of a Nation* (originally entitled *The Clansman* and based on a play, *The Clansman: An Historical Romance of the Ku Klux Klan*) became the biggest box-office success of its era, before the advent of the "talkies," earning upwards of $18 million. Even as film scholars and cultural studies critics acknowledge its technical genius for its time, the racial overtones are nonetheless unavoidable, since the KKK are literally depicted as superhero vigilantes who rescue the South from ignorant and irresponsible black sociopolitical power. Enter McGruder et al., circa 2004. Aaron McGruder, creator of the incomparable comic strip *The Boondocks*, and Reginald Hudlin, the writer/director of a now cult classic hip-hop film *House Party*, convened privately at the 2002 San Diego Comic Book Convention. At this meeting, they developed the idea of East St. Louis seceding from the Union in response to the controversial 2000 U.S. presidential election. They initially developed the idea as a film project and eventually produced it as a comic/graphic novel, realizing that there would be very little interest or monetary support for a complex, satirical comedy about black nationalism. Their project, *Birth of a Nation: A Comic Novel*, explores black nationhood in tandem with an acerbic sociopolitical analysis of U.S. presidential politics. In this essay I briefly explore the remarkable nationalistic and narratological correspondences between D. W. Griffith's classic film, DJ Spooky's (né Paul Miller) audiovisual hip-hop "remix," and McGruder et al.'s phenomenal graphic novel of nearly the same name.

Each of the texts, a film, an audiovisual performance, and a graphic novel, is a distinct medium of artistic expression, and each, in turn, also represents a distinct genre. Griffith's film posits itself as cinematic historical narrative; Miller's performance piece posits itself as postmodern conceptual art; and McGruder et al. present one of the sharpest satirical narratives of the hip-hop generation in the graphic novel, or comic book, form (Kitwana, *Hip Hop Generation*).[1] Taken together, Miller and McGruder's work reflect an important response to the ideologies and notions of nation or nationality reflected in the original film *The Birth of a Nation* (BOAN) and its various, extensive, and attendant discourses and debates. Both of these responsive hip-hop narratives critique, engage, and ultimately reinterpret the original film through the aesthetic lens of hip-hop culture.[2] Mimesis is a guiding concept of representation that helps to situate these three texts within a framework that productively elicits complex interpretations of each separately and in a more integrated sense based upon the ways in which the latter two narratives signify upon, critique, respond to, and distinguish themselves from the former. Within the context of this discussion, mimesis is an iconic form of representation that transcends the differences between media (Mitchell, "Representation," 14). Iconic representation, or mimesis, stresses resemblance; thus it might be prudent to pose several questions to initiate a more general narratological analysis of these texts. First, to what extent does the original, Griffith's *The Birth of a Nation*, resemble "reality" or history? Second, to what extent does the remix, DJ Spooky/Paul Miller's *Rebirth of a Nation*, resemble "reality" and/or resemble Griffith's original? And finally, to what extent does the remake, McGruder et al.'s *Birth of a Nation: A Comic Novel*, resemble reality or resemble Griffith's original film? I employ the terms "original," "remix," and "remake" to distinguish each of these texts along a tentative trajectory of intertextual relationships.

The Original

The subtitle of Melvyn Stokes's recent, exhaustive history of D. W. Griffith's BOAN, "A History of 'The Most Controversial Motion Picture of All Time,'" includes a hyperbolic quote from Roy E. Aitken, one of the film's financiers

(*D. W. Griffith's* The Birth of Nation, 7). While Stokes concedes the outrageous nature of Aitken's publicity-seeking exclamation (i.e., *The Birth of a Nation* may not be "the most controversial motion picture of all time"), he also underscores the film's groundbreaking status. "[It] was the first American film to be twelve reels long . . . the first to cost $100,000 . . . the first to be shown mainly in regular theaters . . . the first to have a specially compiled musical score . . . the first movie to be shown at the White House . . . the first to be viewed by countless millions of ordinary Americans" (3). As an original text from which subsequent remakes and remixes were to be made, Griffith's film distinguishes itself as one of the most influential films of all time. It is an original film, and according to Stokes it was the first "blockbuster." Ironically, on-the-spot and on-the-road edits of the film make it fairly difficult to identify something that could be called an original, or "true print," of *The Birth of a Nation* (Lang, *Birth of a Nation*, 37). D. W. Griffith perpetually edited his critically acclaimed film in successive showings across the country, even changing the original title from *The Clansman* to *The Birth of a Nation*. His constant reworking of and critical attentiveness to *The Birth of a Nation* only subtly suggest his personal sense of the film's historical import. Robert Lang quotes D. W. Griffith's comment on the film in a letter to *Sight & Sound*, 1947:

> I gave to my best knowledge the proven facts, and presented the known truth, about the Reconstruction period in the American South. These facts are based on an overwhelming compilation of authentic evidence and testimony. My picturisation of history as it happens requires, therefore, no apology, no defense, no explanations. (Lang, *Birth of a Nation*, 3)

Over thirty years after its theatrical release, Griffith still defends *The Birth of a Nation* as the mimetic depiction of history, a rendering on film of the Civil War and the Reconstruction era, as well as each moment's attendant sociopolitical issues. As Michele Wallace argues, "*The Birth of a Nation* [is] a masterpiece of the silent era yet widely viewed as antiblack propaganda. The film's continued notoriety challenges all our most beloved notions of the intrinsically moral character of aesthetic masterpieces" ("The Good Lynching and *The Birth of a Nation*," 86).

Based on Thomas Dixon's play and novel *The Clansman* and released on February 8, 1915, *The Birth of a Nation* details the defeat of the South during the Civil War (1861–1865). The film suggests that, in the aftermath of the Civil War and throughout Reconstruction, irresponsible black political power, the looming threat of miscegenation, and the sheer ignorance and laziness of black folk are set to ruin the southern United States. In her essay on the influence of

Thomas Dixon's work on Richard Wright's *Native Son*, Clare Eby suggests that Dixon was "[c]onvinced that radical Reconstruction—which marked the first attempt in the U.S. to incorporate blacks into the body politic—had unleashed the 'beast'" (Eby, "Slouching toward Beastliness," 439). This "beast" can engender at least two interpretations. First, as an originary Eurocentric stereotype of the African and eventually the African American, the bestial depiction on film and in the public sphere (through cartoons, minstrel shows, etc.) signals the subhuman conceptualization of black folk that was the prerequisite to disenfranchisement and the erasure of blacks within the body politic. "In *Birth*, Gus (Walter Long), sometimes known as the 'black brute,' is considered guilty of killing Flora (Mae Marsh), the youngest of the Cameron siblings"—more on this below (Wallace, "The Good Lynching," 88). Thus, at the very moment in history when political white supremacy required them most, images of the African American as ignorant, illiterate, and uncivilized were projected through *The Birth of a Nation*. The regularly referenced scene of black men at a state senate meeting underscores the potency of this stereotype and these kinds of images. In this scene black political representatives are unruly and crude. They prop their bare feet up on desks, have a general disregard for the representative political process, and consume alcohol during the proceedings. "Griffith presents a series of scenes to illustrate how badly blacks behaved after the passage of the Thirteenth Amendment, when they were freed and given the vote, and after the passage of the Fourteenth and Fifteenth Amendments, when they were given free access to public facilities" (ibid., 93). Some of these scenes depicted black folk (actual and in blackface) as "aggressively groveling and grimacing," or pilfering their votes—some not understanding suffrage at all. Others were "shown with picket signs demanding mixed marriages" (ibid.). This was powerful propaganda for the expulsion of blacks from the body politic in the late nineteenth and early twentieth centuries.

Yet the more ominous and enduring interpretation of the bestial depictions in *The Birth of a Nation* asserts the hypersexuality of African Americans. The general fear of miscegenation was the cornerstone of white supremacist violence against blacks during the Reconstruction era. Again according to Eby, "Most ominously, freedom . . . unleashed the Negro male's lust for the white woman, and the white man's response [was] lynching" (Eby, "Slouching toward Beastliness," 440). The quadroon woman's seduction of and subsequent control over Senator Austin Stoneman are particularly subtle examples of the inhuman sexual prowess of the African American. Stoneman is characterized as a powerful politician who supports miscegenation and the repression of Southern political power. In fact, in history Thaddeus Stevens—upon whom Stoneman is based—was the leader of the Radical Republicans, who dominated the

Congress after the 1866 elections and generally directed the policies and planning of Reconstruction.[3] Stevens advocated the continued use of military force to properly reconstruct the South, and he was a vocal proponent of equality and education for freed blacks. In *The Birth of a Nation*, Stoneman espouses similar viewpoints, much to the chagrin of his Southern adversaries. Within the storyworld of the film, Griffith suggests that this powerful white leader is unduly influenced and controlled by his quadroon lover, not coincidentally named Lydia. In history, Stevens never married, but he did indeed live with his domestic servant, Lydia Hamilton Smith, a mulatta with whom he was rumored to have a sexual relationship.[4] According to Michele Wallace, "Lydia's race and questionable moral character are visually marked in three ways: First, although played by a white actress, she wears dark makeup. Second, she is clothed like a gypsy or other colorful ethnic. . . . Third, her gestures are exaggeratedly exotic and elaborate" (Wallace, "The Good Lynching," 90).

The more sinister and/or more blatant depiction of the African American as "beast" in Griffith's film centers on the scenes of rape that occur in both sections of the film. In the first half of the film, during the Civil War section, the Camerons (Southern protagonists) are attacked by a black militia at their home. In addition to ransacking the home, the militiamen attempt to rape all of the Cameron women. The film depicts this desire to rape as a natural consequence of the black militia's violent attack. Fortunately, a heroic cadre of Confederate soldiers saves the women. This theme of forcible miscegenation via black men raping white women is the most sensational achievement of Griffith's film, relying on the ultimate scene (in the second, Reconstruction, part of the film) between Gus, a lascivious former slave, and Flora Cameron—the picture of white feminine beauty.

Gus is played in blackface by white actor Walter Long, and after crudely proposing to Flora—who promptly refuses in fear and disgust—he proceeds to chase her through the woods. Flora decides to leap to her death rather than succumb to the violent fantasies of the depraved Gus. In almost immediate and heroic response, Gus is hunted like an animal by the newly formed Ku Klux Klan and ceremoniously lynched. His dead body is then left at the doorstep of the lieutenant governor, Silas Lynch. "Silas Lynch, the male mulatto, played by a white man (George Siegmann) in brown face, . . . has a wanton appetite for power and revenge and is invited to participate in the Reconstruction government in South Carolina. . . . Lynch's role as a villain is . . . palpable" (ibid.). Through these scenes and enduring images, Griffith establishes a powerful iconography of fear, racism, miscegenation, rape, and political power. This combustible and visual mix of potent imagery reflected just enough of reality to exacerbate the fear-mongering efforts of white supremacist leaders. Not surprisingly, throughout the twentieth century *The Birth of a Nation* was used as a recruitment tool for the organization so heroically depicted in the film.

The Remix

In *Remix: Making Art and Commerce Thrive in the Hybrid Economy*, Lawrence Lessig critically explores competing paradigms for artistic and commercial engagement with media. These paradigms, somewhat at odds with each other, are RO (Read Only) culture and RW (Read/Write) culture. According to Lessig, advances in technology, especially the Internet and the exponential growth in the memory/space capacity of computers, have facilitated the emergence of an RW culture that uses "tokens" of RO culture in order to produce new artistic texts (28–31). Consider how countless computer users excerpt, sample, or quote from previously produced images, films, or music (content easily found online) in order to revise, remake, or remix these RO tokens into completely different artistic texts. Although Lessig is largely concerned with the limitations of current copyright law in accounting for the potential creativity inherent in twenty-first-century RW culture, he also provides a solid operational definition of remix. "[R]emix is collage; it comes from combining elements of RO culture; it succeeds by leveraging the meaning created by the reference to build something new" (76).

   DJ Spooky's one-hundred-minute remix of *The Birth of a Nation*, entitled *Rebirth of a Nation*, is a postmodern DJ performance that attempts to radically recontextualize or leverage the imagery of Griffith's early-twentieth-century classic film for a twenty-first-century hip-hop-generation audience. For Spooky "the subliminal kid," the hip-hop disc jockey (DJ) is a masterful turntablist who samples, cuts, and deftly interpolates vast arrays of texts into audiovisual works of artistic bricolage. The DJ was the founding figure of hip-hop culture. The first hip-hop DJs (DJs Kool Herc, Hollywood, Afrika Bambaataa, and Flash) all isolated and looped break beats from a dizzying range of musical genres. They use(d) previously recorded music, or what Lessig refers to as RO tokens, to produce new music and ultimately new youth culture. In response to the oft-cited reflection on *The Birth of a Nation* by President Woodrow Wilson that it was "like writing history with lightning," DJ Spooky quips: "I wonder what President Wilson would have said of Grandmaster Flash's 1981 classic 'Adventures on the Wheels of Steel'" (Miller, *Rhythm Science*, 84).[5] Spooky honors the creative RW legacy of hip-hop DJs in *Rebirth of a Nation* by extending his repertoire to include film excerpts and other visuals in order to "exorcise" the racial and racist demons of Griffith's film (Gewertz, "'Birth of a Nation'—The Remix").[6] In his

postmodern theoretical treatise, *Rhythm Science*, DJ Spooky explores "the creation of art from the flow of patterns in culture" (back jacket cover description).
He envisions himself, a DJ in the twenty-first century, as a groundbreaking arti-
san similar to Griffith in some intriguing ways.

> The post World War I world, like ours, was one that was becoming
> increasingly interconnected and filled with stories of distant lands, times,
> and places. It was a world where cross cutting allowed the presentation
> not only of parallel actions occurring simultaneously in separate spatial
> dimensions, but also of parallel actions occurring on separate temporal
> planes (in the case of Griffith's *Birth of a Nation*, four plot lines at once).
> These new cinematic strategies conveyed the sense of density that the
> world was confronting. (Miller, *Rhythm Science*, 84)

Inherent in Paul Miller's selection of "Spooky" as his DJ moniker is the dialogic sensibility of his postmodern performance of *Rebirth of a Nation*. He challenged audiences to (re)visit the racist imagery of *The Birth of a Nation* in multiple ways. Throughout the performance DJ Spooky provided a collagelike mix of
music, a soundtrack of twentieth-century tunes including some techno music,
hip-hop, and the blues. In each live show he improvised the musical component
of the performance (sometimes playing original pieces from modern compos-
ers Phillip Glass and Steven Reich), but one of his primary goals was to substi-
tute for one of the original film's greatest ideological assets—its score—a dia-
logically reimagined aural experience for his audience. In the recorded/DVD
version of the remix, DJ Spooky accomplishes this by relying on both his DJ
skills and a full-blown score written and arranged by him and performed by
Kronos Quartet.[7]
    In the live performances, DJ Spooky juxtaposed various stills from the film
with counterimagery. Sometimes this counterimagery took the form of mirror
reflections or reversed black/white coloring, and other times this counterimagery was effected through side-by-side presentations of the film's stereotypes
with modern counterhegemonic images produced by various black artisans (for
example, some versions of the performance showed images of dancers choreographed by Bill T. Jones). The performance played across the country to mixed
reviews. One Harvard viewer captures the ambiguous response thus: "In spite of
Miller's digital manipulations, what remains of Griffith's images still has power
to move us, regardless of how morally and politically repugnant the premises
on which they are based or the ideas they convey, perhaps because nearly a century of cinematic imagery, derived from Griffith's pioneering efforts, have con-
ditioned us to react in this way" (Gewertz, "'Birth of a Nation'—The Remix").

The recorded version of *Rebirth of a Nation* maintains the basic narrative structure of Griffith's original, but in addition to the radical rescoring of the original, DJ Spooky shortens it from over 180 minutes to about 100 minutes, and he frames it with narration. Some of this narration merely advances the story originally intended by D. W. Griffith, but some of the added narration situates *Rebirth of a Nation* within current contexts, including the war in Iraq, the response to the disaster created by Hurricane Katrina, and presidential politics. "In modern twenty-first-century America, *The Birth of a Nation* hangs as a specter over the political process" (Miller, *DJ Spooky's Rebirth of a Nation*—narration). The narrator only intercedes intermittently throughout DJ Spooky's recorded remix, occasionally dropping incisive insights. "The *Rebirth of a Nation* looks at Griffith's vision of America tied together with never before seen close-ups and innovative techniques and turns them on themselves to make a film from the viewpoint of DJ culture. The *Rebirth of a Nation* is a DJ mix applied to cinema" (ibid.). One of the effects of watching DJ Spooky's remix of Griffith's classic is the anachronistic dissonance created by the confluence of his eerie musical score and the powerful magnetism of Griffith's shots. Somehow Spooky's score intensifies Griffith's dramatic inflections. The only other effects employed in DJ Spooky's remix (or edit) of *The Birth of a Nation* are a series of digital effects provided by Panoptic-NYC. These visual effects are varied and difficult to describe—not unlike my attempt to describe the extraordinary effect of Spooky's score.[8] In general, they take the form of shapes—triangles, squares, and/or circles—that are animated and superimposed over/onto certain scenes or characters, usually emphasizing some important aspect of the shot, such as a handshake between Northern and Southern generals, a disenchanted white citizen at a nearly all-black political assembly, or the hand of a black man as he sneaks an extra vote into the ballot box. These cinematic diacritics function in concert with Spooky's narrative frames, and an exceptional collage of music, to remix Griffith's film into a powerful postmodern narrative that at once pays homage to DJ culture, digital media, and the groundbreaking cinematic contributions of *The Birth of a Nation*.

The Remake

Aaron McGruder, Kyle Baker, and Reginald Hudlin's *Birth of a Nation: A Comic Novel* is a hip-hop-generation revelation; it is grounded in urban political realities (socioeconomic neglect, disenfranchisement, crime, etc.), yet its graphic imagery projects only iconic and mimetic figures and/or caricatures of those figures. McGruder et al.'s remake of Griffith's film also takes issue with Griffith's projection of fear and hatred directed at black rule in the South during the Reconstruction era, revisiting African American nationalism via the fictitious secession of East St. Louis from the Union. "Radical Reconstruction, or what Thomas Dixon and many other southerners called 'Negro rule,' followed hard on the heels of Lincoln's assassination" (Wallace, "The Good Lynching," 93). *The Birth of a Nation* suggests that Lincoln's assassination was a critical turning point in the political downfall of the South and, according to the film's twisted logic and racial propaganda, the rise of dangerous black supremacy in the South. McGruder et al. return to the site of a black nation—produced in this instance as a response to disenfranchisement. Although clearly committed to a dialogic discourse with the original, unlike DJ Spooky's *Rebirth of a Nation*, McGruder et al.'s *Birth of a Nation* does not at all rely on the imagery of Griffith's original. The messages and themes symbolically invested in this comic/graphic narrative invite some allegorical interpretation in order to fully excavate the wealth of meanings embedded in the plot, setting, characters/figures, and situations.

The single most allegorical figure of the *Birth of a Nation* comic/graphic novel is the mayor-turned-president of East St. Louis/Blackland, Fred Fredericks. Fredericks is an exceptionally civic-minded mayor of East St. Louis. East St. Louis, a quadrant or section of St. Louis proper, secures its sovereignty from the United States after its citizens' blatant disenfranchisement and the subsequent election of President Caldwell, who bears a deliberate caricatured resemblance to George W. Bush. Note here that the questionable emergence of President Caldwell is a minor impetus for East St. Louis's secession. Like the victimized South depicted in Griffith's film, the citizens of East St. Louis enjoy little or no civic benefits from being a part of the United States. Mayor/President Fredericks bears little or no resemblance to any figures physically or through caricature. However, his name signifies on Frederick Douglass, one of the most prominent figures of American slavery, the Civil War, and the nineteenth century more generally. Douglass's *Narrative of the Life of Frederick Douglass, an American Slave* is one of the most canonized American autobiographies/slave narratives. The doubling of Douglass's first name is an important mimetic invocation of the historical figure in the character of Fred Fredericks. Of course, Fred is not a slave, but like Douglass he is relentless in his commitment to challenging America to live up to its constitutional ideals. When that fails, he is equally committed to the emergence of Blackland as a sovereign state.

Sensing the complexities of newly garnered sovereignty, Fred Fredericks reluctantly delivers his secession speech. He posits himself as a "defender of freedom," not unlike his historical touchstone (Douglass), and, moreover, he likens his work/job to "any other." "[Y]ou gotta get outta bed and do it whether you want to or not" (McGruder et al., *Birth of a Nation: A Comic Novel*, 34). Fred

Fredericks's indefatigable work ethic for freedom (note the nominative alliteration—Fred-Fredericks-Freedom) refigures his character as an embodiment or personification of freedom itself. He is, in short, the allegorical representation of freedom for black folk, which, in the comic/graphic novel, emerges, with Blackland, in a fantastical narrative of black nationalism. Fredericks is also a direct and deliberate challenge to Griffith's Silas Lynch, whose villainy is palpable in the original film. Where Lynch is power hungry, inexperienced, and generally inept as lieutenant governor, Fredericks is reluctant, experienced, and fully capable of handling the challenges with which Blackland is presented.

In general, the figures or characters of *Birth of a Nation: A Comic Novel* are mimetic and allegorical, while the situations, communal responses, debates, and discourses are satirical in nature but often wrestle with parody and the built-in critique of mimicry that Zora Neale Hurston alludes to in her classic essay "The Characteristics of Negro Expression." One particular moment of mimesis (or iconic representation—and its accompanying satire/parody) centers on the decision that must be made regarding the currency for Blackland. In this scene (or these panels) from McGruder et al.'s *Birth of a Nation*, the citizens of Blackland must decide on which figures will represent them on their own currency.[9] James Brown, Malcolm X, and Harriet Tubman are all under consideration here, amongst others. One of the more powerful concepts to emerge from this brief comedic study in iconic representation for the African American community is that all of the figures listed or mentioned (except for Blackland's own Fred Fredericks) were all at some point in their lives literally and figuratively outlaws to/from/of American culture and society. In fact, for the most part, these figures' technical and symbolic outlaw status is central to their emergence in the public sphere as black heroes. In a more subtle way this contemporary currency representation also gestures toward black political representation in the Reconstruction era—especially as it is degradingly depicted in Griffith's original film. That is, when black folk represent themselves and/or choose their leaders, they can, will, and have supported political figures (or social heroes) who exhibit criminal and/or socially corrupt behavior. This fact loses all of its cultural meaning without the historical context of black folks' relationship to the law and the criminal justice system (Jim Crow, lynching, slavery, and more currently the prison-industrial complex). But the joke here might be on McGruder et al. anyway, since their parody of black currency representation so cogently echoes D. W. Griffith's critique of "Negro rule" (i.e., it is prone to ignorant, whimsical decision-making).

McGruder et al. cap this fantastic scene with a fight between two surrogates for hip-hop culture's most enduring icons: Biggie Smalls/Notorious B.I.G. and Tupac Shakur. Both of these rappers (who in reality were brutally gunned down in public spaces and whose murders have not been solved) have become icons for the hip-hop generation partially because of their talent, partially because of the media's overblown coverage of their complex public conflict, and partially because they were murdered in the public sphere. Moreover, their murders are still, over ten years later, unsolved. Thus they are icons also for the thousands of black men who have been murdered (by other black men), but whose deaths have become unremarkable and unresolved. As the fight escalates between the surrogates over which rapper (Biggie/Tupac) should be the face of the nickel, readers are left to contemplate the instability of monetary signifiers and the fervor with which young people attach their own identities to hip-hop iconography. Of course, the fight ends in a shoot-out. Thus, in one page of panels, McGruder et al. parody inner-city violence and the pendulum-swinging significance of dead presidential currency representation. Although the critique of the social interactions of inner-city African Americans seems to mirror Griffith's classic antiblack propaganda, McGruder et al. are attempting to construct a mirror for the hip-hop generation: a mirror in which young African Americans might see the residue from *The Birth of a Nation* in the internecine squabbles projected into the public sphere via twenty-first-century American popular culture.

Another important signifier of Blackland is the national flag. The citizens ultimately and in diplomatic and democratic fashion select a red, black, and green flag, with a white Jesus superimposed over the traditional black nationalist colors. More on the Jesus piece in a moment, but the panels that reflect the discussion construct an interesting satirical narrative of cultural and generational ideology in the African American community. The first flag considered, an Afrocentric simulacrum of the American flag, garners negative looks from the mostly older black audience. For the second flag, an image of the continent of Africa superimposed over the traditional black nationalist colors, McGruder et al. repeat the response-panel from the previous flag—thus indicating that the audience sternly disapproves. The final flag, a Kente cloth Nike symbol superimposed over the traditional black nationalist colors, elicits smiles and approval. This response is possibly due to the design (a Kente cloth Nike symbol)—insinuating the consumerist underpinnings of black nationalism—or it may be due to the fact that this flag "comes with a generous donation from Nike" (McGruder et al., *Birth of a Nation: A Comic Novel*, 58). Although the ultimate decision to use the Jesus flag occurs "off panel," the selection is nonetheless iconographically complex. The black nationalist narrative of "the black Jesus" has been wrestled with throughout the history of African American artistic production, with particularly interesting episodes in the TV series *Good Times* and in the lyrics of Kanye West's "Jesus Walks."[10] The white Jesus

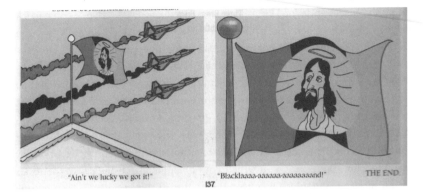

"Ain't we lucky we got it!"   "Blacklaaaa-aaaaaa-aaaaaaaand!"   THE END
137

6.1. *From Aaron McGruder et al.,* Birth of a Nation

superimposed on the traditionally black nationalist colors of the Blackland flag also tacitly concedes white Christian dominance over any possibility of African American sovereignty. Thus the idea that Blackland would select a white Jesus for the flag typifies the kind of mimetic irony that McGruder et al. invest in their rereading of black nationalism.

Maybe the most complex and suggestive mimetic connection between McGruder et al.'s *Birth of a Nation . . .* and the original film centers on the opening images/scenes of both texts and their subsequent and distinct engagements with gender and sexuality. One of the opening scenes of D. W. Griffith's *Birth of a Nation* features a minister in a predominantly white church ushering in several African American children. The children are obviously poor, and as he leads them through the aisle to the pulpit, one white congregant shudders in disgust, presumably at the body odor of one of the children. Aside from the obvious racialized undertones of the scene (i.e., "all black people smell bad"), this particular representation obscures the very real "funk" of the poor folk who lack access to the amenities required for personal hygiene (i.e., clean running water, affordable soap, etc.). McGruder et al. signify on this scene by opening their graphic novel with a ten-day sanitation strike that leaves all of East St. Louis in a similar funk. Here, though, the lack of structural civic responsibility and organization is on full display, and Fredericks, the mayor of East St. Louis—soon-to-be-president of Blackland—must assume the institutional slack and pick up the garbage himself.

If, as literary theorist W. J. T. Mitchell asserts, "[e]very representation exacts some cost, in the form of lost immediacy, presence or truth, in the form of a gap between intention and realization, original and copy," then the gaps between the original *Birth of a Nation* and the remake are telling (Mitchell, "Represen-

116

Table 6.1.

THE ORIGINAL (BOAN)	THE REMAKE (BOAN)
The Church Scene of Smelly Disgust	Uncollected Garbage in E. St. Louis
The Quadroon Seduction	The Mulatto Influence
White Female Sexuality Triangulation	The Misogyny of Black Nationalism

tation," 21). Table 6.1 lists several of these representations that in turn solidify the mimetic relationship between Griffith's and McGruder et al.'s works. Other examples include the constructed licentious nature of mulattas: in Griffith's film, Lydia, a quadroon woman unduly (and through sexualized interactions) influences the Stoneman/Stevens figure, convincing him to support miscegenation-oriented legislation. The mulattas in the McGruder et al. remake (Donna and Kabilah/Shannon) are depicted as secretive sexualized objects with enormous influence over the principal leaders of Blackland. Shannon, who is Fredericks's love interest, has a dual identity as Kabilah, an upstart black nationalist who rushes to Blackland as soon as she and her cadre of pseudo–black nationalists learn of East St. Louis's secession. She ultimately embraces her true identity, signaled by her finally letting Fredericks know that her name is not Kabilah but Shannon Randall. Donna, apparently another mulatta, attracts the gaze of Fredericks, but she is also likely involved with billionaire John Roberts. Donna ultimately infiltrates an Arab country in order to secure its support for Blackland. Both Donna and Shannon influence the patriarchal rule of Blackland and ultimately assist in protecting the sovereignty of Blackland as a nation. They are both manipulative and subversively powerful without actually holding any office. This abiding intersection between race, sexism, and the black and white fears of miscegenation puts into bold relief the well-documented misogyny of black nationalism and the rampant (and often violent) triangulation of white female sexuality during Reconstruction and in the ruthless lynching practices of the nineteenth- and twentieth-century American South.

Even with the healthy recurring skepticism about mimesis in literary and artistic production, the original *Birth of a Nation* is not a dead-end representation, just as it is not an historically mimetic text, despite its earnest claims to represent the reality of Civil War and Reconstruction era Southern experiences. It has, over time, become a platform for additional and additionally dense artistic significations or remixes. The signifyin' mimetic texts (DJ Spooky and McGruder et al.) shift representational resources of technology, history, and black political power toward a twenty-first-century paradigm of nationalist and socioeconomic discourses that tend toward political satire, even as they elide the abiding misogyny that inhabits too much of hip-hop culture and black nationalism. In conclusion, here again Mitchell is incisive: "Even purely 'aesthetic' representations of fictional persons and events can never be completely divorced from political and ideological questions. . . . representation is precisely the point where these questions are most likely to enter the literary work" (Mitchell, "Representation," 15). Thus Fred Fredericks, and the various panels/pages of *Birth of a Nation: A Comic Novel*, as well as DJ Spooky's *Rebirth of a Nation*, represent aesthetic and mimetic reflections on the themes and ideology of D. W. Griffith's *The Birth of a Nation*, and as a result a potent political discourse emerges to unveil the ways in which race, sexuality, and political power continue to interact and reverberate in the twenty-first century.

- -

NOTES

1. In his seminal work *The Hip Hop Generation*, Bikari Kitwana defines this generation as those born between 1964 and 1985 who subscribe to hip-hop culture as a central frame through which they experience life. For these hip-hop-generation constituents, certain events and historical developments formulate the zeitgeist of their lives. These include: living in a post-civil-rights, post-racial-segregation America; the rise of the prison-industrial complex; the war on drugs; the emergence and spread of HIV/AIDS; and the unsolved murders of Tupac Shakur and The Notorious B.I.G.

2. Hip-hop culture is generally defined by its four foundational elements: DJing; MCing, or rapping; b-boying, or breaking; and graffiti and/or visual art. Note here that Miller is DJ Spooky and that McGruder's use of language clearly reflects the signifying aesthetics of the MC and the visual art of his graphic novel captures brilliantly the hip-hop aesthetics depicted in the most elaborate graf art.

3. See Mildred Bryant-Jones's "The Political Program of Thaddeus Stevens, 1865."

4. See Fawn M. Brodie's *Thaddeus Stevens, Scourge of the South*. It corrects the historical record as to Griffith's/Dixon's false representation of Stevens as Stoneman in *The Birth of a Nation*.

5. DJ Grandmaster Flash is one of several pioneers of hip-hop culture. He revolutionized the practice known as scratching—when a DJ physically ruptures a phonograph record, producing a scratching sound—and he is generally considered a forefather of the practice known as turntablism. "The Adventures of Grandmaster Flash on the Wheels of Steel" is an excellent example of both his abilities as a mixer/remixer and of DJ Spooky/Paul Miller's notion of rhythm science.

6. For a full review of DJ Spooky's 2005 live performance of *Rebirth of a Nation* at Harvard University, see Ken Gewertz's "'Birth of a Nation'—The Remix: DJ Spooky Presents New View of Contentious Classic," published in the March 17, 2005, issue of the *Harvard Gazette*.

7. Kronos Quartet consists of David Harrington (violin), John Sherba (violin), Hank Dutt (viola), and Jeffery Zeigler (cello). They appear in the film courtesy of Nonesuch Records.

8. I highlight this ineptitude here only to strongly encourage that readers watch DJ Spooky's *Rebirth of a Nation*. My analysis here simply cannot adequately reproduce the experience of watching it either live or on DVD.

9. In some of my other work on hip-hop culture (Peterson 2006) I reflect extensively on the sociolinguistic phrase "Dead Presidents," a synecdoche for money in hip-hop and AAVE (African American Vernacular English) parlance. I will not rehearse that here, but one conclusion that can be drawn from the dead presidents discourse is that the notion of dead presidential representation on paper currency, and the lack of presidential representation for some of the residents of America's inner cities, are inextricably linked through a series of mimetic representations.

10. I'm thinking here of the *Good Times* episode where JJ paints a picture of a black Jesus, who just so happens to look like Ned the Wino, and of Kanye West's infectious single (and powerful video) where he claims not to be concerned about Jesus's "facial features."

7 LOST IN TRANSLATION
Jessica Abel's La Perdida, *the Bildungsroman,* and "That 'Mexican' Feel"

PATRICK L. HAMILTON

P UBLISHED SERIALLY BY Fantagraphics between 2001 and 2005, and collected by Pantheon Books in 2006, Jessica Abel's graphic narrative *La Perdida* has met with widespread acclaim. It earned her the 2002 Harvey Award for "Best New Series." One reviewer praised the novel as a "realistic drama for adults told in a straightforward manner," and as a "focused examination of the relationship between foreignness and being 'native'" (Arnold, "Lost in Mexico"). Another lauded Abel for "successfully portray[ing] characters both on the fringes of society, and those who wish that they were" (Anonymous, Rev. of *La Perdida*, 3). Abel and *La Perdida* have garnered accolades, too, from within the comics community and from writers outside it: Scott McCloud, author of the seminal *Understanding Comics*, and contemporary novelists Susan Choi and Sherman Alexie contribute quotations to the back cover of Pantheon's collected edition. Abel herself stands at the forefront of contemporary graphic narrative, coauthoring with her husband the textbook *Drawing Words & Writing Pictures: Making Comics from Manga to Graphic Novels* (First Second, 2008) and similarly serving as series coeditor for the 2008 volume of *The Best American Comics,* published by Houghton Mifflin.

Much of the praise for *La Perdida* centers on its apparent critique of what Choi describes as the protagonist's "catastrophic folly" (back jacket cover). The narrative tells the tale of the half-Anglo, half-Mexican Carla Olivares, who recounts her yearlong sojourn in Mexico City that began with her desire to connect with her father's Mexican roots and ended with her deportation back to the United States after she became unwittingly embroiled in a kidnapping plot. Carla's journey is born out of equal parts her dissatisfaction with her Anglo culture and identity, and her belief in the power of Mexican culture to compensate for this lack. The novel illustrates how such belief is misguided in the way it reifies Mexican culture. For Carla, Mexico is "a new delight, more intense, more satisfying than normal ways of doing and feeling . . . ethnicity becomes spice, seasoning that can liven up the dull dish that is mainstream white culture" (hooks, *Black Looks*, 21). Carla's reification of Mexican culture as "spice" or accentuation persists throughout the narrative of her younger self. Consequently, Carla's narrative is an antibildungsroman in how her *Bildung* ultimately fails.[1] Carla persists in her naïveté and ignorance, a failure to develop or transform that is at the heart of *La Perdida*'s ostensible critique of its protagonist.

However, Abel's construction of *La Perdida*—specifically, her juxtapositions of Carla's older and younger selves and linguistic shifts over the course of the narrative—undermine this critique. While Carla's recounting of her experience depicts her to be as "lost" as she was when first crossing into Mexico, Abel's prologue implies Carla's transformation both linguistically and visually. Also, Abel herself exhibits reification parallel to Carla's in her text's linguistic construction. In addition to the text's retreat from a bilingual representation and recourse to a monolingual translation, Abel, like Carla, treats her use of the Spanish language, and in particular Spanish slang, as "spice" to grant a sense of authenticity to the narrative's portrayal. In the end, *La Perdida* reveals problematic underlying assumptions mirroring those of Carla's journey. Derek Parker Royal, in his Introduction to the recent special issue of MELUS on multiethnic graphic narrative, describes how the "figures that make up the comics rub up against reality in ways that words cannot, revealing the various assumptions, predispositions, and prejudices that author-illustrators may hold" (7). In the case of *La Perdida*, Abel's construction of the narrative "rubs up" and grates against, and ultimately undoes, its critique of cultural relativism and ignorance.[2]

La Perdida signals its correspondence with the novelistic mode of the bildungsroman from the very start of its narrative. Carla opens her first-person account of her experiences with the following confession: "I arrived in Mexico two years ago today, February 23rd. What I was thinking when I decided to go—it's no longer at all clear to me. That is, I can remember, but it's like peering into the mind of a stranger" (11). Such a confessional stance is a trapping of the bildungsroman mode, particularly as practiced by Chicana authors: these novels "tend to be more confessional in nature, emphasizing the reexamination of the past through the recollection of past experiences in order to arrive at an understanding" of the self (Eysturoy, *Daughters of Self-Creation*, 4).[3] Furthermore, the mode does not depict "solely a search for identity per se," but "rather an exploration and articulation of the process leading to a purposeful awakening of the female protagonist" (ibid., 3–4). Carla's narrative likewise concentrates on not only its presumed goal but her process of achieving that goal, fumbling and catastrophic as it may be. Similarly, such novels emphasize "the education of the self emerging from the interaction between the self and the world" (ibid., 4). For Carla, that self is her Anglo-identified self, and that "world" is Mexico, and specifically Mexico City. She further confesses to her audience how she no longer recognizes her past self, with its "ideas and plans that seem now to be entirely based on misconceptions" (Abel, *La Perdida*, 11), a disconnect that demonstrates how Carla sees herself as in fact having been educated by her experiences.

Yet Carla's presumption of her transformation founders upon her narrative's representation of those experiences. As a result, Carla's account of her experiences in Mexico City can best be described as an antibildungsroman. Whereas the traditional bildungsroman, or "novel of formation," depicts "the development of the protagonist's mind and character . . . into maturity," Carla's experiences and her reflection on the same seem intended to exhibit her failure to so develop (Abrams, *Glossary of Literary Terms*, 193). She remains, as the graphic novel's title indicates, "lost." Much of her failure stems from how she persistently exoticizes and thus reifies Mexico's people, particularly her sexual partners, and culture. Consequently, Carla never veers from the position of "tourist" while in Mexico, remaining isolated and disengaged. Such constant reification and positioning prevent Carla from achieving any "authentic self-fulfillment" in spite of her claim (Eysturoy, *Daughters of Self-Creation*, 4).

The initial impetus behind Carla's journey reveals the underlying assumptions fostering her reification of Mexican culture. Her stated motives betray an "imperialist nostalgia" that always filters her various interactions and renders them inauthentic (hooks, *Black Looks*, 29). Carla explains, "I thought that I went because I was sick of the USA, sick of everybody. I wanted to find my Mexican roots. Somehow it seemed I would like them better than my Anglo ones" (Abel, *La Perdida*, 11). In this statement, Carla "desires 'a bit of the Other' to enhance the blank landscape of whiteness" (hooks, *Black Looks*, 29). Carla reifies "Mexico" as both better and more exotic than her Anglo culture and identity. In comparison to her as-yet-unknown Mexican roots, they appear impoverished and lacking. Having been raised exclusively by her Anglo mother, Carla has no direct sense of her Mexican heritage. However, she still imagines that heritage in a compensatory or accentuating role. As a result, Mexico only exists to serve her purposes, making her, metaphorically, the colonizer ("conquistadora") that Memo, a pseudosocialist Mexican whom Carla befriends, repeatedly accuses her of being.

A similar reification of "Mexican" persists in Carla's intimate relationships during her stay. Carla has two sexual partners in *La Perdida*: her Anglo "ex-some-thing" Harry Powell and Oscar, a Mexican poser-DJ and wannabe drug dealer. Initially she voices dissatisfaction with Harry: "Harry's not my type; I'm not into blond upper-crusty frat boys." Yet, she manages to overcome the "massive chip" she has on her shoulder "about East Coast blue bloods like Harry" (Abel, *La Perdida*, 13, 14). Carla soon reveals what overcomes her discontentment with the WASP-ish Harry. "I knew before I met him that he was planning to move to Mexico. . . . That was half the attraction. That's why I even got involved with him in the first place. . . . It was the Mexico thing that intrigued me" (ibid., 12–13). Carla's attraction to Harry benefits from his simply traveling there, his Anglo drawbacks mitigated by this merest of associations. In particular, it is at least in part the "mystery" Carla perceives behind Harry's sojourn to Mexico that motivates her own. This perception of "mystery" or "intrigue" likewise under-pins Carla's relationship with Oscar. She describes how the fact that they "could barely communicate with each other" and how "his looks . . . made him seem extremely mysterious and intriguing" (ibid., 50). The same alluring mystery Carla perceived in Harry is even more explicitly a factor in this later relation-ship. Her various "[e]ncounters with Otherness," filtered somewhat with Harry but less so with Oscar, "are clearly marked as more exciting, more intense . . . The lure is the combination of pleasure and danger" (hooks, *Black Looks*, 26). Driving her attraction to both men is Carla's reification of "Mexico" and "Mexi-can" as mysterious and intriguing, and such flattened conceptions preclude the possibility of authentic change or development.

Demonstrating Carla's interfering disengagement and disaffection is her per-sistent representation as a tourist while in Mexico. For one, Carla's tourist status allows her to ignore much of the reality around her, as well as to only perceive that which coincides with her flattened-out imagination of the country. Such an effect occurs almost immediately upon her entering the city, as she stumbles upon Parque México:

> I felt like I'd found the doorway to the part I recognized from my imagina-tion, where the hard truth about the crime rate, and the pollution, and the disappearance of traditional culture, just didn't apply. . . . I had this imme-diate feeling that everything would be OK, that I would find the Mexico I was looking for. (Abel, *La Perdida*, 15–16)

It is Carla's imagination of Mexico that she searches for and finds here; the reali-ties of Mexico—the crime, pollution, and cultural deprivation that Carla lists—recede from her mind and perception. Carla displays a similarly narrow perspective when she visits the home of her "hero," Frida Kahlo. She exclaims about the "passion for Mexico, and for the Mexican people," that informs Kahlo's work and life (ibid., 19). Those aspects of Kahlo's life—her love for Diego (the "fat frog") and her politics—that Carla finds displeasing are simply ignored. As she says about Diego, "I sort of tried not to think about him too much" (ibid.), and the same can be said about whatever else disrupts Carla's postcard-image sense of Kahlo and Mexico in general: she just ignores it. But in ignoring it, Carla again reduces the authenticity of her interaction. She becomes locked in a solipsistic cycle, only interacting with and appreciating those aspects of Mexican culture and society that fit with how she already imagines them, while disengaging from the rest.

This touristic sensibility continues throughout Carla's experiences in Mexico. It is reinforced by a journalist for a free press organization when Carla accompanies Harry to a job interview. The journalist rattles off a litany of dangers to watch out for that echoes those realities Carla earlier put out of her mind: corrupt police, air pollution, earthquakes, economic depression, duplicitous cab drivers, and kidnappings. Here, Carla is instead told to indulge herself in these realities. They are what make Mexico and its capital a "vibrant, exciting" place; she advises Carla not to "lock yourself in your house . . . and hope it goes away," but rather to "enjoy the city, it's a wonderful place" (ibid., 32). Similarly, after Harry boots her out of his apartment, she moves to a new neighborhood that is not "as safe or insulated from raw Mexico City . . . It was old and noisy and highly earthquake prone and full of constant activity and I *loved* it" (ibid., 66; original emphasis). Whereas before these realities failed to mesh with Carla's conception of Mexico City, they now are subsumed within it as one more part of Mexico's larger attraction.

And still coupled with this touristic reification of Mexico into the "exotic" is an ignorance and disconnection from the "real" Mexico around her. The bulk of her time is spent amongst the American "ex-pat" community Harry introduces her to. Her second night in the city, Harry takes her to one such party, where "there were no Mexicans," and she spends the night talking with the jaded among Harry's friends (ibid., 21–22). Later, she meets up with the ex-pats at a Mexican bar, where they spend their time discussing William Burroughs, Jack Kerouac, and Allen Ginsberg (ibid., 55–57). Though she calls Harry out on the inauthenticity of his experience, Carla remains blissfully ignorant of her own, even once Harry reciprocates her critique with his own: "You think because you go to ART galleries and the fucking PYRAMIDS you know what's going on in this country? You fucking poseur. You tourist" (ibid., 57). Even Carla's interactions with "actual" Mexicans are profoundly superficial. She associates mainly with two Mexican men—the previously mentioned Memo and Oscar—but their activities together are limited to either going to parties and drinking and/ or getting high, or hanging out at Carla's apartment and drinking and/or getting high. Carla's fatal ignorance is driven home by the arrival of her brother Rodrigo, who grew up with their Mexican father, at the start of the novel's third section. Rod and his skateboarding, Internet entrepreneur friends in Mexico live "in a kind of parallel-universe Mexico City" in relation to Carla's (ibid., 122). Rod, for example, takes her to a restaurant right near Carla's apartment that she never saw before, betraying her blindness and ignorance to her actual surroundings. Carla's specific ignorance of something so close by her is emblematic of her larger and continued ignorance toward the "real" Mexico, eclipsed as it is by her touristic disengagement from both country and city.

All of Mexico City eventually gets reduced to a spectacle—a "social relationship between people that is mediated by images"—that Carla disaffectedly participates in (Debord, *Society of the Spectacle*, 12). In Carla's case, her "social relationship" with Mexico City and its people is mediated and interfered with by the "image" created by her reifying illusions. The result is disengagement and disaffection. She displays both these qualities most prominently when she learns of Harry's kidnapping in the paper, an event that drives approximately the last quarter of *La Perdida*'s plot. To her, the event is "so weird and scary" and "just unreal . . . like an action movie" (ibid., 153, 156). Here, Carla reduces the "reality" of Harry's kidnapping to a filmic image. And the vicarious thrill provided by this image in the continued coverage of Harry's disappearance comes to inflect her sense of her own life: "Sure it was tragic, but you know, life or death struggle and all—it made my life more dramatic and exciting by proxy" (ibid., 153). Once again, Carla vacates the realities of the situation—its tragedy, its life-or-death consequences—flattening it into yet another addition to and compensation for her otherwise dull life and identity. But the drama and excitement do not last long. She becomes bored with the "fabulous case of the missing capitalist pig" (ibid., 162); she cares more about the plant she fails to water than the details trickled out about Harry's case (ibid., 167). Only when Memo and Oscar reveal themselves as involved in the kidnapping, and hold Harry and Carla both prisoner in Carla's home, does the reality of the situation overwhelm the illusions Carla built up. But even then, its impact is profoundly self-directed. It reveals to Carla her "wrongness," robs her not only of her freedom but also what she perceives as her status as "victim," when she has only been the victim of her own assumptions and illusions. Even to these "realizations" of Carla's, there are limits. She continues to sleep with Oscar, even as he assists in holding her prisoner, accompanying her to her job as an ESL teacher, surveilling her every move and interaction. She similarly expends more effort toward saving Oscar, when she fears the others are setting him up to take the fall for the kidnapping, than she does trying to save Harry. Both efforts are fruitless: the latter amounts to a single failed attempt; the former ends in Oscar's execution by his fellows.

Carla's past experiences end with her deportation back to the United States exactly one year to the day from when she first arrived in Mexico City. Her *Bildung* ends in failure. Carla remains as naïve and un-self-aware as she was at the beginning of this journey—despite her own claims to the contrary. In the graphic novel's epilogue, Carla laments her isolation and her disengagement as the cause of all the tragedy: "And because I refused to understand who my friends really were, and what was happening before my eyes, Oscar is dead, Harry is damaged, I'm banished, and I'll have to live my life with the knowledge that I may not have pulled the trigger or done the crime, but it wouldn't have happened without me" (ibid., 254). She hints here at a realization that has somehow changed her. But in the novel's present, Carla still exhibits profound isolation and disengagement. She remains completely anonymous in a bulky coat, ski hat, and scarf, and completely disappears from Abel's visuals in the final two and a half pages. More problematic still is the present-day Carla's desire to return to her younger self. The narration in the final pages has Carla imagining her younger self, pursuing her, only to lose track of her. "Before I know it, she's gone from sight, from understanding" (ibid., 255). Carla is similarly "gone" from the reader's sight and understanding; her closing words—"I wish I could find her again, that girl" (ibid., 256)—indicate her explicit desire to regress to her younger, naïve self. Such a desire prevents the reader from seeing Carla as having developed, and Abel's graphic novel as a whole seems intended to critique Carla precisely for this failure.

However, *La Perdida*'s apparent critique of Carla for her persistent naïveté and ignorance is undermined by how the narrative and visuals in the present contradictorily signal her transformation. Like Carla's own statements differentiating her past and present selves, Abel's visual representations of the same speak to her having gone through a process of *Bildung* in spite of the superficial nature of her experiences. Furthermore, how Abel linguistically signals these changes in the text's own construction demonstrates a reification of Mexico and its culture parallel to Carla's. Even as *La Perdida* attempts to critique Carla for her narrow-mindedness and willful ignorance, then, it exposes the same underlying assumptions in its own representation.

Carla's previously mentioned claims for just such a transformation are manifested most fully in the novel's prologue and epilogue. When talking about the motivation behind her journey, for example, present-day Carla explains how the idea that her Mexican roots could compensate for her Anglo ones now "makes no sense." Similarly, Carla describes her recollection of these experiences as "peering into the mind of a stranger," a statement that again signals that she at least feels transformed by these experiences (ibid., 11). Carla draws a similar distinction between her present and past selves in the novel's epilogue. The mistakes of her younger self are now "so clear" and "like a map, [with] many clearly marked roads" (ibid., 255). She further explicates the wrong paths her confused younger self followed: "I thought the rules were different in Mexico, but they're not different. I didn't judge because I thought I wasn't qualified to judge, but as it turned out, that was just an excuse not to be engaged, and not to act right" (ibid., 254). Despite acknowledging her own disengagement and self-isolation whilst in Mexico City, Carla still makes an implicit claim for a greater self-awareness resulting from these experiences and in spite of their shallowness.

More troubling, however, are the ways in which Abel's own construction of the narrative similarly alleges Carla's transformation. Much of this contradiction stems again from *La Perdida*'s seven-page prologue and its visual juxtaposition of Carla's older and younger selves. In the present, Carla enters Guadalupe's, a Mexican restaurant, in Chicago. She orders a Coke and three broiled pork tacos in Spanish and, left alone at her table, reminisces with a grin about a similar moment from her time in Mexico City. The panels representing this earlier meal depict Carla as a far cry from her present self. She fumbles and fails in her attempt to order a taco: she uses the word for "pig" instead of "pork," uses the verb for "to like" *(gustar)* instead of "to want" and ends up saying "I like me, a pig taco please sir" rather than "I would like." She similarly fails to apprehend how the Mexican server mocks her, and ultimately requires rescue from Harry, though not before he labels her a "rube" and a "tourist" for how she clumsily holds and eats the taco (ibid., 5–6). Juxtaposed as this flashback is with Carla's present, it clearly indicates how Carla has been transformed. She is no longer such an ignorant rube in the present, but rather orders confidently in Spanish that blatantly contrasts with the Mexican waitress's halting, phonetically spelled English: "Do you wan' somting to dreenk?" (ibid., 4).

The transformation is further suggested by the expression on Carla's face in panels five and six of page four, followed again by the same as she munches her tacos in panel four of the subsequent page. She appears self-satisfied and pleased as she thinks back, amusedly, on her earlier experience and self. Indicated thus to the reader as well is how "far" Carla has come from the ignorant American she once was. Now she is culturally sophisticated. Now she is adept.

But such an alleged transformation is girded by the same misconceptions and reifications Carla has already exhibited. Before, as she herself acknowledged, she thought she could compensate for her lackluster Anglo identity and culture through exposure to and incorporation of Mexican culture. In this

7.1., 7.2. La Perdida

moment and its juxtaposition, Abel represents Carla as having done essentially that. To achieve this representation, though, Abel ends up reducing and flattening out such longed-for cultural understanding by equating it with ordering and eating tacos. To use bell hooks's terms, Abel has Carla literally "eat the other" in this sequence, and thus figuratively does so herself. Another moment from the novel's prologue is similarly demonstrative. When Carla leaves the restaurant, she sees a man resembling one of Oscar's drug pals and exclaims, "That *cabrón* looks exactly like Ricardo" (ibid., 7). Here, Abel "peppers" Carla's English with a touch of Spanish slang (the term for "fucker"). Again, the intent here seems to be to indicate how Carla has had a transformative interaction with Mexican culture, one that has left her authentically changed. But those changes, or their representations to be more precise, are as profoundly superficial as the experiences upon which they are based. They, in fact, make Abel complicit with Carla's original motivation: Abel has accentuated Carla's Anglo identity with just enough of a smattering of Mexican culture and language to compensate for the former's deficiencies. In doing so, Abel demonstrates in her construction problematic assumptions similar to those in which Carla persisted throughout the novel's narrative.

Further implicating Abel in such assumptions are her linguistic choices in the construction of *La Perdida*. In the end, Abel ends up appropriating the Spanish language as accentuation in a way similar to Carla's. This is not, however, how the graphic novel begins; instead, the use of English and Spanish alters over the course of the narrative. In the first section, comprising 63 pages of the 250-plus-page narrative, dialogue spoken in Spanish remains in Spanish in the word balloons, with translations in English under each panel.

The panel that depicts a boat trip Carla takes with Memo, Harry, and others dramatically exemplifies the effect of this. The vast majority of this dialogue occurs in Spanish, which is used not only by the native Mexican characters but also the American expatriates, with the notable exception of Carla, whose Spanish is still fairly weak at this point. In effect, Abel centers Spanish as the normative language. English is marginalized or, in fact, pushed beyond the margins, the literal panel borders, and thus decentered. Accordingly, the non-Spanish-speaking reader is made uneasy here. Such a reader must work harder than the Spanish speaker to follow the dialogue, having to shift between the dialogue and the translations, which at times can appear cluttered. Too, the page itself is bilingual in how it presents both languages on the page and slides back and forth between them.

But whatever strategic decisions Abel's utilization of this linguistic device might appear to signal, they disappear after the opening section and thus for the bulk of the narrative. From that point on, all dialogue spoken in Spanish is rendered into English, with nothing marking such dialogue's translation. Dialogue spoken in English remains in English, though Abel surrounds such dialogue with arrow brackets. The result is a bit of linguistic whiplash. The reader must imagine the unmarked English as Spanish and the marked English as English. But there is a further and at least as troubling effect: Spanish, formerly predominant on the printed page of *La Perdida*, virtually disappears, except for the occa-

7.3. La Perdida

sional untranslated slang term. Once a narrative marked by bilingual pages, *La Perdida* becomes resoundingly monolingual.

Abel's linguistic decisions ultimately reveal further the problematic assumptions and misconceptions she shares with her fictionalized protagonist. Besides recentering English as the normative language despite the novel's Mexican setting, she similarly deploys Spanish as accentuation in how she, like Carla, uses the occasional bit of Spanish slang in otherwise wholly English dialogue. Abel justifies her use of Spanish in "A Note on the Use of Spanish in This Book," which appears as part of the novel's front matter. From her initial effort to write the dialogue as "spoken; that is, in English when it's in English, and in Spanish when it's in Spanish (with 'subtitles')," Abel describes how she "dispensed with subtitles and simply 'translated' the dialogue" into English because "the vast majority of dialogue is meant to be spoken in Spanish" (ibid., ix). There is a curious logic here: that the dialogue actually occurred in Spanish is justification for its translation into English. While the sheer amount of Spanish requiring translation, had Abel continued with her original approach, is possibly prohibitive, it is unfortunate that such verisimilitude as the opening section attempted became too inconvenient to continue. Furthermore, she goes on to explain her occasional use of untranslated Spanish slang: "However, throughout the 'Spanish' dialogue I've sprinkled words actually written in Spanish, particularly where the words have a particularly Mexican feel" (ibid.). In describing how she herself "sprinkles" Spanish dialogue amongst the English translation, Abel replicates Carla's own hooksian reification of "Mexican" as "spice" or accentuation. Further reifying is her recourse to "a particularly Mexican feel." Such a statement cannot help but recall the "intrigue" and "mystery" Carla likewise associated with "Mexican," particularly the men with whom she herself associated that were even tangentially connected to the culture. Such parallels problematize the narrative's and Abel's critique of Carla for how she fails to achieve any sort of *Bildung*. What Abel seeks to critique Carla for, her ignorance toward and reification of Mexican culture, she herself duplicates in her graphic novel's constructions.

La Perdida, in its undoing of its own purposes, demonstrates a fault hooks criticizes as characterizing U.S. mass culture: it "both publicly declares and perpetuates the idea that there is pleasure to be found in the acknowledgement and enjoyment of racial difference" (*Black Looks*, 21). The work purports to question the culturally relativist stance of its protagonist and perhaps even express, through their absence in Carla, the "thirst for another knowledge, unprejudiced striving," and "supple open-mindedness" that are the popular manifestations of cosmopolitanism (Brennan, "Cosmo-Theory," 662–663). However, Abel's construction of her graphic novel proves contradictory to these ideals. Far from "dismantl[ing] those very assumptions that problematize ethnic representation," Abel's *La Perdida* reproduces them (Royal, "Introduction," 9).

NOTES

1. By the term "antibildungsroman," I mean to indicate how Carla's *Bildung*, or formation, fails. This usage is distinct from other applications of the term to texts that parody the conventions of the bildungsroman mode. See, for example, Miles, who discusses how writers such as Franz Kafka, Thomas Mann, and Günter Grass burlesque the form, as well as Trachtenberg on Philip Roth and Steinberg and Hallstein on James Joyce.

2. The temptation might be to attribute *La Perdida*'s own problematic cultural relativism to the fact that Abel, an Anglo writer and artist, depicts the experiences of a Chicana protagonist. However, such an attribution is not the intent of this analysis, and the issues of Abel's own ethnic identity and its impact on her representation similarly lie outside its scope. Rather, the limitations of *La Perdida* as a text identified here stem from how they conflict with what appear to be the narrative's aims.

3. Eysturoy identifies this definition with Chicana bildungsromans that feature older, more mature protagonists rather than children. Carla, in her twenties, clearly belongs to the former category. Also, while Abel herself is Anglo, unlike the novelists Eysturoy discusses, her protagonist is half-Mexican and thus her narrative fits well with Eysturoy's definition.

SAME DIFFERENCE

Graphic Alterity in the Work of Gene Luen Yang,
Adrian Tomine, and Derek Kirk Kim

JARED GARDNER

A LTHOUGH ASIAN AMERICANS have been working at the highest levels
in writing and drawing mainstream superhero comics for some time now,
Asian American characters have remained largely invisible in the pages of these
comics. And yet, the past decade or so has seen the emergence of independent
and alternative Asian American comics creators interested in exploring what
happens when an Asian American—long the target of virulent racist cartoon
stereotypes—is the hero of a comic book. In what follows, I want to examine
the work of three Asian American comics creators, Gene Luen Yang, Adrian
Tomine, and Derek Kirk Kim, in undertaking these experiments—experiments
that seem in many ways to make about as much sense as trying to put out a fire
with gasoline. Yang has most recently had to confront these challenges when a
character, Chin-Kee, from his book *American Born Chinese* (2006) was featured
on MySpace, resulting in a torrent of hurt and confusion from readers who felt
betrayed by Chin-Kee's concentration of generations of Asian stereotypes. An
example is a panel in which Chin-Kee is eating at the school cafeteria with his
cousin Danny (114) (Figure 8.1).

On MySpace, images such as these were greeted with horror by readers who
had not yet read the book. Out of context, as a single panel, on a MySpace page,
how could Chin-Kee be read otherwise? And yet, as Yang reminded his readers
on his publisher's website, he had "yanked [Chin-Kee], every last detail about
him, straight out of American pop culture."[1] In fact, the image is a direct quotation from an editorial cartoon by Pat Oliphant, where Uncle Sam is served

8.1. *From Gene Luen Yang,* American Born Chinese

"crispy fried cat gizzards with noodles" by a Chinese waiter. Yang's question, then, was whether one can deploy a racial stereotype without empowering it, reinforcing it. And if Asian faces are always read as Chin-Kee, can the Asian American comics creator tell stories of Asian Americans without him?

LIKE ALL PEOPLE OF COLOR, Asian Americans have historically been read through the lens of contradictory stereotypes and presumptions. In the postwar years, especially, these have often been framed (as contemporary racism often is) as "compliments," in this case regarding Asian Americans as the "model minority" (insisting, in the same breath, on a racial homogeneity among an incredibly diverse population of immigrants and their descendants). These "flattering" portrayals emerged in the early 1960s as a way of scolding the "problem minorities" and the civil rights movement. The devastating consequences of this stereotype have been spelled out in numerous studies, most recently in a report by the National Commission on Asian American and Pacific Islander Research in Education (*Facts, Not Fiction: Setting the Record Straight,* 2008).

Of course, as this report makes clear, this new stereotype of Asian Americans as "model minorities" was formulated less than a generation after the forced relocation during World War II of more than 120,000 Japanese Americans for being "enemy aliens," only forty years after Asian Americans were explicitly targeted as undesirable aliens in the 1924 Immigration Act, and less than a century after the very Chinese immigrants who were exploited to build the

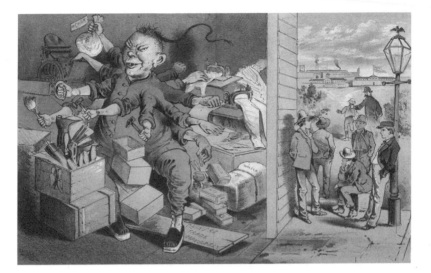

8.2. *"What Shall We Do with Our Boys?"* The Wasp (*1882*)

transcontinental railroad were defined as the nation's first "illegal immigrants" by the Chinese Exclusion Act of 1882. These earlier stereotypes of the Asian American as bestial, violent, and savage seem at first glace to run in opposition to the postwar fantasies of the quiet, studious, and robotlike Asian American, but they are never far apart. For example, in his story "Thoroughbred," published in 1895, Frank Norris imagined a Chinese mob as rats bent on the destruction of the native. The dominant stereotype today of the Asian American as the inscrutable model minority has authorized a mounting hysteria on the part of today's self-proclaimed native students (and their parents) regarding a new kind of mob taking over: Asian American children programmed by their parents for the Asian Invasion, ruthlessly stealing spots in elite universities and in the halls of power from other (white) children.[2] In other words, the late-nineteenth-century nativist fantasies of the mob of rats single-mindedly bent on the destruction of Anglo-Saxon culture and the twenty-first-century fantasy of model minorities seeking the destruction of American opportunity are all of a piece.

And throughout the generations, comics have done yeoman's work in institutionalizing this reading of the Asian problem. In fact, the nineteenth-century cartoons addressing the Asian problem look remarkably similar to those one can find today in college papers around the country. For example, San Francisco's *The Wasp,* one of the leading pioneers in the early comics of the nineteenth century, made Chinese Americans one of its central subjects, playing up images of the city overrun by swarming invaders, jobs stolen by monstrous—and monstrously efficient—aliens, and institutions overturned.

Contemporary images look remarkably similar and are especially prevalent in school newspapers, where editorialists and cartoonists have increasingly articulated images of Asian American students as mechanized alien robots (Stephen Davis, "The Adventures of Antman") and even issued "satirical" calls for "war" against Asian American students (Max Karson, "If It's War the Asians Want . . . ," *Campus Press*, February 18, 2008).

Single-panel comics especially lend themselves to the work of stereotyping. As Chris Ware says, "If you treat comics as a visual language and trace their origins, they point back, essentially, to racism" (*Dangerous Drawings*, 41). But as Ware and other contemporary graphic novelists have demonstrated, sequential comics have a unique and contrasting ability to *destabilize* racial stereotype. Indeed, it is worth noting that the cartoon stereotypes used to inscribe specific readings of racialized bodies were first formulated in the eighteenth and nineteenth centuries, when comics were almost entirely single-panel, static images. And it cannot be entirely a coincidence that at precisely the period of the greatest wave of new immigration into the United States—predominantly from Eastern Europe and Asia—the *sequential* comics form first emerged in the United States.

There are many reasons, of course, why we begin to see more nuanced and complex portrayals of racial and ethnic "Others" in mainstream American comics in the early years of the twentieth century. For one thing, many of those working in early newspaper comics, the dominant medium for comics after 1900, were themselves newer immigrants or the children of recent immigrants. Further, increased immigration both into and within the urban centers that were the publishing sites of the major newspaper comics of the day meant that both creators and their readers had daily experience with racial and ethnic difference as never before in U.S. history. But, I would argue, we should not ignore the significance of the formal properties of the medium itself in playing a significant role in the beginnings of a shift away from cartoon racism toward what we might call "graphic alterity."

For example, Frederick Burr Opper, himself a son of a German-Jewish immigrant, created in 1900 the first celebrity of the new comic strip form in Happy Hooligan, an Irish-American tramp whose simian features and heavy dialect openly reference generations of cartoon representations of the Irish. And yet, as I have argued elsewhere, the effect for Opper's readers of watching Happy Hooligan every day bravely attempt to do the right thing, only to be once again beaten by the police and thrown in jail for a crime he did not commit, was to forge a deep identification with Happy and inspire contempt for those who were always ready to convict him as the hooligan his name proposes him to be.

Yet Opper was himself no progressive where anti-Irish discrimination was concerned: his earlier work for *Puck* magazine in the late nineteenth century in single-panel cartoons utilized all the conventions of the stereotype that had been deployed on both sides of the Atlantic for decades to read the Irishman as subhuman, grotesque, and comical. While it is possible that some of Opper's own attitudes changed over the course of his life, a more convincing explanation for the change in Opper's cartoon Irishman lies in his move from single-panel cartoons to the sequential comic strip. His "King of A-Shantee" (1882), after all, does not look terribly different from his later Happy Hooligan: both wear pots on their heads, smoke ratty pipes, wear tattered pants. But where the "King of A-Shantee" serves only the joke that is his title, Happy over time and between the panels transforms into something else entirely.[3]

".IF MOTHER COULD ONLY SEE ME NOW.!"

8.3. *Frederick Burr Opper,* Happy Hooligan, *circa 1906*

The difference lies in the formal properties of sequential comics: their distilled frames of time and the spaces between them—the "gutter," as the blank space between the panels is formally known. A single-panel cartoon gag of an ethnic or racial stereotype is contained by its frame; it does the work of stereotyping as the term originally was defined: printing from a fixed mold. It is static and resists ambiguity, directing the reader to very specific ways of reading. The "King of A-Shantee" is funny because he imagines himself a "king," because he believes his miserable living conditions endow him with human dignity. The effect of the single-panel racist cartoon is to force readers to read the next Irishman they encounter in precisely these terms: to laugh at his claims to dignity or even humanity. Reading that same image in sequential comics becomes, inevitably, a more complicated and unruly enterprise.

Comics (single-panel *and* sequential) rely on stereotype and caricature—on individual characters distilled to iconic characteristics. But once two panels

PUCK'S GALLERY OF CELEBRITIES.

THE KING OF A-SHANTEE.

8.4. *Frederick Burr Opper, "The King of A-Shantee," Puck (1882)*

are put together, narrative is inevitable. As visual culture theorists from Eisenstein to McCloud have demonstrated, two radically dissimilar images in different times and space juxtaposed in sequential panels require of their readers the work of imaginatively filling in the time and space that connect them. As McCloud argues, it is the gutter, or the space between the panels, that represents the empty space to be filled in by the reader in the act of closure, forging the connections required to make meaningful this highly compressed narrative form (see McCloud, *Understanding Comics*). Indeed, of all modern narrative forms, comics are the most compressed, the most dependent on ellipses and lacunae; comics, that is, must always show and tell only a fraction of the information required to make narrative sense of the information being presented. They are, as many comics creators and theorists have pointed out, a profoundly collaborative narrative form (a fact that helps explain the highly charged relationship between comics creators and their readers). But the space between panels is not the only site where readers are required to exercise over and over again the act of closure required to make meaning: other gaps emerge that require significant conceptual and cognitive work on the part of the readers.

Arguably the most significant of these is the tension between the two primary systems of communication in graphic narrative: image and text. As we well know, image and text do not communicate information in identical ways— and as Gotthold Lessing rightly argued over two centuries ago, one can never be made equivalent to the other. For Lessing and his contemporaries, this revelation required the segregation of image and text into separate and discrete aesthetic and academic disciplines (a segregation that still largely remains in force today). But there are good reasons beyond the force of Lessing's dictates as to why text and image have been segregated into two separate but equal aesthetic categories. And there are reasons why their combination always instills a certain degree of discomfort.

In the single-panel comic this discomfort is easily managed in the service of the joke. The "King of A-Shantee" is funny because of the distance between the word "king" and the image of the Irishman. It is precisely such disjunction, for example, that Gene Luen Yang plays on in introducing Chin-Kee in a single-panel splash page (Figure 8.5). Here the joke is in Chin-Kee's assertion (in a grotesquely exaggerated dialect) that everyone loves him, even though from the start he is set out as an object not of love but of scorn and ridicule. The joke here works in precisely the same way as it does in Opper's "King of A-Shantee": the disjunction between the character's blind self-image (a blindness figured in Chin-Kee's case by his hyperbolic squint) and the realities of how the rest of us perceive him.

But if the single-panel comic can put the gap between word and image to work in the service of racist stereotype, this gap—once combined with the space between the panels and the vital role of individual readers in making up the difference—is precisely what makes the sequential comic so resistant to racialist work. This is not to say that there are not comics created with racist intention: obviously from the beginning there have been (and continue to be) a wide range of comics that make racist arguments, that deploy racial stereotypes in the service of an explicitly racialist logic. But because of the ellipses

8.5. *From Gene Luen Yang,* American Born Chinese *(2006)*

and lacunae at the heart of the comics form, such arguments always are at risk of going astray—as likely happened when Opper translated his nineteenth-century "King of A-Shantee" into a twentieth-century sequential form.[4]

IN TRUTH, HOWEVER, Yang's Chin-Kee would seem at first to be the counterargument to my assertion that the work of racist stereotyping is inevitably undermined by the ambiguities and collaborations between creator and reader inherent in sequential comics. After all, it is not as if Chin-Kee becomes *less* an object of ridicule once he is set in sequential motion; the fundamental nature of his initial single-panel introductory joke does not significantly change in the repetition. He remains a monstrously exaggerated concatenation of every popular cultural stereotype of Asians and Asian Americans over the last two centuries: we see him arriving at his cousin Danny's house for his annual visit with his luggage packed in oversized Chinese food containers (Yang, *American Born Chinese*, 48), after which he immediately begins salivating at the sight of Danny's wished-for girlfriend and her "bountiful Amellican bosom" (50). If this is an example of the many stereotypes that have been imprinted on the Asian body by U.S. popular culture in the nineteenth and early twentieth centuries, shortly after we see Chin-Kee playing out the postwar stereotypes with equal facility. "It would behoove you all to be a little more like Chin-Kee," the teacher tells the class over their barely repressed laughter after Chin-Kee has provided the correct answer regarding the three branches of American government: "Judicial, Executive, and Regisrative!" (111). By the time Chin-Kee starts doing his William Hung impersonation, performing "She Bangs" on the library table (203), Cousin Danny has had enough, and Yang seems to invite the reader to empathize with him as he finally loses his temper and begins slapping Chin-Kee, telling him to stop "ruining my life" and "go away!"

Of course, this is a book where we have already seen the consequences of such blows. *American Born Chinese* is fragmented not only by the inherent properties of the comics form, but by the structure of its narrative. It moves back and forth between three seemingly discrete stories: the story of the Monkey King, the story of Jin Wang, and the story of Cousin Danny and Chin-Kee. The first story begins with the first blow, as the Monkey King unleashes his mighty anger after being humiliated in front of the other gods for being "still a monkey." But his beating of the other gods does not heal the wound their words have opened: the Monkey King returns home to his royal chamber and discovers there, for the first time, "the thick smell of monkey fur." He dedicates himself to transforming himself into someone the gods will at last take seriously: putting on shoes, changing his stature, mastering new powers. Despite all his efforts, he is still greeted each time with laughter by the other gods, forcing him to react once again with violence. Eventually he is confronted by Tze-yo-Tzuh (a god transplanted to the Buddhist myth from Yang's Catholic upbringing), who buries the Monkey King under a mountain of stone until he is finally willing to assume his true nature and thereby free himself.

The second tale, of Jin Wang, tells the story of a young Chinese American boy's experiences at a predominantly Anglo-American school, where he encounters all-too-familiar assumptions about his family's culinary practices, his ability at sports and other all-American activities, and his romantic prospects. When a new student, Wei-Chen, recently arrived from Taiwan, joins the class, Jin reacts with horror. An F.O.B. (fresh-off-the-boat) Asian student will only remind his classmates of all he had worked so studiously to make them forget: that he himself is foreign, not one of the guys. Yet, over the years, it is Wei-Chen who finds his way in the new school more easily, making friends and then actually finding a girlfriend, Suzy Nakamura, while Jin continues to pine hopelessly after Amelia Harris. In many ways, of course, Jin's dilemmas are typical schoolboy stuff: a schoolboy crush and the agony of summoning the confidence to take the risk of making it public. And with Wei-Chen's help, Jin does find the confidence at last, and Amelia responds encouragingly to his tentative advances. But of course, where this typical coming-of-age story differs for Jin from his Anglo classmates is with the burden of being always, finally, a "chink" in the eyes of his peers. No sooner does he start going out with Amelia than the popular boy, Greg, asks him to stop going out with her: "I just don't know if you're right for her."

Stunned by the request from someone he thought was his friend, Jin initially acquiesces, but soon he is fantasizing about different responses he *might* have given, including a well-deserved punch in the jaw, and his confidence (represented by subjective cracks of lightning in the background) begins to mount again as he goes to confront Amelia and stand up for his desires. But as soon as he sees Greg, lightning literally emanating from his golden curls and the unspoken word heavy in the air between them, Jin's confidence dissipates instantly. Retreating in defeat, he meets Suzy at the bus stop, and when she speaks the word out loud everything goes horribly wrong. "Today," she says, "when Timmy called me a . . . chink, I realized . . . deep down inside . . . I kind of feel like that all the time" (187). And with that articulation of what Jin could not bring himself to acknowledge about himself, the lightning returns, and in his confusion over the emotions she has inspired, Jin makes the fatal mistake of attempting to kiss Suzy, a betrayal of both of his friends. Instead of acknowledging the injury he has caused, however, Jin internalizes the racism, turning his hateful words on his best friend: "Maybe I think she can do better than an F.O.B. like you," he tells Wei-Chen. With these words and the blow that follows, Jin's transformation is complete, and he wakes up the next morning now finally wearing the face of all he aspires to be: the bland, blond-haired Cousin Danny, his new identity.

Thus, as the novel moves toward its conclusion, the fragments that make up the whole are brought together, forcing the reader to rethink everything up to that point. With the realization that Cousin Danny is in fact the older Jin, now transformed into his ideal, the character of Chin-Kee is thrown into a different kind of relief, as is his relentless embarrassment of Danny (forcing Danny to change schools every year in order to escape the stigma of being Chin-Kee's cousin). Even before we discover (with a blow that knocks Chin-Kee's head literally off) that Chin-Kee is actually the Monkey King himself, we are already prepared for the (pun intended) punch line.

Thus even this extreme case, which Yang seems to have set for himself almost as a test of his medium, demonstrates the ways in which sequential comics destabilize racialist logic. Racism may share with comics some fundamental grammatical elements: caricature, stereotypes, condensation. But racism requires precisely that which sequential comics make impossible: unequivocal meanings, and a stable definition of us and them. Comics offer no such promise to their readers, as we have already addressed, and further, unlike more efficient narrative forms such as film or the novel, comics allow—and often even require—an unruly reader who can and will double back, skip to the end, flip between pages, rereading once, twice at a sitting. The Chin-Kee we read the second time, as indeed we are expected to, is a very different character than the gross spectacle we encountered (through Danny's privileged point of view) the first time through the book—just as the Monkey King we encounter at the book's end is very different than the angry, resentful deity we met in the book's opening pages. "You know, Jin," he concludes, "I would have saved myself from five hundred years' imprisonment beneath a mountain of rock had I only realized how good it is to be a monkey" (223).

AT FIRST GLANCE, it might well appear that *American Born Chinese* is something of an exception among works by the new generation of Asian American comics creators. After all, few address issues of identity and stereotype with the kind of directness Yang brings to bear. But just as the revelations at the end of *American Born Chinese* require a rereading of the book's three narratives, so too does Yang's story demand of us a return to earlier works by this generation of talented younger Asian American creators in order to see the ways in which many of the same themes and strategies are deployed, albeit in more subtle ways.

For example, in "Hawaiian Getaway" (1999) by Adrian Tomine, twenty-something Hillary Chan faces many of the same issues that confront the younger Jin. But outside of the cruel confines of the schoolyard the racism she encounters takes on a more insidious and unspoken form. The word Suzy and Jin realize they have lived with every day is now a quiet, relentless hum beneath the surface of Hillary's daily life, so quiet she cannot even begin to articulate it to herself. As the story begins, Chan has just been fired from her job as a phone operator for making the wrong kind of small talk with a celebrity customer. Her inability to master small talk is a source of constant frustration to her, and it is exacerbated by the seeming effortlessness of those around her in striking up random conversations with each other. "Sometimes I feel like there's a sign floating above my head that says something like 'Warning: avoid contact with this person,'" she tells us. "I was told once that I look 'naturally stand-offish,' which I could not understand."[5] When, immediately after articulating this thought to the reader, we watch Hillary's silent standoff with a coffeehouse cashier, when we see the (suspicious? resentful?) backward glance of the other customer whose flirtations Hillary's presence has interrupted, we are being invited to read more into the silences she encounters than Hillary herself seems prepared to.[6] That she is read by others as stand-offish, as distant and unreadable, has of course everything to do with the assumptions those around her have made about her based on her name, her appearances, perhaps even the traces of the Mandarin accent of her mother, from whom she has run as far away as she possibly can. But even if she cannot acknowledge it, Hillary has nonetheless internalized this reading of her, and so finds herself increasingly isolated, angry, desperate.

Cut off from her one regular line of human interaction in her job as phone operator, Hillary regresses, holing up in her apartment and making random prank calls to strangers at the phone booth down below her window. Over time the calls get nastier, as she directs her own self-loathing at the people below, insulting them, threatening them, mocking them. The themes worked out in "Hawaiian Getaway," one of Tomine's longer stories, are familiar ones throughout his work: isolation, the need for community and contact, and the simultaneous deep distrust of community and other people—the inevitable gaps and misunderstanding in all human interaction. These themes arise also in his stories that don't feature Asian American characters, but we would be wrong to assume that those stories have nothing to say about the experience of being Asian American. One of the predominant strategies in Asian American comics, and especially in the work of Tomine, in confronting the legacy of the Asian American stereotype—as inscrutable, mysterious, and unreadable by mainstream America—is to point out the universality of this inscrutability, the impossibility of ever comprehending, truly, another person.

Although infinitely more adept socially than Tomine's Hillary Chan, Nancy, one of the Korean American protagonists in Derek Kirk Kim's first graphic novel, *Same Difference* (2003), has found herself engaged in remarkably similar behavior. Shortly after her roommates have forced upon her painful memories of her high school self (as, for example, a member of the ping-pong team), twenty-something Nancy confesses to her best friend, Simon, a more recent, shameful secret. She has been taking on the identity of the former tenant of the apartment to answer the overwrought and vaguely disturbed love letters of one Ben Leland. The results of her game now lie spread out before them in an overflowing correspondence from Leland, who turns out to be from Simon's hometown. Simon is aghast at her for playing with an emotionally vulnerable stranger for her own fun. But he is feeling guilty himself, having just run into Irene, a blind girl, once his best friend in high school, whom he long ago unceremoniously abandoned when he found out she had romantic feelings for him. And so he allows himself to be convinced that it would be fun to go back to his hometown and spy on Ben.

The trip proves to be not nearly as fun as Nancy had imagined, however. Back in his hometown, Simon must confront his high school self, as he first meets some old classmates and then runs into his former best friend, Irene. All have gotten on with their lives in different ways, Simon realizes, while he remains stalled: "still the same pathetic loser weaving juvenile lies those 7 years ago. Am I any different now?" (79). Simon has finally come to the realization that his attraction to Irene and his abandonment of Irene both originated from the same source: her blindness. Her lack of sight made her the one person at his overwhelmingly white high school who did not see him as first and foremost Asian—and for a teenager desperate to fit in, this was a liberating gift. But her disability was also a stigma in the eyes of his peers, and in this way she represented everything he was trying to escape: the mark of difference, Otherness, inscrutability. Nancy, meanwhile, finally spies the object of her games, and to her surprise Ben Leland turns out to be a middle-aged grocery clerk, and Asian American. Seeing him, the game is no longer any fun, as Ben is a reflection of everything Nancy most fears for her own future and most fears about her own present self. The novella ends with an apology letter to Ben that we are not invited to read, and with the suggestion that maybe both Simon and Nancy have arrived at a place where they might finally begin to progress beyond their high school selves.

Problems of identity and experience in Kim's and Tomine's stories are not as straightforward as those Yang spells out in *American Born Chinese*. In his most recent (and longest) narrative, *Shortcomings* (2007), Tomine concludes with a similarly unreadable letter—this time from Ben Tanaka to the friend he is leaving. At the end of a long and miserable breakup, Ben (who had hitherto been unwilling to countenance anyone's judgment or motivation that did not accord with his own) can at least say in defense of his ex, "We all have our reasons" (107). The reader, of course, is left wondering about those reasons. But in lieu of explanation, the reader receives, in conclusion, seventeen silent panels: a fragment of the Brooklyn Bridge, seemingly disconnected from the islands it binds together; an unanswered knock on the door; a letter that we are not allowed to read. The sequence culminates in a final series of panels showing Ben staring out a plane window as it slowly turns to white, a blank slate. Tomine's minimalist realism does not have the luxury that Yang's magic realism does of promising that one might escape from the mountain of rock simply by being true to oneself. But as with Simon and Nancy, we do have a sense that Ben had learned something—or, more appropriate, unlearned something—and become willing to accept the possibility that prejudgment might be replaced by the release of judgment ("We all have our reasons"). Ben is at least willing to let go the need

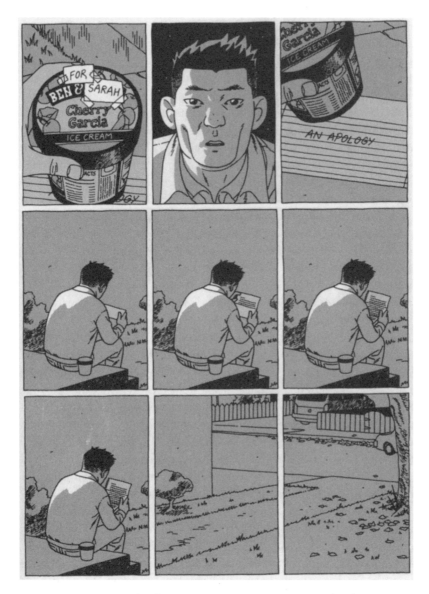

8.6. *From Derek Kirk Kim,* Same Difference and Other Stories *(2003)*

to label everyone he meets by type and category and start over in the blank space at the end of the novel.

The blank space at the end of these novels, of course, represents precisely the interactive space opened up by the comics form: Nancy's apology, Ben's farewell note, the blank field of stars, or the empty pane of the window, all are texts for the reader to fill in, drawing from what we have learned about our characters. Reading these stories of isolation, cruelty, humiliation, and masquerade, we see common threads that run through them, shared experiences—but in the end we are asked to complete the story. The authors ask that our encounter with these characters be something like Nancy's encounter with Ben Leland—forcing us to pick up a pen and start writing ourselves into the story, taking active responsibility for the fun we have had by reading, watching, looking into other people's windows and lives (reminding us how very like Hillary and Nancy we are). Even the somewhat more didactic *American Born Chinese* ends with a similar moment: a final page in which Jin and Wei-Chen are sitting together talking once more, a conversation we are not invited to listen in on. If the comics creator must surrender a remarkable degree of authorial control in working in this medium, turning to readers at every panel to help forge the connections and fill in the blanks, these works all conclude by putting on readers the responsibility, literally, for ending the story—drawing on, and drawing in, their own lives.

It is worth pointing out that none of these books offers what Tomine's Ben Tanaka mockingly calls a "big 'statement' about race." They all differently confront the experience of growing up Asian American, being read always by dominant society through the lens of a century's worth of stereotypes and racist assumption. But they don't promise that cultural identity offers a safe haven or an easy answer. Instead, each of these authors similarly (and differently) turns to the sequential comics form to confront and destabilize racial stereotype, using the very tools that have been historically used to forge those molds in the first place. And they similarly (and differently) use graphic narrative's necessarily interactive nature to force the reader into a position of taking an active role in making meaning out of what can't be spoken: the conclusions, the road map as to how to move forward. In all cases, the creators are aware that the ways in which readers take up this charge will differ. They will differ, certainly based on whether or not the reader is herself Asian American. But they will also differ for a whole range of other reasons that the author cannot predict, any more than Ben Tanaka can finally know the reasons for his breakup. "We all have our reasons," and for all of us the reasons of others remain ultimately inscrutable, mysterious. The best we can hope for is to know our *own* reasons, and to begin to own them, as Nancy and Simon seem to do at the end of *Same Difference*. If we are all different, we are also the same for *being* different (as Kim's playful title reminds us), and the inscrutable Asian becomes no longer the model minority but the universal model of the painful and beautiful alterity of other people.

If the single-panel comic is the ultimate medium of stereotyping, it could be argued that the sequential comic is the most powerful (in part because least susceptible to authorial discipline) medium for embracing the radical consequences of an alterity that disables stereotype and the easy readings of the hegemonic gaze.[7] The sameness of difference and the difference in sameness are what these Asian American graphic novelists all gesture toward in similar and different ways, and what we do with the blank panels with which we are left at the end is the power and the responsibility that they each pass on to us as readers.

NOTES

1. "Gene Yang on Stereotypes," May 1, 2007, http://firstsecondbooks.typepad.com/mainblog/2007/05/gene_yang_on_st.html.

2. As with all stereotypes, the realities, of course, are very different. Despite, and indeed because of, the model minority stereotype, Asian American students increasingly find it harder to get admitted to elite universities, and once admitted they are far less likely to receive needed help and support than other students. And of immediate impact for the writers and artists we will be talking about, assumptions that Asian Americans are *always* science and engineering students lead those who pursue careers in arts and humanities to be seen as doubly alien: the model minority who doesn't even fit the model. And no one knows this reality better than an Asian American *cartoonist*—one who has chosen one of the least profitable and least culturally respected professions.

3. In fact, Happy Hooligan became not a subject of the joke, but an object of admiration, such that his birthday became an event regularly acknowledged by national and civic leaders.

4. See Jared Gardner's "Reading out of the Gutter: Early Comics, Film, and the Serial Pleasures of Modernity," forthcoming.

5. Adrian Tomine, "Hawaiian Getaway," in *Summer Blonde: Stories* (Montreal: Drawn & Quarterly, 2003). "Hawaiian Getaway" was originally published in Tomine's serial comic *Optic Nerve #6* (1999).

6. As Sandra Oh nicely reads this scene, "Given that Hilary's [*sic*] order is unremarkable, the explanation for this attitude can be attributed to the visual, recasting Hilary's problem not as one of language but of vision" ("Sight Unseen: Adrian Tomine's *Optic Nerve* and the Politics of Recognition," 137).

7. For a discussion of the ways in which the graphic narrative form's engagement with alterity has been put to use by graphic novelists confronting issues of disability, see Susan M. Squier, "So Long as They Grow Out of It: Comics, the Discourse of Developmental Normalcy, and Disability" (2008).

A MULTICULTURAL COMIC BOOK TOOLBOX

9 "IT AIN'T JOHN SHAFT"
Marvel Gets Multicultural in The Tomb of Dracula

ELIZABETH NIXON

"MULTICULTURAL" AND "MARVEL" are not usually included in the same sentence, at least not in an affirmative way. Though Marvel introduced Luke Cage, the first black superhero with a series all his own, in 1973, it has been dismissed by critics on the multicultural front. Marvel has been charged with modeling Cage and its other black superheroes on a watered-down version of John Shaft and failing to do anything more complex. (See Jeffrey Brown, *Black Superheroes, Milestone Comics, and Their Fans.*) *Luke Cage: Hero for Hire* is indeed, at least initially, very much indebted to Shaft, right down to the way the protagonists are framed at the outset by billboards, movie signs, and other markers of city life. However, even during the time of Luke Cage's debut, Marvel authors and illustrators, such as *The Tomb of Dracula*'s Marv Wolfman and Gene Colan, were increasing Marvel's multicultural repertoire. During its successful seventy-issue run between 1972 and 1979, *The Tomb of Dracula* moved beyond Shaft impersonations and used a variety of visual and verbal combinations to make readers question borders imposed between nations and races.

The Tomb of Dracula not only represents characters with a wide variety of ethnic and racial backgrounds, but also uses sophisticated verbal and visual techniques separately and in juxtaposition to make readers inhabit many characters. By providing a multitude of perspectives, both visually and through word bubbles and the narrator's prompting, *Tomb* encourages its audience to cross boundaries erected between people on the basis of nationality or ethnicity. It also questions authoritative assertions about what makes someone truly British or American. One of *Tomb*'s strictly visual means of encouraging its audience to inhabit a character occurs when the audience sees what is pictured in the panel through a character's eyes. In issue #5, for example, though Taj Nital is incapable of speaking and we often do not have access to his thoughts, we do see out of a coffin through his eyes, sharing the danger from his perspective and imagining his thoughts and feelings. *The Tomb of Dracula* also sometimes uses second-person narration to encourage readers to adopt, to some degree, the identities of characters from a wide variety of cultures. The narrator addresses the audience as a character, beginning an issue by addressing "You, Frank Drake," for example, and continuing on to explain what you feel when you pick up a lamp or feel a spider crawling up your leg. While the narrator uses the second person more often with Drake, he also encourages identification with characters who are not American, blond, or blue-eyed, in an attempt to prevent readers from imagining any of the characters, from Frank Drake to the mute Indian Taj Nital, and even Dracula, as entirely "Other."

I am not asserting, however, that *The Tomb of Dracula*'s blurring of national and racial borders makes it politically correct. Taj Nital, for example, who is called the "mute Indian" by both the narrator and Dracula and is referred to on one occasion as fellow vampire hunter Rachel Van Helsing's servant, is literally the subaltern who cannot speak as a result of having been attacked by vampires back in India. Verbal expression (or the lack thereof) is also presented as the primary feature that marks *Tomb*'s other minority vampire hunter as different. Shaft's specter haunts the vampire hunter Blade, though the resemblance is more verbal than physical. Unlike earlier comics that distorted black bodies and made them alien, *Tomb* is laid out in a way that suggests that, despite characters, and even the narrative voice, frequently referring to his blackness, what really distinguishes Blade is the way he speaks, a marker of difference he shares with many other black comic book characters of the era. (Stephen Krensky's *Comic Book Century* points out that when it was no longer seen as permissible to make light of black bodies, many comics turned to marking African American characters by means of their "ghetto" dialect.)

Blade frequently drops his g's and sprinkles his speech liberally with "brother" and "dig." *The Tomb of Dracula* makes it clear that the way he speaks is distinctive, often having him speak in a panel before appearing in the next, teaching characters within the comic, as well as the flesh-and-blood audience, to anticipate his appearance based on his manner of speaking. Blade's speech prepares readers to expect a black, urban, American man despite his having been born and raised in London. *The Tomb of Dracula* comments on this directly in issue #17, introducing Blade off-frame with "pin the tail on the donkey, Fang-Face—'cause that's exactly what's comin' off tonight," and having Dracula tentatively ask "Blade?" to which the response is "It ain't John Shaft, red eyes!" However, even though Douglas Wolk dismisses Blade as yet another Shaft-wannabe and the character conforms to the stereotype of the way black people speak, the British Blade being frequently identified by means of his black American accent is one of the ways in which *The Tomb of Dracula* asks readers to question what elements constitute national and racial identities.

Tomb begins with a journey across borders. The series starts with the formerly wealthy Frank Drake, an American blond-haired, blue-eyed descendant of Dracula's, reading excerpts from Dracula's grandson's diary and finding the inspiration to set off for Transylvania in order to turn Castle Dracula into a tourist trap. Readers follow Drake across the pond and, along with Drake and his companions, have vampire lore explained to them by the locals. While having readers travel with characters and assuming that they share ignorance of their surroundings is a common way to motivate exposition, *Tomb of Dracula* takes further steps to make readers feel that they are indeed "with" the characters. Inside Castle Dracula, for example, bats appear to be flying out of the panel and at the reader at the same time as characters are being attacked by bats. Readers are then even more explicitly placed in a character's shoes when they are encouraged to identify, to a degree, with Frank Drake in issue #2. Readers are addressed as "you, Frank Drake" and told that memories of being attacked by a newly awakened Dracula in the castle and the subsequent death of Frank's girlfriend "burn, stinging your eyes almost as much as the heat from your handheld lantern." Being addressed as Drake and being told what "our" emotions are gives us more insight into the character and encourages us to see from his perspective while at the same time observing him.

Second-person narration in comics is in many ways similar to second-person narration in nongraphic fiction. James Phelan stresses that second-person narration does not make either the narrative audience (the audience the narrator envisions) or flesh-and-blood audience relinquish their roles as observers, even though it can make readers identify across gender lines and other boundaries and is meant to increase emotional involvement in the narrative world. (See Phelan's "Self-Help for Narratee and Narrative Audience: How 'I' and 'You' Read 'How.'") *The Tomb of Dracula* is a good illustration of how second-person narration involves both observer and participant roles. At the same time as we are told that we feel the heat from the handheld lantern and are being sent down a dark tunnel, we see Drake's chiseled face and the lantern in his hand, making it harder, thanks to our position as visual observers, to imagine ourselves as Drake. While including some degree of visual information about the character at the beginning of the issue would help the audience picture the person they are meant to be identifying with, addressing the audience as "You, Frank Drake" while they see through his eyes would make them less conscious of the observer role. They would be free to imagine their own reactions instead of relying on observation of his body language and facial expressions.

The participant versus observer pendulum swings closer to the observer role the more fully a character is fleshed out. Phelan observes that it is harder for readers to participate as "you" in fiction when there is a lot of information about the "you" that contradicts the readers' realities ("Self-Help," 350). Scott McCloud observes a similar phenomenon in *Understanding Comics*, noting that more realistically drawn characters are harder to identify with than faces that are just circles with eyes, a nose, and a mouth. Drake, along with most of the other characters in *Tomb*, is drawn in a realistic style. It is not quite photo quality, but close. In addition to having definite features, he also, in the scenes where he is "us," is often highly characterized. He speaks many lines of dialogue, prepares to commit suicide, and calls Taj a "Rudyard Kipling reject," all of which work to give him a well-defined personality that might be difficult for flesh-and-blood audience members to identify with. However, as Phelan also points out, readers are capable of swinging back into experiencing roles when the use of detailed characterization diminishes; it would be easier for us-as-Drake to imagine ourselves with a deadly spider crawling up our legs than in scenes that reveal more about his personality.

Though it would be more than a challenge to map what all real readers feel when directly asked to identify with a Drake who prepares to commit suicide and makes insensitive comments, it is possible to analyze what they are encouraged to feel by examining the extent to which the narrator endorses Drake's actions and opinions. However, it is difficult in several cases to ascertain whether or not the narrator agrees with racist remarks made by the characters. Like the layout of the panels, the narrative voice shifts and blurs, blending with the voices of different characters and leaving readers in suspense as to which values the narrator will prompt them to adopt at any given point. (While several issues of *Tomb of Dracula* are narrated in part by characters, I am referring here to the series' primary narrator, who is not a character.) Initially, the narrator appears to hold, and encourages readers to share, Drake's one-dimensional view of Taj. Taj cannot speak, and readers are not given direct access to his thoughts as compensation for his inability to express himself verbally, even though *Tomb* makes use of the thought bubble convention for other characters. Instead, the narrator uses the third person to speak for Taj on the rare occasions that his feelings are considered. In addition to being rendered voiceless and thoughtless, Taj is often pictured on the fringes of the panel and is implicitly compared to the good-hearted Monster of the Moorlands in issue #6. Early in the issue, Taj uses his hands to signal a location, and the monster later uses his fist to thank Rachel

Van Helsing and Drake for "calling him a man." Taj appears in the panel directly following a close-up of the monster's hand signal for man, signaling a connection between a mute Indian man and a speechless monster.

Interestingly, readers are encouraged to experience Taj as a more fully rounded character at the same time that Drake, the character whose experiences we are most often encouraged to identify with, undergoes an experience that complicates the idea of racial boundaries. In issue #28, we go from seeing Taj as essentially impenetrable to being asked, via the same type of second-person narration we have seen with Drake, to put ourselves in his position. We-as-Taj do not entirely see from his perspective. On the second page, for example, even when the angle allows us to recognize "our" hand reaching out to tilt "our" wife's chin up, we later see Taj's face on the same page looking horrified. However, we do occasionally see through Taj's eyes, and the narrator addresses us as Taj: "You are uncertain of the meaning in your wife's words as you stare through the bamboo curtain—but you are not unsure of what you see, and that makes you sick!" Even though we often observe Taj here, only really seeing from his perspective when he is comforting his wife or about to drive a stake into his son, we are not placed outside of him any more than we are placed outside of Drake. Prompting us to inhabit Taj to the same extent that we have been encouraged to identify with Drake suggests that being a mute and being Indian do not have to render someone opaque. The Taj we see arguing with his wife and agonizing about what to do with his vampire son is a far cry from the one-dimensional "Kipling reject" given to us in the beginning.

At the same time as readers begin to inhabit Taj, Drake, whose experiences

9.1., 9.2. The Tomb of Dracula, *Issue 28*

we are most often encouraged to share, is possessed by Brother Voodoo's spirit brother when he needs help fighting zombies. Issue #31's layout suggests that it is no accident that readers are prompted to become Taj at the same time as Drake is possessed in Brazil. For several issues, whole pages are split between Taj in India on the left and Drake in Brazil on the right, with readers having to unconventionally read down the page rather than across. The narrator calls attention to the color difference in the Brazil section, explaining that Drake, the "blond-haired victim," is now protected by Brother Voodoo, "master of black magic." Readers see the possessed Drake fighting off attackers at around the same time as readers, possessing Taj in the sense that we see through his eyes, hold a stake over his son. The positioning of both possessions indicates that readers are once again meant to share Drake's experience to some extent. Given the way the panels and story sequences are linked, the suggestion appears to be that having been in Taj's shoes enables readers to relate to Drake's experience of being part of an "Other," indicating that we are ultimately meant to identify with him even when we are given access to other characters. However, though the use of second-person narration in Taj's case may relate to Drake's possession by another "Other," readers experience Taj in the second person for several pages before there is even a hint of Drake, indicating that it is also an important experience in its own right. It is to be one of the last experiences of Taj. At the Brazil sequence's conclusion, Brother Voodoo looks out of the panel while addressing Drake, indicating that the reader has once again taken on Drake's perspective. Taj has just left the series, electing to remain in India with his wife after the death of their son. We finally see his words while he is composing a note of explanation to Rachel Van Helsing. His first words are words of farewell. Nevertheless, Frank's life-saving possession by a black spirit and the readers' experiences of Taj indicate that racial and national borders are not impenetrable.

In addition to challenging the boundaries between people of different races and nationalities, the *Tomb of Dracula* team works to undermine exclusionary notions about what the "real" Britain looks like, both in terms of its people and its neighborhoods. Big Ben and Parliament stand for London in the parts of *The Tomb of Dracula* where readers follow Drake. *Marvel Preview* #3 and *Vampire Tales* #8, which are in *The Tomb of Dracula* universe but feature Blade, question the idea that the only "real" London is the one associated with Anglo institutions and traditions. (Notably, in un-PC style, Marvel elects to have the black vampire hunter originate from and investigate crime in the city's slums.) These issues reveal the London beyond the public monuments to examine what the city has in common with the rest of the world. However, the narrator does not begin either issue by unfurling a cross-cultural banner. It is initially unclear whether or not readers are meant to view the untouristed areas, at first pre-

sented as slums, as positives even if they are more authentic. As the issues progress, however, the idea of an idyllic "old Britain" represented by the monuments
and sought after by xenophobes is undermined.

The narrator begins *Preview* #3 by articulating a point of view Enoch Powell would have agreed with, noting that London, "mother of Empires" and "the
city that ruled the world," is a "city much like other cities. Life's changed, death
has changed. These days, it seems like you can die in London as easily as in the
South Bronx." *Vampire Tales* #8 begins on a similar, though slightly less negative, note. The narrator explains that "tourists never trod this squalid London
side-street—it has no sights, no thrills, no exotic excitements to write home
about . . . it is a slum and like any home-grown slums, its back alleys are infested
with disease." Presumably, then, having areas that tourists do not see is not really
something to be proud of after all, at least not if the areas contain disease.

However, *Preview* #3 and *Vampire Tales* #8 ultimately discredit the idea that
nontraditional, non-Anglo London can only be discussed in terms of crime
and disease. *Vampire Tales* #8 retreats from its earlier vision of squalor and filth.
Readers see Blade in the shower, which is "warm and soothing," and are told
that the brothel near the alley smells like jasmine, providing a counterpoint
to the narrator's earlier statement about squalor and filth in the area. *Preview*
#3 uses a similar strategy, introducing pro-Empire ideas and then dismantling
them. The issue indicates that, though violence in the present is very real, it is
nonsensical to cling to an idyllic version of what Britain was like in the past. Just
after the narrator bemoans the lack of safety post-Empire, for example, we see
an "authentically English" man dressed in period clothing using what appears
to be a dueling sword in a fight with Blade. Considering the introduction to
London at the beginning of the issue, readers unfamiliar with Blade might be
tempted to side with the gentleman wearing traditional garb. Were he not a
vampire. Blade clearly defeats a period-clothing-wearing representative of the
days of Empire, a representative who is, appropriately enough, a vampire. *Preview* #3 further undermines the idea that an older, more traditional Britain was
less violent and something to be missed when Blade remembers saving an old
man from an attack by what appear to be Teddy Boys. It turns out that they were
vampires, not Teddy Boys, but another link between the idea of "English" and
"vampire" has been made. It seems that the violence referred to by the narrator
in the beginning comes from those associated with "Englishness."

It is important to remember that it was not just a black vampire slayer who
defeated the aristocratic-looking representative of "traditional England." It was
a black *British* vampire slayer, one who speaks with an American accent but still
says "mum." Blade represents a new Britain, one that boasts jazz clubs that one
might expect to have difficulty locating outside of major American cities. Yes,

Marvel may be perpetuating some stereotypes by having Blade frequent a jazz club in addition to working and living in the ghetto. Similar stereotype-perpetuating accusations can be made about the *Tomb of Dracula* series as a whole. However, though these comics can be incredibly un-politically-correct and simplistic, they offer sophisticated means of asking readers to look for cross-cultural connections. *The Tomb of Dracula* is never uncomplicated; readers are never sure which point of view the narrator will encourage them to adopt next and are frequently unsure of the narrator's own opinions. Second-person narration that is combined with images that do not always correspond with the character's viewpoint invite reader identification with a number of different people. At the same time, readers rarely fully relinquish the observer role, which raises questions about whether or not full identification with another, any Other, is possible. *The Tomb of Dracula* asks its audience to "read [and see] across identity borders" (see Phelan, "Reading across Identity Borders," 39), while at the same time questioning which elements of identity require borders in the first place. *The Tomb of Dracula*'s Empire-questioning content, along with its narrator's changing viewpoints, second-person narration, and changing visual perspective for readers, means that part of the suspense is generated by uncertainty as to what the audience is supposed to think about nationality and identity. *The Tomb of Dracula*'s design raises both goose bumps and questions.

10 INVISIBLE ART, INVISIBLE PLANES, INVISIBLE PEOPLE

EVAN THOMAS

THIS ESSAY WILL INVESTIGATE three varieties of the invisible: the invisible art, an invisible plane, and invisible people. Ever since comic creator and theoretician Scott McCloud dubbed comics "the invisible art" in his famous book *Understanding Comics*, I have been stuck to the term. It underscores the importance of the gutter—so easily dismissed in French as a *blanc*—in the generation of meaning in comics. The gutter, in fact, contributes an entire plane of meaning to comics that employ it. The "invisible plane" I reference with my title is a mythical vimana, a flying chariot from which Grant Morrison and Philip Bond's *Vimanarama* draws its name. *Vimanarama* is a book that features the "invisible people," the marginalized.

These three varieties of the invisible are interesting in their interrelations and forced inferences. Thierry Groensteen, comics theoretician and critic, has investigated a system of meaning that is completely unique to comics, arthrology, characterized by approaching them on the level of panels and their interrelations. This approach—as opposed to classical ideas dichotomizing comics as image and text—opens *Vimanarama* to a wider range of meanings. These elements of comics don't have the strictly linear relations of mechanical reading, and so can operate around and through narrative. I will demonstrate that examination of these elements in *Vimanarama* reveals the space in which the marginalized speak. The marginalized are characterized by their mobility, and while one character in *Vimanarama* is minimized in the classical narrative, he influences other areas of narrative. Groensteen's investigation into alternative spaces provides significant insight to reading *Vimanarama*, and furthermore, opens that comic up for alternate readings.

For now, some background in the critical situation of this essay is necessary. After some definitions and an introduction to the relevant terms from Groensteen's *System*, McCloud's hypotheses—privileged here for their popularity and accessibility—will serve as a traditional sounding board for Groensteen's more recent theories concerning interpanel relations.

First, I identify image and text as the "classical" instruments of comics narration. As Thierry Groensteen identifies, this dichotomy began at the latest with the father of modern comics, Rodolphe Töpffer, who "saw in the text and in the image two equal components of comics, which he defined from their mixed character" (Groensteen, *System*, 8). Comics for Töpffer were a site of cooperation between two preexisting art forms. Simple linear associations of image and text constitute what Groensteen calls "mechanical meaning," and I use this term for immediate linear meaning (124). This notion of comics as a simple pairing of text and image is quite limited in light of what Groensteen calls the "truly specific processes and techniques" of comics—ideas including arthrology, braiding, and gutter (23).

These truly specific processes and techniques find their formal definition in *The System of Comics*, beginning with *arthrology*. Broadly, it is the study of relations between panels in comics. Groensteen comes to emphasize the importance of panels first from abstaining from the debate concerning the "minimum signifying units" and second by taking the opposite starting point: looking for the largest systems of collaboration in comics. In this way, Groensteen arrives at an interest in what he calls the *system* of comics: "The comics panel is fragmentary and caught in a system of proliferation; it never makes up the totality of the utterance but can and must be understood as a component of a larger apparatus" (4–5). The neologism "arthrology"—from the Greek for "articulation" (viii)—is specific to two kinds of panel interrelation (13).

Restricted arthrology studies the relations between panels on the linear level, commonly in sequence in a strip. Two topics I would consider relevant to restricted arthrology are word balloons and gutters, because they strongly influence transitional relations in the short range of comics. *General arthrology* addresses the relations between panels at a distance. One phenomenon studied within general arthrology is that of *braiding*, linkage between panels through non-narrative correspondences (ix). Panel placement and interrelation are the chief structure of space on the comic page and across comics pages, and they can be used to force inference.

The phrase "forced inference" is inspired by Groensteen's discussion of the capabilities of the gutter, a subject of interest in restricted arthrology. The importance of the gutter, which is the unframed area between panels, is as widely recognized as the space is plain. It is first and commonly observed that the gutter passes idly while the reader actively constructs the transition between panels. Groensteen summarizes a series of critical insights as this: "Comics exist only as a satisfying narrative under the condition that, despite the discontinuous enunciation and the intermittent monstration, the resultant story forms an uninterrupted and intelligible totality" (114). Similarly, McCloud writes, "Here in the *limbo* of the gutter, *human imagination* takes two separate images and *transforms* them into a single idea" (McCloud, *Understanding Comics*, 66; emphasis added). While it is granted for now that smooth linear transitions between frames are the work of the reader, *Understanding Comics* presses the issue further.

McCloud argues, with some success, that the work of the reader is more than that, that the gutter between panels constitutes a complete break from narrative authority. Stepping beyond the idiosyncrasies of the gutter, McCloud suggests—delighting in his power as a creator—that elements of story that are embedded in the gutter are by definition indefinite: "I may have drawn an *axe* being *raised* in this example, but I'm not the one who let it drop or decided how *hard* the blow, or *who* screamed, or *why*. . . . To kill a man between panels is to condemn him to a thousand deaths" (68–69; emphasis added). He posits that there is "blood in the gutter" because the death between the panels "was *your special crime*" (69; emphasis added).

I will consider his perspective as a close relative of Benoît Peeters's *cases fantômes*, or "ghost panels," hypothesis, which also considers the operations between frames to be wholly the reader's construction. Peeters asserts, in the case of McCloud's example, that the reader mentally constructs an intermediate panel of the axe murder. Both ideas assert a very independent reader—taking over as a comics creator—projecting ideas between the frames. If this is the case, then the workings of the gutter are very independent from the surrounding panels: is this so?

Thierry Groensteen considers Peeters's theory with little interest. He concedes that "ghost panels" are feasible in the long passages which are cherry-picked by advocates, but asserts that the "ghost panel" hypothesis has not been demonstrated on the scale of two panels, the minimum of moving parts for such an effect. He advocates the opposite view: "The comics image is not a form that, subjected to a continual metamorphosis, would be modified by investing successive frames (between which it would be permissible to reconstitute the missing moments)" (Groensteen, *System*, 112). Furthermore, he finds that an interpolated panel in Peeters's famous example would actually disrupt continuity rather than uphold it: "within this supplementary image the link between the two other panels of this syntagm would have been much less happy" (175).

In a prime example touted by Peeters in favor of his theory, the very independent reader model misfires.

Not only do the very independent reader models of McCloud and Peeters lead to unsatisfactory readings, but also in their logical extremes they suggest readings formed with minimal coherence to the text. The strong emphasis on the absence in these theories leads to readings based more in fantasy than the text (by text I mean here the sum of the markings that comprise a comic, including but not limited to written language). Instead, Groensteen argues for the strength of the text:

> Maybe, you will say to me, but the term "gutter" (*blanc*) lends itself metaphorically. We use it to designate "that-which-is-not-represented-but-which-the-reader-cannot-help-but-to-infer." It is therefore a virtual, and take note that this virtual is not abandoned to the fantasy of each reader: *it is a forced virtual*, an identifiable absence. The gutter is simply the symbolic site of this absence. (112; emphasis added)

Groensteen's premise here—that the inference that activates comics is a forced inference—invaluably opens comics to new voices and new readings. The gutter is not an abdication of narrative authority, but instead the application of a different narrative tool.

This approach to comics—a top-down analysis looking for articulations within the system—guides Groensteen's theory of word balloons. "Although it is unusual to consider them this way," he apologizes, "the word balloon participates in the constitutive spaces of the comic—as do the frames enclosing a narrative text" (67). Because balloons are not nearly as dependent on frames and panels for placement and structure, they are privileged in Groensteen's *System* similarly to panels. Balloons, like panels, can act on the level of restricted arthrology (67). Consequently, these, too, construct alternate readings and forced inferences.

One of the immediate consequences of arthrology is that meaning is constructed outside of or in between the linear passage of story. If this is the case, then reading for arthrological tools will locate related panels and passages at great distance in the story. This is precisely what is found in *Vimanarama*, in the case of a sort of "bookend" pairing that surrounds the linear story.

In the first part of the pair, Ali requests of a deep and shining vortex, "I think I'm going to need some help to save the world" (Morrison and Bond, *Vimanarama*, 1). This page occurs just before the two-page title spread, starring Ben Rama and Sofia, thereby preceding the introduction and two of the most vital characters. Much later in the story, after Ali has died and the romance

designs of American illustrator Jack Kirby. *Vimanarama*'s hero from the Hindus is a mirror image—albeit a chromatic reverse—of Jack Kirby's character Orion, one of the New Gods. Similarly, the craggy coal-like faces, rectangular mouths, and modernist armor of Ull-Shattan and Ull-Blizz allude to Darkseid, Jack Kirby's ashen-colored villain. Third, this strong American influence on the linework plays a counterpoint to, and strengthens, the airy pre-Semitic script that surrounds the Ultrahadeen. The bold lines of *Vimanarama* outline and emphasize the curling writing that emblazons entrances to other dimensions, the land of the dead, and a tunnel under Bradford. These bold lines simultaneously emphasize the Eastern and the Western influences on the iconic art.

These linework effects combine to demonstrate the heterogeneity of the Other. In either the English working-class world of Bradford or the Vedic Indian revisionism of the Ultrahadeen, Ali is too X for Y. His track jacket and Proton rapper poster (Morrison and Bond, *Vimanarama*, 93) exclude him from Ben Rama's peaceful, prayer-filled utopia, and his existential doubt excludes him from his brother's pragmatic life as the manager of Kandivali Gulley. Ali is unquestionably an unrepresented actor in either of the hierarchies in which he participates.

Next, while Ali clearly possesses the ability to speak, it's often comically sublimated by the Ultrahadeen and their devices. After a prayer-bomb from Prince Ben Rama destroys the devils ravaging London, Ali tries to share with Sofia his feelings toward her:

> Because it just started and . . . we never got to know one another and . . . well, I just wanted to say something before . . . so sure God hated me but then I saw you in the torch light and you were the most beautiful . . . I just wanted to be with you and no one else for the rest of my life. (63)

Here we see his speech as fragmented and diminished because of the CLANNG-GNNGN RUMMMBLE of an Ultrahadeen Taj Mahal on mechanical spider legs. After all the cacophony, Sofia understandably responds, "Sorry? What?" (63) (Figure 10.3). This instance is typical of Ali's experience for the entire book. In one of the few moments his father consults him—"What [am I going to do] about my back shop?"—the shining Prince Ben Rama appears in the sky and interrupts, "Fear not. All will be made well" (50). As Ali explains the situation, "This world of angels and devils and spaceships. I've been left out of the whole *thing*. Every time I open my mouth a flying *man* turns up" (64; emphasis added). The devils of Ull-Shattan articulate the indifference of the superbeings to listening to the complaints of humans. While decapitating a room of British politicians, Ull-Shattan mocks, "Let uszz debate with these maggutzz"

10.3. *From Grant Morrison and Philip Bond's* Vimanarama

(43). Throughout *Vimanarama*, the godlike beings from six thousand years past thwart Ali's attempts to speak.

While Ali is linguistically muted, he is also ignored in the other half of the classical dichotomy of comics representation, pictorial image. Iconically, the narrative ignores Ali during his most poignant and important decision. While Ali hangs himself, frames of the devil Ull-Shattan and Prince Ben Rama are featured instead (67–68). Rather, his suicide is only captured long after the fact with the image of a pair of feet suspended over a bed (70). His single most important action is fragmented, interrupted, and nearly excluded. Ali's marginalized station means his perspective is ignored in both the linguistic and iconic halves of the classical comics composition.

Instead of visual or linguistic self-representation, Ali is given rare moments of free indirect discourse. The standby definition comes from H. Porter Abbott, who describes the "free indirect style [as] narrative representation of a character's thoughts and expressions without . . . some of the grammatical markers" (Abbott, *Cambridge Introduction to Narrative*, 191). In comics, narrative representation arrives through several media. It follows that these moments of free indirect discourse come in three varieties in *Vimanarama:* verbal, scenic, and arthrological.

In verbal free indirect discourse, Ali receives punishment that is wholly incongruous with the remainder of the plot. On the first page of Act Two, a bright vimana piloted by the devils lights the Parliament building aflame. A pair of Harrier jets rocket toward it and an armored group of the British army approaches the half-demolished Big Ben, and yet a tank commander leans around the hatch to point at the chaos and shout, *"Now look what you've done, Ali!"* (Morrison and Bond, *Vimanarama*, 39; emphasis added). Strangely enough, in the rest of the narrative, Ali's nephew Imran is responsible for releasing the devils. As Ali's father remarks, "How can anyone say *Imran* was responsible for releasing this army of flying devils? Look at his big brown eyes" (47; emphasis added). Given the incongruity with the remainder of the story, the paternalistic scolding of the tank commander is a moment of free indirect discourse, courtesy of Ali—who spends this period of the story half-curled in a corner, half-hidden in the high collar of his Adidas track jacket (47).

Toward the beginning of Act One, at a point when Ali still considers himself the hero of the family story, he announces, "Ali to the rescue" in a two-page splash full of Bollywood allusions. This moment develops in the background as scenic free indirect discourse. As Ali utters this sentence, the scene pictured on the bottom of the previous page—a quintet of schoolgirls playing sports in the street and a pair of officers examining a cell phone (5)—is transformed into a choreographed spectacle. The schoolgirls now dance in sync, and the pair of officers perform a romantic proposal in effigy, using the phone as a precious offering and a pair of handcuffs as a coyly offered fetish. Residents along the street lean out of second-story windows to witness the spectacle, smiling despite the rain. Clearly, Ali's self-affirmation of superheroic posturing transformed this scene from a rainy day in England to an overblown extravaganza.

A simple example of free indirect discourse through arthrology borrows Ali's point of view as the panel frame. While Ali peers into the hole in the back of the shop caused by the floor collapse, the frame bends around the arc of his flashlight (14). This frame-image interaction braids the next two pages, as the arthrology at the top of each page continues to mimic Ali's perspective with the flashlight (15–16). Of all of these instances of free indirect discourse, the final analysis of arthrology holds the most promise.

Arthrology emboldens and manifests Ali's plot, unrepresented by and large in the classical tools. In separate passages of *Vimanarama*, arthrological idioms can augment messages related in the image and text or they can signal meaning entirely independently of the text. In *Vimanarama*, the latter appears before the former. Ali signals his intent to kill himself without either of the classical tools, and later when this message is directly stated, restricted arthrology underscores the meaning.

A strip at the beginning of Act One—domain of restricted arthrology—is askew, with a discussion of suicide and responsibility. Ali's sister, Fatima, leaves for the airport to pick up "the lovely Sofia" and trusts her son Imran to his grandfather, Ali and Fatima's father. She asks, "You'll look after Imran, won't you, Dad? It won't be like our *goldfish?*" to which her father responds, "The fish had suicidal tendencies *long* before I got there, Fatima" (10). Predictably, marginalized Ali says exactly one word during this exchange—"Urrr . . ."—but something more is happening on the level of restricted arthrology. Unlike every other strip on the rest of the page and the reverse page, the strip featuring this exchange is not rectangle-justified. Instead, two panels of discussion between Fatima and her father slope downwards from left to right; the third and final panel in the strip is rectangular and justified to the corner of the page (10).

The downward slope ends with a single panel of Ali humming in a hospital lobby and playing with a rope; this image is isolated horizontally by a massive gutter and vertically by a crooked pair of frames (10). The compound effect of white space and guiding lines is to draw the reader's line of vision directly to this image of Ali in the hospital lobby. From this point, it's obvious to follow the advice of Groensteen:

> When one encounters a layout deemed ostentatious, it is necessarily opportune to interrogate it, in a second level of analysis, about the motivations that the cartoonist has obeyed in the elaboration of the page. In order to proceed in this evaluation, one must necessarily compare the layout of the page to its iconic and narrative contents. (Groensteen, *System*, 99)

Fatima describes Sofia as "lovely" and her father disavows suicidal tendencies, and both of these signal something diachronistically. Ali will reveal in two pages that "*If* [Sofia]*'s ugly I'm hanging myself!*" (Morrison and Bond, *Vimanarama*, 12; emphasis added). Until that moment, however, Ali's ultimatum is his personal secret, meaning that the syntagm of the downward-sloping discussion is unheralded (Figure 10.4). Instead of serving linear narrative, this sequence represents something significantly different. The arthrology here favors Ali's internal response to the discussion of suicide to the extent that it's free indirect discourse from Ali's vantage.

Indeed, while Ali has only an "Urrr . . ." and a tune during this passage, he is differently empowered to report through restricted arthrology. The arthrological report he provides dramatically shifts the meaning of the linear sequence from a mundane discussion of "who's on first" to a chilling omen of Ali's suicide.

Ali's ultimatum further dictates arthrology when he reveals the noose and announces his intent to Omar. After this, Omar collapses and Ali rides his bicycle home in the strictly linear narrative. Arthrologically, frames whirl and scatter around the noose. The noose extends an inch into the gutter and grows a massive white space around itself. Inside this mammoth gutter is Ali's noose, the failure of his arranged marriage, his journey to the land of the dead, and his reincarnation. These two scenes related to the ultimatum provide enough evidence of collaboration between margin and arthrology to strengthen the case for the marginalized voice.

All of the readings as of yet have demonstrated the power of restricted arthrology. General arthrology, too, is an autonomous system. Furthermore, the next two readings of general arthrology demonstrate the collaborative possibilities

10.4. *From Grant Morrison and Philip Bond's* Vimanarama

between arthrology and classical tools to establish and embellish meaning. First in this set of passages is Ali's voyage to the land of the dead. There, his face and neck are diffracted into eight different panels that do not mimic reality or even represent the same face. The eight panels of Ali float at different angles to one another and show different attributes of him in different palettes: Ali as a teenager, a child, a baby, a skeleton, and all in different levels of saturation and coloring. Apropos of the surreality of the scene, Ali asks his self, "How did *you* get here? I mean . . . how . . . did I?" (73).

This passage calls to memory a quotation from Thierry Groensteen:

> The comics image, whose meaning often remains open when it is presented as isolated (and without verbal anchorage), finds its truth in the sequence. Inversely, the gutter, insignificant in itself, is invested with an arthrologic function that can only be deciphered in the light of the singular images that it separates and unites. (Groensteen, *System*, 114)

This is the guiding insight of a margin-centered reading of arthrology. Comics utterances which are fragmentary, interrupted, and muted find meaning in sequence. The process of developing this sequence, in turn, invests the interstitial spaces with meaning. In the case of Ali's visit to the land of the dead, this sequence of interpanels is an example of braiding. The passage in question appeared on the first page of Act Three, and on the final page of Act Two, Ali stands in the same space—a grassy field in front of a glowing rotunda and minaret, filled with a floating flock of mirrors and bubble-images of embryos— and submits the request, "I think I'm going to need some help to save the world" (Morrison and Bond, *Vimanarama*, 71). Read as a sequence, these two pages answer their own requests. How did Ali arrive in the land of the dead? By searching for help to save the world. Who will help Ali save the world? Ali, Ali, and Ali.

This reading, which takes the braiding as a cue to sequence and collaborative meaning, is supported by the twist at the end of *Vimanarama*. Ultimately, Ali is revived as a reincarnation of Prince Ben Rama, who died slaying Ull-Shattan and the devils with the Horn of Jabreel. Ali becomes the help that he needed to save the world, which is foreshadowed with a braided reading of his two scenes of fragmentation in the land of the dead. Clearly, then, an arthrological reading of *Vimanarama* is more than a critical novelty. Arthrology works here to establish a new meaning, missing from text and image. The next image demonstrates the ability of arthrology to embellish meaning.

Surrounding Ali's voyage to the land of the dead is a braided pair of pages that reference love and reincarnation. The motive force that pushes Ali toward suicide is Ben Rama. On the page in which Ali abandons his hopes of winning Sofia over Ben Rama, he tells her, "Go to him." The four panels of Ali's resignation form, inside the gutter, the image of the swastika. *Vimanarama* repeats this pattern just before Ali is reincarnated, but rotating in the opposite direction. In the Hindu tradition, the former appearance represents the evolution of the universe and the latter represents the involution of the universe. The relevance of this imagery to Ali's death and resurrection as the new Ben Rama is obvious. Ali's suicide was an evolution, opening another space in the story. The land of the dead is quite literally a new ground in which Ali, Omar, and their father can collaborate despite geographical separation. Ali's assumption of Ben Rama's life is the in-folding, synthetic resolution to the love triangle. The two diverging story arcs are unified with this reincarnation. These two scenes form the antithesis and thesis of *Vimanarama*, but the link is signaled only in the gutter.

This pairing represents a critical piece of evidence in favor of Groensteen's arguments. What is immediately visible between these two scenes is that braiding on the level of general arthrology signals symmetry in the story. This confirms what appears in *The System of Comics*:

> By its nature, a story develops in length in a linear and irreversible manner. . . . With respect to comics, this disposition finds itself constantly embattled, and in certain measure neutralized, by the properties that we have seen in the panels. The network . . . also exists in a dechronologized mode, that of the collection, of the panoptical spread and of coexistence, considering the possibility of the translinear relations and plurivectoral courses. (147)

Within the pages of *Vimanarama*, action is definitively reversed with the network described here. Arthrology in this example works in collaboration with the linear element of story.

What's more is that this arthrological element expounds the experience of the marginal. Arthrological tools allow for Ali's last words, "Go to him" (Morrison and Bond, *Vimanarama*, 65), to resonate and so provide an iconic counterpoint to his transformation. If the passage of Ali's revival were limited to classical tools, it would instead represent Ben Rama's final glowing sacrifice. Instead, thanks to the tools provided by Groensteen, *Vimanarama* ends much more strangely, and in such a way that the marginalized voice surfaces.

I set out to demonstrate within the pages of *Vimanarama* that the margins could find another space to speak. To do this, I first differentiated what comics have been found to do, classically, from what they can do. Groensteen's investigation into comics' unique processes and techniques showed a separate set of storytelling mechanisms. What I call the "bookends" of the story clearly demonstrate the viability of his linear story–busting tools. The marginal people's mobility allowed for those disenfranchised in one paradigm to be empowered in another. While the machinations of the Ultrahadeen crowded Ali's voice off the page, there were other ways for Ali to tell his story. Ali snuck his story in as best he could through free indirect discourse in image and text, but arthrology shows more promise. The simple flashlight frames licensed extended readings into scenes surrounding Ali's suicide, and these in turn revealed much more story outside of the frames than inside. Then arthrology proves its ability to supplant dialogue by assuming the form of word balloons. Because the strength of arthrological systems has been demonstrated, it becomes clear that Ali's braided passage in the land of the dead embellishes the image and text, correlating information that is unlinked by classical tools. Finally, I show that the swastika arthrology adds significance in such a way that the story of the marginalized, rather than the elite, passes through the pages of *Vimanarama*.

This finding carries great significance for multicultural comics. The silence, the heterogeneous Other, the marginal are represented in readings that reach beyond classical tools for arthrological insight. The fragmented, invisible art makes visible the invisible citizens of the world.

11 WONDROUS CAPERS
The Graphic Novel in India

SUHAAN MEHTA

THE GRAPHIC NOVEL is a relatively recent phenomenon in India, and the existing body of work has little in common with the flourishing mainstream comics industry. The most widely read Indian comics series is Amar Chitra Katha (ACK), with around four hundred titles in over twenty languages. The philosophy of ACK is that comics must tell what is pleasant and avoid what is unpleasant (Pritchett, "The World of Amar Chitra Katha," 80). ACK steers clear of polemic, ironing out creases in the fabric of national integration and presenting a highly selective view of India to a young audience. This approach finds little sympathy with India's leading graphic novelist, Sarnath Banerjee. In an interview with Samit Basu, Banerjee commented: "There should be a five-year ban on anything on Hanuman,[1] for the sake of Hanuman. And while you are at it, *The Mahabharata* and *Jataka Tales*, only for five years. Let us explore some other stories. I feel these tales have done what cricket has done to hockey and what Bollywood has done to other cultural forms that could have come out of India" (par. 27). The work of Banerjee and his contemporaries signals a decisive break from ACK's airbrushed view of India's past and present. More broadly speaking, the Indian graphic novelist has created an alternative space by accommodating voices that habitually fall outside the realm of Indian socio-politico-cultural discourses. In the pages that follow, I will argue that the Indian graphic novel problematizes monolithic notions of home, identity, and history of marginalized peoples[2] by presenting the reader with a range of interpretive choices.

The countermainstream dimension of the graphic novel sets it apart from comic books. Charles Hatfield clarifies the distinction between the two in the American context. Hatfield writes that the graphic novel is an offspring of the comic book industry and owes its life to the direct market's specialized conditions in the 1980s. He notes, "It was the comic book shop that gave the genre its economic spark" (*Alternative Comics*, 30). The comic book shop provided a hub for readers to buy and creators to sell alternative comic books. This spurt in innovative work led to greater commercial and critical attention for an emerging literature. "Alternative comic books and graphic novels are at the core of this development" (ibid.) and form the centerpiece of Hatfield's study. Sarnath Banerjee's company Phantomville, which exclusively publishes graphic novels, occupies a similar position to American independent publishers and their comic books. Banerjee commented to Samit Basu, "Mainstream publication houses work under many restrictions, one of which is the profit motive. . . . Our aim is to train [visual storytellers] and publish their books. In a royalty-oriented publishing house this is almost impossible to achieve" (par. 18).

Banerjee's *Corridor* and *The Barn Owl's Wondrous Capers*, Orijit Sen's *The River of Stories*, Naseer Ahmed and Saurabh Singh's *Kashmir Pending*, and Amruta Patil's *Kari* all attempt to chart new territory. To analyze the complex interactions between text and reader in each of these works, I shall turn to the critical frameworks provided by Hatfield in *Alternative Comics* and, more briefly, by Eugene Kannenberg in "Form, Function, Fiction: Text and Image in the Comics Narratives of Winsor McCay, Art Spiegelman, and Chris Ware."

Charles Hatfield's attention to reader response is particularly valuable to my analysis. Hatfield's premise is that the fractured surface of the comic page, with its varied images, shapes, and symbols, offers plural interpretive options, creating an experience that is "radically fragmented and unstable." This discontinuity urges the reader to be actively involved in the inferential process: "Various ways of reading—various interpretive options and potentialities—must be played against each other" (Hatfield, *Alternative Comics*, 36). These interpretive options revolve around four kinds of tensions, those between:

1. Image and word: One glosses, illustrates, complicates, or ironizes the other;
2. Image and image series: The author evokes an imagined sequence by creating visual series on the one hand, and the reader sutures the given series into a narrative sequence on the other;
3. Sequence and surface: an image can function both as a moment in an imagined sequence of events and as an atemporal element within a static design;

4. Content and the material dimensions of a text: comics in the long form can exploit material qualities (design and technique) to communicate or reinforce meaning(s) available in the text. (see ibid., 36–67)

The interaction between the verbal and visual that Hatfield analyzes is developed further by Eugene Kannenberg. He argues that the appearance of the text in comics conveys a wealth of information about a narrative. He identifies three key relationships between the graphic qualities of comics lettering and their consequences:

1. Narrative qualities: How the text influences the order in which discrete images combine into an aggregate narrative whole and the order in which text should be read;
2. Metanarrative qualities: How the text can convey information such as sound/tone of voice, characterization, pacing, and thematic resonance;
3. Extranarrative qualities: How the text can draw attention to its status as a particular type of work or as an example of an effort by a specific cartoonist. (see Kannenberg, "Form, Function, Fiction," 25)

These multiple parameters create a rich critical framework that can be profitably used to analyze the works mentioned above.

Struggle for an Independent Homeland

Orijit Sen's *The River of Stories* and Naseer Ahmed and Saurabh Singh's *Kashmir Pending* foreground the struggle of peoples for an independent homeland against repressive state apparatuses.[3] *The River of Stories* is a thinly veiled critique of the Narmada Valley Development Project,[4] which has resulted in displacement of *adivasis* (indigenous people).[5] Vishnu, a young reporter, stumbles into the Rewa Andolan (Save the River Rewa Movement, or the Rewa Movement) while preparing a story on migrant workers. He learns that workers who scrounge for low-wage jobs in cities are *adivasis* who have been evicted from forest reserves. The Rewa Andolan's objective is to protect the *adivasi* way of life threatened by the government's decision to build a dam on the river Rewa. *Kashmir Pending*, on the other hand, is a young man's chronicle of the Kashmiri independence movement. The book throws into relief the disillusionment of certain Kashmiri youth, the highly politicized environment of Kashmir, the bitter factionalism among warring groups, and the endless cycle of violence that plagues the valley.

11.1. *Invoking legend to preserve a way of life: from Orijit Sen's* The River of Stories

THE RIVER OF STORIES

In Sen's work, a center-spread "Rewa: A map of stories" shows how home for *adivasis* is associated with rich legends of nature. At the top of the spread, there are panels of people protesting against the construction of the Rewa dam, and at the bottom, there are close-ups of the legendary singer of *adivasis*, Malgu gayan. These are laid out against a background of the river Rewa and its adjoining forests, hills, and villages.

The map is an instance of the undivided polyptych that invites both synchronistic and serial readings. The atemporal dimension of this page is embodied in Malgu gayan's song of the river. For centuries, as this legend goes, the river Rewa has been a life-giving force. There are also stories associated with each temple, forest, and village along the Rewa. For example, Andaruo is a "Shrine of the sacred turtle of the spring where the Malgu sang the song of Kujum Chantu" (47). Manigam is a site "where the people of the Rewa valley pledged never to desert their lands and waters" (49). The dynamic aspect of this spread, on the other hand, is suggested by the forward movement of the river and images of collective solidarity—the near-circular arrangement of panels on this page bears this out strongly. The protestors identify with the river Rewa's trajectory as they chant in unison: "What started as a trickle / has become a stream / What was a single stream / has been joined by a myriad / streams! What was once / a rushing current has become / a broad river! And I dreamt / what is today a river / will tomorrow join / the vast sea!" (49). Sen shows the close relationship of the synchronic and the serial by the arrangement of text on the page. He cues readers to begin with the legend of Rewa, by using a large balloon for his opening lines, and then move to the top of the page, where various people are animatedly discussing the significance of the movement. The close link between a timeless legend and an ongoing conflict suggests that the Rewa Andolan is a struggle for preserving a way of life.

KASHMIR PENDING

Naseer Ahmed and Saurabh Singh's *Kashmir Pending* also deals with people fighting for an independent homeland. The secessionist movement in Kashmir has led to deep resentment against successive Indian governments, creating fertile ground for indoctrination of impressionable youth in the "armed struggle" for Kashmir's "liberation."[6] *Kashmir Pending* is the story of one such individual, Mushtaq, who turned to violence for securing freedom for his people.

The relationship between experiential and material dimensions of a graphic novel is key to understanding how group identity is constructed in *Kashmir Pending*. Hatfield writes that the "ligne claire," or clear-line tradition, popularized by Hergé privileges smooth, continuous linework, simplified contours, and bright, solid colors, while avoiding frayed lines, exploded forms, or expressionistic rendering. Hatfield's notion of the "ideal union of style and subject" (*Alternative Comics*, 60) has been spoofed in the work of Joost Swarte, Daniel Torres, and others for masking the difference between character and setting and per-

11.2. *Mourning a son, a friend, a martyr: from Naseer Ahmed and Saurabh Singh's* Kashmir Pending

petuating racist stereotypes. These cartoonists have drawn on the inherently "ironizing tension between Hergé's 'ligne claire' and a roughhewn graphic technique." The tension often expresses "a violent and absurdist worldview that represents a subversion of the cultural and ideological reassurances proffered by the Clear Line" (ibid., 61). Moving on to *Kashmir Pending*, there are two transformational moments in the protagonist Mushtaq's life—the deaths of an innocent bystander, Jabbar, and Mushtaq's friend, Aziz. Jabbar's death in the crossfire between Indian troops and militants merits close stylistic reading.

Though Saurabh Singh's artwork does not share Swarte and Torres's radical edge, his departure from the "ligne claire" has considerable bearing on our interpretation of the episode in question and *Kashmir Pending* as a whole. Singh represents the collective outpouring of grief and anger at Jabbar's death by depicting mourners in dark green with anguished faces and downcast eyes. This is in contrast to the Indian troops who appear in low-angle shots and strike confrontational poses with frontal gazes. Facial expressions of the Kashmiri people vary from anger to resignation. These emotions are accentuated by extreme close-ups, pronounced lines on foreheads, dark, narrowed eyes, and partially concealed faces. A large number of frames depict mobs of angry demonstrators with upright arms, tense muscles, and open mouths, often bathed entirely in shades of red, orange, and yellow. The use of color bears out the prevailing mood: "It seemed as if all of Srinagar had turned up to witness this moment of grief. Eyes brimmed with tears and anger" (Ahmed and Singh, *Kashmir Pending*, 37). The artwork in *Kashmir Pending* has definite aesthetic and ideological purposes. It gets the reader to reflect on both subjective and objective realities of characters. And by privileging the perspective of the Kashmiri people, it alerts its audience to a significant blind spot in dominant discourses of Indian nationalism.

The Sexual Minority: *Kari*

Whereas *The River of Stories* and *Kashmir Pending* sensitize the reader to struggles for home, Amruta Patil's *Kari* focuses on how a member of a sexual minority[7] copes with her isolation in an urban landscape. In a gloss on her protagonist, Patil writes, "I am beginning to enjoy the feeling of being on sound mute. No one understands what I am saying. I understand no one . . . Liberating! And necessarily solitary! Kari's experience is the same, but a little worse. Her visual language is impermeable and too foreign for most" ("Lost," par. 1).

Kari's contradictory accounts of events in her life destabilize a one-to-one correspondence between text and image in the novel. The existence of her former lesbian partner, Ruth, is suspect. Besides Kari, the only other person who

Bearded Man grunts, and we know that grunts are at a premium.

'Great TV possibility,' he says. Then he gives us an immense hug each. 'I have great regard for you two bloody jokers.' Laz and I are both blushers and we duly blush. We have cracked Fairytale Hair.

It needs to be mentioned that when I looked for the road to Alexa and Manuel's house the next morning, it was not there. I have seen it since, once or twice, but I can never be entirely sure when I will find it next.

11.3. *Elevating Kari's lover to a work of art: from Amruta Patil's* Kari

There are more cats in Alexa's backyard.
They are all very dusty, the whites turned sooty, the gingers turned grey. None
as beautiful as Bostiao in the tree, but beautiful nonetheless. Because of
Bostiao, I get to meet Alexa and her husband, Manuel, who is blind and plays
the violin like a particularly haunting dream. I have scrambled eggs in their
balcony and talk about Goa, where Alexa and Manuel's ancestors lie buried.

Needless to say, I am very late getting into work. But there is a happy buzz
in my heart that will surely turn into a small blue thing in Ruth's palm.
Bead, maybe. Or bauble or marble or egg.

11.4. *Cracking advertising campaigns and looking for missing roads: from Amruta Patil's* Kari

has spoken to Ruth is her mother, when she asks, "Why does this Ruth call so often?" (Patil, *Kari*, 029). All the other evidence suggests that Ruth is a figment of Kari's imagination. Ruth visits Kari's apartment only when her roommates are away. Kari likens her lover to a fairy-tale character: "The house fit her perfectly, like a crystal slipper" (026). And the most discordant note is struck when Kari says of her doting housemaid Kusum Tai, "She'd believe in *a* Ruth more than any of the others" (095; emphasis added). The blurring of lines between fact and fiction is also seen in the contingency of physical spaces and Kari's farfetched claim that she bought a boat to unclog the choked sewers of Mumbai. However, in each case, the accompanying visuals seem to confirm Kari's dubious claims.

The resulting dissonance between the verbal and visual components of the text suggests that Kari's subjective world is a utopian space in an alienating environment. Ruth is drawn almost always in full-page colored portraits. The accompanying text is often a highly lyrical description of the most intimate moments between Kari and Ruth—"No one else could call a colt a flower" (026) or "there is a happy buzz in my heart that will surely turn into a small blue thing in Ruth's palm" (045).

These moments are the closest the reader comes to ekphrastic poetry; they elevate Ruth to art. On the other hand, though the heterosexual couples in *Kari* are flesh-and-blood characters, they are one-dimensional figures that spout clichés. Similarly, Alexa and Manuel's house, which mysteriously disappears the next day, is an oasis in an industrial wasteland. The fact that the image of Alexa and Manuel's house may not have a real-world equivalent is secondary; given its fragility we'd rather that it exist solely in Kari's mind. Similarly, Kari's role as a boatman has to be read metaphorically for her compassionate nature. The visual spread of Kari as a boatman may only be Kari "trawling the drains dream after dream" (041), but this nebulous identity helps her make meaningful connections with people otherwise left to die. Amruta Patil privileges a dissonant verbal-visual equation over a stable one-on-one correspondence so that her protagonist can find respite amidst the sewers, pubs, and land sharks of Mumbai.

History from the Margins: *The Barn Owl's Wondrous Capers*

If *Kari* is an account of Mumbai's underbelly, Sarnath Banerjee's *The Barn Owl's Wondrous Capers*, henceforth called *The Barn Owl*, interweaves legend and history within the urban spaces of London, Paris, and Kolkata (formerly Calcutta). Banerjee's work is remarkable for its exploration of Kolkata's myriad spaces, its commentary on the idiosyncrasies of the Bengali community, and its metadis-

THAT'S HOW I KNOW THE CUP SIZE OF MADAME GRAND'S CORSET, AND THE BLEACH USED BY THE PRESENT LADY HASTINGS FOR HER FACIAL HAIR.

HOW COLONEL WATSON SPRAYS ISHPAHANI ROSEWATER ON HIS PELVIC AREA

AND SIR PHILIP FRANCIS USES SPANISH FLY AS A PRECAUTION, TO AVOID ANY MISADVENTURES THAT MIGHT OCCUR DUE TO OVER-EXHAUSTION FROM HIS HECTIC NOCTURNAL AND SOMETIMES DIURNAL ACTIVITIES.

ALL DAY I TRADE, BUT AT NIGHT I DUTIFULLY RECORD THE SCANDALS OF THE CITY. A HABIT THAT IS PERVERSE, YET REWARDING.

11.5. *Recording the scandals of a city: from Sarnath Banerjee's* The Barn Owl's Wondrous Capers

course on storytelling. He employs several sophisticated narrative techniques in keeping with the book's rich content. The focus of this essay limits my commentary to one of the many dimensions of *The Barn Owl*.

In the novel's preface, Banerjee signals the indebtedness of his work to the myth of the Wandering Jew. The subsequent pages tell the tale of another wanderer—an unnamed narrator resembling the writer—who is looking for his late grandfather's book in present-day Kolkata. The two tales intersect in the character of Digital Dutta. Dutta is caught in the cycle of perpetual return for stealing a book—the very book that the unnamed narrator is looking for.

While Abravanel's Jewishness does not make him a marginalized figure, given that India has had no history of anti-Semitism, he does offer a unique nonmainstream view of colonial India. The book announces its departure from historical facts in the epigraph: "[It] is inspired by history / but not limited by it" (Banerjee, *Barn Owl*, iv). Scandal, rumors, and gossip form the blueprint of Abravanel's historiography. This irreverent take on history is also seen in the book's artwork; the illustrations depict all the officers of the East India Company in an unflattering light: Big noses, glazed eyes, and oval heads. The rough edges of the colonial rulers are magnified through the foibles of their hirelings.

The rendition of history in *The Barn Owl* can be understood through the significant tension between narrative breakdown and closure. According to Hatfield, "'breakdown' and 'closure' are complementary terms, both describing the relationship between sequence and series: the author's task is to evoke an imagined sequence by creating a visual series (a breakdown), whereas the reader's task is to translate the given series into narrative sequence by achieving closure" (*Alternative Comics*, 41). This interplay between breakdown and closure is seen at work in Banerjee's treatment of India's colonial history. Abravanel calls attention to what is ostensibly the "biggest spectacle of mid 18th-century Kolkata" (Banerjee, *Barn Owl*, 4), but really a little-known duel between two officers of the East India Company, Warren Hastings and Philip Francis.[8] The basic challenge for the reader is that the context of this event is not adequately defined. The prelude to this book begins with the Crucifixion and leaps spasmodically to 1228, 1601, 1740, 1743, 1864, and 1914. The reader learns only at the very end that these dates mark different avatars of the Wandering Jew. At the beginning, though, there is a significant gap between these temporal frames and eighteenth-century Calcutta. The narrative leading up to the battle between Hastings and Francis is significantly clearer, but it is frequently interspersed with various digressions and completed at the close of the book.

These narrative ellipses are designed to exploit playfully the fragmented nature of most historical discourse. If Abravanel is to be believed, Hastings and Francis's mutual dislike does not stem from their differences over administrative matters, but a mole on a lady's bosom: "Discerning Readers, please cast a second glance at Madame Grand's left bosom, not in its entirety, only at the delicate mole that is to be a source of future conflict, resulting in the ill-fated morning under the murderous twins" (ibid., 6). This candid approach to sex is characteristic of the bawdy humor used to undermine the authority figures who populate the text. Francis's attraction for Madame G's mole and Hastings's purported jealousy are not entirely a figment of Banerjee's imagination, though. Scholarship reveals that stories of Madame Grande's connection with Hastings and Francis were making the rounds. In *Echoes from Old Calcutta*, H. E. Busteed writes of the Francis-Hastings duel, "Some believers in 'cherchez la femme' (searching for the lady) doctrine have pressed this combat into service as one more proof of its universal application" (109). He references Charles de Rémusat, who notes: "Ce récit prouve que *contrairement à des suppositions souvent répetées* la beauté de Madame Grand fut complètement étrangere aux démêlés de Hastings et de Francis" (This account proves that *contrary to often repeated assumptions* Madame Grande's charms had nothing to do with the wrangling between Hastings and Francis and she wasn't the provocation for their duel) (quoted in ibid., 109). Rumor, however, is fodder for Abravanel; so Hastings's misgivings toward Francis are attributed to the latter's promiscuity and not their difference over important policy matters. In Banerjee's words, "The history itself is manufactured, but the rigor, the process of gathering information, is where the history comes in. . . . I want to bring in the truth, but not give it the status that it receives elsewhere" (quoted in Mehar, "Of True and False Histories," par. 4).

Abravanel's dutiful recording of scandals makes him both a storyteller and an ethnographer. He presents a tableau of the most intimate details from the dark armpits of history: Madame G's corset, the cup size of which is known to Abravanel; Ishapahani rose water that a Colonel Watson sprayed on his pelvic area; and Sir Philip Francis's Spanish fly, which he used to avoid misadventures during debauchery (Banerjee, *Barn Owl*, 22). Before his duel with Hastings, Francis's past appears before him in the form of various images. A print ad for Egyptian cigarettes is juxtaposed with a painting of a group of Britishers looking upon a "darker" Indian woman clad in a sari. These moments have a narrative function, but more importantly they afford a quirky snapshot of India's colonial past.

THE IDEA OF READING GRAPHIC NOVELS as an intellectual activity is even more alien in India than in North America and Europe. Like their Western counterparts, the pioneers of the Indian graphic novel face challenges in getting recognition and visibility. However, the late debut of the graphic novel in India has also worked to its advantage in some ways. One of the cultural side effects of globalization has been that English is being embraced even more readily, and India now sees itself less in opposition to the West than it did in the past. Consequently, creative minds can think beyond the "post" of postcolonialism and not be pigeonholed into resisting different "isms." In this essay, I have attempted to show that the Indian graphic novelist has tremendous latitude, which is only beginning to be explored.

NOTES

1. Hanuman is an anthropomorphic deity depicted as an ardent devotee of Lord Rama in one of the two founding epics of the Hindu civilization, *The Ramayana*. He appears also in two ACK titles, *Hanuman* and *Hanuman to the Rescue*. Banerjee takes a dig at mainstream culture's obsession with regurgitating tales from Hindu mythology.

2. I use the term marginalized largely as shorthand in referring to aggrieved minorities in India, while being fully aware that both marginality and minority escape easy definition. Pilar and Udasco's recent study concluded that there is no agreement in social science literature about the meaning of the concept of marginality ("Marginal Theory," 11). Cullen and Pretes concurred in their assessment, saying that marginality continues to be elusive, and a clearer understanding of the term was necessary for the concept to be useful in the social sciences ("Meaning of Marginality," 215). One encounters similar problems with the idea of minority, particularly in the Indian context. The Indian constitution provides neither a definition nor a set of principles by which a particular group constitutes a minority (Sinha, "Minority Rights," 365). Sinha's paper addresses the issue of marginality on a case-by-case basis.

3. Louis Althusser's discussion of the ideological and repressive state apparatus is an apt framework for understanding how dissent has been silenced by the Indian law-and-order machinery. In "Ideology and Ideological State Apparatuses," Althusser writes, "The State is thus first of all what the Marxist classics have called the State apparatus. This term means: not only the specialized apparatus [like] the police, the courts, the prisons; but also the army, which intervenes directly as a supplementary repressive force in the last instance, when the police and its specialized auxiliary corps are 'outrun by events'; and above this ensemble, the head of State, the government and the administration" (1487).

4. The government of India planned to build 30 large, 135 medium-sized, and 3,000 small dams to harness the waters of the Narmada and its tributaries. The proponents of the project claimed that it would provide large amounts of water and electricity required for the purposes of development. Opponents of the dam questioned the basic assumptions of the Narmada Valley Development Plan and believed that its planning was unjust and inequitable and that the cost-benefit analysis was grossly inflated in favor of building the dams. The social activist Medha Patkar, who makes a brief appearance in Sen's book, founded the Narmada Bachao Andolan (Save the Narmada Movement) for the

rehabilitation of *adivasis* ousted by large dams along the Narmada River. On October 18, 2000, the Supreme Court of India allowed construction on the Sardar Sarovar Dam up to a height of 90 meters. The judgment also authorized construction up to the originally planned height of 138 meters in 5-meter increments, subject to approval by the Relief and Rehabilitation Subgroup of the Narmada Control Authority. The Narmada Bachao Andolan, however, continues to function as a watchdog to ensure that the government does not renege on its promise of rehabilitation to displaced peoples. For more, see Narmada.org.

5. The 67.7 million people belonging to "Scheduled Tribes" in India are generally considered to be *adivasis*. In most of the precolonial period, the *adivasis* were notionally part of the "unknown frontier" of the respective states and governed themselves outside of the influence of the local ruler. This changed with the idea of private property, introduced by the British in 1793, leading to the forced restructuring of the relationship of *adivasis* to their territories and other people. Through colonization of forests, which began formally with the Forest Act of 1864 and was codified completely in the Indian Forest Act of 1927, the rights of *adivasis* were reduced to mere privileges conferred by the state. See Bijoy, "The Adivasis of India."

6. Under the partition plan provided by the Indian Independence Act of 1947, the state of Kashmir was free to accede to India or Pakistan. The Maharaja of Kashmir decided to accede to India, signing over key powers to the Indian government— in return for military aid and a promised referendum. Successive Indian governments have not upheld the conditions on which Jammu and Kashmir were brought into the Union. The political pact originally ruled that only limited clauses of the Indian Constitution could apply to the state, a commitment observed in its breach. This has fueled the separatist movement in the state, which has often been harshly suppressed. International human rights groups have accused the Indian army of massive violation of civil liberties. Successive Pakistani governments in turn have stoked the flames of rebellion by abetting cross-border infiltration for their own vested interests. In a *New York Times* article, Salman Rushdie wrote, "Pity those ordinary, peaceable people, caught between the rock of India and the hard place that Pakistan has always been! . . . the present-day growth of terrorism in Kashmir has roots in India's treatment of Kashmiris, but it has equally deep roots in Pakistan's interest in subversion. Yes, Kashmiris feel strongly about the Indian 'occupation' of their land; but it is also almost certainly true that Pakistan's army and intelligence service have been training, aiding and abetting the men of violence" ("Kashmir, the Imperiled Paradise," par. 2 and 10). However, despite the resentment it must be noted that there is no collective will for self-determination in Jammu and Kashmir, which have a diverse population of Muslims, Kashmiri Pandits (Hindus), Buddhists, and Sikhs. For more, see Chandhoke, "Exploring the Right to Secession."

7. In India homosexuals face persecution and discrimination on a daily basis. Article 377 of the Indian Penal Code prohibits relations against the order of nature and allows the state to prosecute individuals caught in homosexual acts. In 1998, there was a flare-up against lesbianism in India following Deepa Mehta's lesbian-themed film *Fire*. The depiction of Hindu women indulging in lesbianism was labeled an obscene provoca-

tion, a denigration of womanhood, and an attack on Indian culture. However, in a landmark judgment in July 2009 the Delhi High Court nullified Article 377. This ruling has been welcomed by gay rights activists in the country, but has received stiff opposition from various groups belonging to the religious right. June 29, 2008, was an earlier watershed moment for the homosexual community in India, as the first gay pride parades were held in the cities of Kolkata, New Delhi, and Bangalore. An article in *The Hindustan Times*, "At Home with Homosexuality on City Campuses," on April 22, 2008, revealed that there are people who are trying to create an environment free of bias against any particular sexual minority.

8. According to Lord Macaulay, Warren Hastings, the then–governor general of Bengal, strongly opposed the unlimited authority of the English judiciary over the people of India decreed by the Regulating Act (1773). This would undermine his own position and let people far removed from India's complexities decide its fate. To avoid confrontation with the higher ups, Hastings bribed the chief justice, Eliah Impey, in return for Impey's assurance that he would scale back his judicial powers. Hastings's position was challenged by Sir Philip Francis, one of the four councillors appointed to assist the office of the governor general. In his book, H. E. Busteed gives a different version of events. Quoting Francis's biographer, Busteed says that Hastings was provoked by Francis's repeated interference in his war with the Maratha forces despite assurances to the contrary (*Echoes*, 109). Either way, Hastings felt he had to act, and in a minute at the Council Table declared, "I do not trust to Mr. Francis's promises of candor, convinced that he is incapable of it. I judge of his public conduct by his private, which I have found to be void of truth and honor" (quoted in Macaulay, *Warren Hastings*, 62). This provoked Francis into challenging Hastings to an armed duel, a challenge the latter readily accepted.

CHRONOLOGY, COUNTRY, AND CONSCIOUSNESS IN WILFRED SANTIAGO'S *IN MY DARKEST HOUR*

12

NICHOLAS HETRICK

IN MANY WAYS, Puerto Rican American Wilfred Santiago's *In My Darkest Hour* (2004) seems destined for this volume on multicultural comics. Having noted the author's name and dedication—"To you, Mami"—and read the epigraph from seventeenth-century Spanish playwright Pedro Calderón de la Barca, we find protagonist Omar Guerrero waking up to read a few pages of Gabriel García Márquez's *Chronicle of a Death Foretold* in Spanish before saying good-bye to his Cambodian girlfriend Lucinda. From the prefatory and paratextual material to the first five pages of the novel and beyond, *In My Darkest Hour* seems to invite a decidedly ethnic reading. Yet as this novel teaches us, seeming and being are rather slippery things. Instead of fronting ethnicity as a central thematic concern, Santiago's bold aesthetic experimentation emphasizes the relationship between form and content, specifically with respect to the representation of consciousness. Ultimately, this experimentation gives rise to the novel's chief concern: to call relations between real and unreal significantly into question.[1]

In My Darkest Hour is, essentially, the resolutionless chronicle of bipolar Omar's misery. In brief, the plot consists of a string of troubled relationships, episodes of depression and mania, and substance abuse and self-loathing—all brought to a close by news of the September 11, 2001, terrorist attacks at novel's end sending Omar into yet another downward spiral. More interesting (and less bleak) than the story itself, however, is the fact that Santiago provocatively casts 9/11 as an intensely and primarily *private* event in the storyworld. Indeed, the

few pages following this news consist almost entirely of Omar's private reflections on paranoia and isolation in its wake. In this "psychological turn" of sorts,
Santiago turns still-common rhetoric of collective shock and bereavement in
9/11's wake on its head, instead focusing on Omar's subjective, interior response
to the news.

This inversion of content—which foregrounds the impact on an *individual*
of an iconic, emphatically *social* event, rather than focusing on its effect on a
community or nation—is mirrored by an equally striking formal innovation
in consciousness representation. Throughout the book Omar's psychological
state is discernible not primarily by his thoughts or speech presented in balloons or captions, but by the layout, color scheme, and style of art on a given
page or in a given frame. Rather than relying on plot events, speech, or thought
balloons to show readers Omar's interior state, Santiago roots the formal landscape of *In My Darkest Hour* in its protagonist's (largely nonverbal) subjectivity,
and thus provocatively conflates "the world out there" with Omar's interiority.
Taken together, these innovations constitute what I would suggest is the most
compelling and important element of the novel: its exploration of the nature
and complexity of a post-9/11 American consciousness in which, according to
the novel, the reciprocal relationship between private and public makes it difficult if not impossible to separate the real from the unreal. Far from indicating
contentment with this indeterminacy, however, Omar's confusion—and ours as
readers—regarding reality and unreality both reflects and results in the anxiety
and depression that dominate not just Omar's mood, but ultimately the mood
of *In My Darkest Hour* as a whole.

One of the novel's outstanding accomplishments, then, is its innovative
engagement of the relationship between public and private identities—most
notably, perhaps, the way nation influences not just social identity, but the very
nature and operation of consciousness. By projecting subjectivity onto the
landscape of the page with his striking and sometimes disturbing art, Santiago
productively reflects on the dialectic between self and surroundings, inviting
renewed consideration of what it means to live in a country and with a mind in
which, at times, it becomes difficult or perhaps impossible to determine what is
actual and what is imagined, as well as what is private and what is public. This
consideration is forced particularly by projecting Omar's consciousness onto the
panel in ways that trouble a conventional comics reading practice whereby readers maintain a relatively clear distinction between the diegetic world and characters' subjectivity. In particular, comics readers typically (and rightly) default
to speech bubbles and captions to understand the interior states of characters in
the storyworld. While these devices are important in *In My Darkest Hour*, they
are not the primary means by which Santiago reveals Omar's inner life.

Comics critics and theorists rightly point out that speech balloons give readers direct access to the contents of thinking agents' minds, even as those contents are not directly accessible to other agents in the storyworld.[2] To be sure, the balloon, which both is and is not part of the scene depicted in a given panel, is a distinctive feature of comics, and offers the comics artist a unique opportunity to present thoughts directly. It is not, however, the only—or perhaps, for that matter, the most interesting—way to do so, as *In My Darkest Hour* demonstrates. In seven separate sections, the novel breaks into essentially panelless, darkly shaded and shadowed, impressionistic sketches of grotesque bodies and body parts, surrounded by variously legible handwriting consisting mainly of accusatory and self-deprecating phrases and insults we must assume come from Omar's memory or subconscious (in his depressive episodes); or else into erratic handwriting on lined paper, accompanied by yellow-wash art (in what appears to be a sustained manic episode).

12.1. *From Wilfred Santiago's* In My Darkest Hour

12.2. *From Wilfred Santiago's* In My Darkest Hour

In these episodes, Santiago uses not speech balloons but art—including font and text presentation—to represent Omar's consciousness; but, importantly, the pages in this style are *not* presented predominantly from Omar's point of view or through his eyes. To the contrary, other characters are sometimes present in these scenes (especially the sustained manic episode), and in others, Omar's body is represented from an external vantage point, in profile or from above, indicating that the image is presented by something or someone apparently other than, or at least in addition to, Omar's own consciousness. Challenging the natural and logical intuition that speech balloons are the most accessible way to render consciousness, Santiago brings direct representation of subjective states out of the province of interiority (i.e., speech balloons) and allows them to affect, literally, the shape and feel of the storyworld—even when other characters are present. Consequently, Omar's subjectivity actually

the search for meaning despite, as he sees it, the essential isolation and meaninglessness of the human condition—and this existential angst sets the tone for the rest of the novel.

Having aligned us with Omar's perspective and forced on us some weighty considerations about humanity and significance in the "prologue," Santiago moves to complicate the plot's chronology in the next scene and for the duration of the novel. In the second scene we find Omar working at a greeting card shop called Touchstone, but with a ponytail, in contrast to the short hair he has in the opening pages. We deduce, knowing as we do that hair grows from short to long, that we are witnessing a scene—and here only witnessing, since we have no access to anyone's thoughts—that either takes place before or long after the opening scene. Since Omar's substance abuse, depression, and existential angst follow him throughout the plot, the task of sorting out *In My Darkest Hour*'s chronology is ultimately quite difficult. And while chronology is not my primary concern here, these complications do point toward the way Santiago, in both content and form, experiments with representing consciousness. Consequently, I want to point out a few of the problems readers encounter in any efforts they might make toward reconstructing plot events in their order of occurrence in contrast to their order and manner of presentation in the book. From there, I will examine what these chronological/temporal problems might suggest about narrative and consciousness representation in general.

Santiago provided his account of *In My Darkest Hour*'s chronology in an interview with Newsarama.com's Daniel Epstein:

> The actual story of the book is Omar getting up in the morning, going to work then he goes home and falls asleep watching TV. But the book in itself is not a storyline but rather, what it's like to be inside this guy's head and how he confuses reality with his dreams. Either his disorders [*sic*] a result of his environment or biologically [*sic*] or alcoholism. At least Omar isn't starving and he's alive. He tries to see it that way but the whole book is showing these constant images that Omar has no control over. They are dreams and memory so Omar feels like a bomb about to explode. He has great despair because of that. In the times we are living in we all feel that despair and isolation. (Epstein, "Wilfred Santiago Talks *In My Darkest Hour*")

Earlier I described Omar's unvoiced thoughts that appear in the novel's opening panels, mentioning that his thoughts are similarly presented at the end of the novel. Here Santiago clarifies that everything in between the first 8 and final 3 pages—that is, 117 pages—dwells somewhere in Omar's psyche, but not in the diegetic world of the novel's opening and closing. It is not clear from this description how much of the material between the framing opening and closing is "really" from Omar's past and how much constitutes his "dreams." Further, even if we separate the sections according to the style of art and label them as either emotional impressions or real memories, the verbal accompaniment to the impressionistic sections could still come from Omar's memory—"There you are! You worthless fat . . ." and so on. Notice as well Santiago's language, particularly in the statements that Omar "confuses reality with his dreams" and "tries to see" that he "isn't starving and he's alive," yet "the whole book is showing these constant images that Omar has no control over." That is, Omar's harrowing and confusing "dreams," a category that seems to include memories, figure so dominantly in his consciousness that he feels "despair and isolation" as he seeks to live outside his own mind. That Santiago foregrounds Omar's problem of "confus[ing] reality with his dreams" suggests that the frame narrative is indispensable to a well-developed understanding of the novel, even as that diegetic level constitutes only a small fraction of the novel's contents.

Even in more apparently lucid moments, Omar's reflections on his past, present, and future prove problematic. For instance, in the latter portion of the novel, actual pages from Omar's journals appear on the pages of Santiago's novel—one from the apparent manic episode (see Figure 12.2 above), and another, in distinctly different handwriting, from a later time at which Omar and his girlfriend Lucinda reunite. In the latter entry, he reflects in the present tense on his situation: "Today is a very special day. We are moving in together. . . . There's a lot of skepticism in me about all this, but what are my options? I have to do something. I do feel a little intimedeted [sic], now that she's about to become a history professor." An earlier entry actually finds a present-tense Omar reflecting on a memory of something he is not sure actually happened, and the journal page is accompanied by images readers cannot identify as certainly being the product of Omar's imagination or dreams, or as actual memories of real events. With these entries, readers seem to gain access to Omar's present reflections on his current situation; but if we are to take Santiago at his word, these selections are presented to us as part of Omar's memories from the "present" of the novel's opening pages. Further, that opening scene's "present" is one in which Omar is confused, under the influence of several substances, and contemplating suicide. It seems Omar is split into at least three perceiving positions at once: the center of consciousness that encompasses the whole novel, the central character in the temporally jumbled plot, and also a third agent who reflects on these events from different temporal locations. There is no "real" Omar to be found, and Santiago uses several registers to create such confusion: Omar as framing narrator at the opening of the novel; Omar as reflective homodiegetic narrator in his journals; and Omar on the page as experiencing agent in the events depicted in the art.

In the same essay I mentioned above, Dan Shen points out that a homodiegetic—within the storyworld—narrator's "I" function qua narrator and "I" function qua character tend to blur the distinction between story and discourse, since at any point such a narrator can be:

1. Telling about events in her/his past—where the distinction remains relatively clear;
2. Telling about a present situation—where the distinction is slightly less clear; or
3. Expressing judgments/thoughts/feelings about past and current events—where the distinction becomes even less clear. ("Defense and Challenge," 238–241)

My above account of Omar's reflections demonstrates that at different points in *In My Darkest Hour*, Omar as narrator and as character functions in each of these ways at different points—and at times, apparently more than one of these ways at the same point. All of this is to say that Santiago's novel highlights the particular suitability of comics to challenge and exploit the possibilities different storytelling techniques offer artists.

Such troubling of chronology as we find in *In My Darkest Hour* has implications even beyond its potential to help us understand consciousness in narrative. For instance, it is significant for our understanding of narrative generally. Again, instead of understanding the specific events of Omar's life and his subsequent response to those specific events, Santiago conflates public and private— Omar's response to his life, and that response's interrelatedness with memories and psychological content—in order to render the experience of contemporary America as at once and inseparably both public and private, bound up with experiences and associations that outstrip the immediate circumstances. Such conflation is in keeping with recent accounts of narrative fiction and storytelling, such as Richard Walsh's recasting of the fundamental distinction between *fabula* and *sujet* in *The Rhetoric of Fictionality*. Contrary to conventional narratological wisdom that says readers of fictional narratives come to stories structured in a certain order, with certain emphases and omissions, and in turn reconstruct the events being narrated in order to understand what "really" happened, Walsh argues persuasively that fictional texts are part of a triangulation involving the story as presented on the page, the events of the storyworld as they happened, and readers' encounters with the narrative. In reading story and discourse this way, Walsh "inverts the logical priority of fabula to sujet. The reader's engagement with sujet does not enable the *reconstruction* of fabula, but its *construction*" (67; emphasis added).

Taking such an approach to a work like *In My Darkest Hour* highlights the important point that understanding the world of the novel is not a matter of understanding, say, 9/11 and then understanding Omar's response to it—planes slam into World Trade Center towers, and then Omar responds—but of understanding both event and response as part of a vast psychological landscape that cannot be separated into distinct segments consisting of external events and internal responses to those particular events. This is also consonant with observations like those of Erin McGlothlin, who notes the irreducibly recursive relationship between past and present in Art Spiegelman's *Maus*. Such a relationship, McGlothlin argues, is particularly important in comics, where the past has significant implications for the way the present is represented not only in terms of verbal storytelling, but of visual representation in comics panels ("No Time Like the Present: Narrative and Time in Art Spiegelman's *Maus*").

The preceding investigations of chronology and consciousness in *In My Darkest Hour* can further be conceived of as part of an effort already begun by comics scholars like Jan Baetens and Philippe Marion. Baetens and Marion in particular are interested in examining visual aspects of comics "*as one single field*" and also as "*'communicative'* or rather *'narrative'*" ("Revealing Traces," 145; emphases in original). Much more recently, Johanna Drucker has begun a more comprehensive investigation of the ways "graphic devices," including page numbers, headers, and chapter headings "can be read as an integral part of narrative texts" and "model the discourse field in ways that constraint [*sic*] or engineer the narrative possibilities for a reader" ("Graphic Devices," 121, 124). Though Drucker is primarily interested in calling attention to seemingly paratextual apparatuses that often remain under readers' radars, her account of graphical elements as influential in readers' understanding of how they are to move through a narrative, as well as Baetens's and Marion's claims, has import for my discussion of Santiago's novel. Or perhaps better, I would argue that Santiago's novel lends support to these scholars' work. If *In My Darkest Hour* conflates private and public, real and unreal, by destabilizing the boundaries between image and text, then such a work obviously requires an approach to comics that seeks to understand image, text, and graphic devices generally as part of a comprehensive narrative system that together guides the interpretive and aesthetic experience of it.

In the interview I quoted above, Santiago said, "Omar feels like a bomb about to explode. He has great despair because of that. In the times we are living in we all feel that despair and isolation" (Epstein, "Wilfred Santiago Talks *In My Darkest Hour*"). Considering the historical-cultural moment in which *In My Darkest Hour* emerged, it seems that Santiago's disruption of the image/text distinction, coupled with his description of Omar, evinces what Terry Kading describes in "Drawn into 9/11, But Where Have All the Superheroes Gone?" Though Kading's concern is with superhero comics, he argues that 9/11 constitutes a kind of "super-villainy" the United States has not seen outside the comic book genre, perhaps ever, perhaps excepting only Pearl Harbor. But while in superhero comics the hero comes to rectify the wrong perpetrated by the supervillain(s), no parallel superresponse has come in the contemporary United States. Omar seeks, as Santiago suggests others living in the contemporary United States do, some kind of certainty and stability, but finds only confusing and unsettling dreams and emotions. Consequently, his life is blurry and aimless, and we along with him remain utterly uncertain about what is real, both empirically and psychologically.

NOTES

1. James Phelan's categories of mimetic, thematic, and synthetic components of narratives (and readers' interest in narratives) are helpful here. These categories refer, respectively, to: interest in characters and the storyworld as similar to one's own experience and world (thus emotions, desires, and the like are of interest); interest in cultural and ideological issues the narrative addresses; and interest in the narrative as an artistic and artificial construct. See pages 5–6 in *Experiencing Fiction: Judgments, Progressions, and the Rhetorical Theory of Narrative* for a brief introduction to these categories. To use Phelan's terms, I am arguing that *In My Darkest Hour*'s synthetic component maintains the highest degree of interest and importance for its overall effect, and in fact draws forth its most important thematic concerns.

2. For example, see David Carrier, *The Aesthetics of Comics*, especially Chapter 2, "The Speech Balloon; or, The Problem of Representing Other Minds." See also McCloud's *Understanding Comics* and Thierry Groensteen's *The System of Comics*.

13 FINDING ARCHIVES/ MAKING ARCHIVES

Observations on Conducting Multicultural Comics Research

JENNY E. ROBB AND REBECCA WANZO

Creating Canons

As the study of comics has grown as an academic field, scholars, librarians, and curators have worked to define the canon(s) of graphic storytelling. While the word canon is rejected by some scholars as a means of making value judgments that exclude a variety of texts produced by "Others," the value of a living canon—one that changes over time—is that it tells the story of what various communities find important. Canons are a means by which people communicate because they share a common language and set of references—which is integral to something like superhero comics. These texts constantly refer back to the work of other comic book creators and of other decades in crafting stories of their present. Internal referencing has become more decipherable because of the fan-scholars who have encyclopedic knowledge of popular culture and fill Wikipedia and other websites with information that can make these comics more intelligible to those who have not been reading them for decades.

Thus canons are important to comics, but some canons are more difficult to construct than those in the Marvel and DC universes. Constructing a canon of multicultural or multiethnic texts, for example, raises a host of questions. What groups would be included? Would we define a "multicultural" canon as U.S.-based, since the multiculturalist enterprise has a particular genealogy as a U.S. theory emphasizing a diversity of voices, largely racial and ethnic, in the construction of a pluralist national identity? Is it important simply to preserve as much as we can of these graphic narratives, as opposed to confining preservation to the "important," as such texts are rare and even more vulnerable to disappearing into the ether than other comics (a medium in which so much is routinely lost)? Does the canon include the representation of racial and ethnic minorities, texts produced by racial and ethnic minorities, or both? Rather than being grounded in claims about authentic narrative voice, should the archive be open to texts that are addressing ethnic and racial experience in the United States that are not necessarily created by racial or ethnic minorities? To truly understand this canon, should we include racist representations, as they so often—given the referential nature of comics—haunt the storytelling of those who are trying to challenge that visual history?

People do not have the same answers to these questions; thus the variety of canons available can only add to the richness of the field. Answering these questions helps in the exercise of shaping canons of multicultural comics. Canons are important to the study of multicultural comics, since fewer resources are devoted to comics featuring racial and ethnic minorities. Through collecting, preserving, and researching these comics, librarians and scholars make an argument for their importance. Given the relative youth of the field, shaping canons, and more importantly, archives, is an enterprise in which everyone doing or facilitating research in the field can participate. Curators, librarians, online archivists, and scholars are partners in creating and maintaining archives of graphic storytelling. In a discussion of why it was important to write about women cartoonists, cartoonist Trina Robbins commented that "if you are not written about, you are forgotten."[1] The same imperative governs the work of people doing multicultural comics—much of this work will be forgotten (or will never be known) if interested communities do not collect these texts and write about them.

This essay provides a primer to those interested in beginning research into multicultural comics in the United States. While there is a rich history of graphic storytelling around the world, we situate the construction of the "multicultural" as part of a project with a specific U.S. genealogy. Multicultural projects emphasize varied cultures and place emphasis on the non-Eurocentric in order to be inclusive of what is often left out of narratives about national identity. To that end, we discuss tools and resources for studying graphic storytelling that focuses on race or ethnicity. For example, we would see the Jewish comic as one that takes up the issue of cultural experience, a debatable approach as Jewish creators have been deeply influential in the development of U.S. comics but have not always explicitly made the Jewish experience part of their work (although many have argued for the allegorical importance of said experience in comics featuring Anglo-American characters). In our construction of the lines of the multicultural, we, like the others in this volume, are contributing to the project of defining the field. However, the lines drawn here do not mark incontrovertible boundaries. In fact, we invite contestation in the ongoing effort to define the canon(s) of multicultural comics and cartoons.

Embracing Alternative Sources of Knowledge: Beginning the Search

A new student to comics, who might have been inspired by reading Kyle Baker's *Nat Turner* or parts of Gilbert and Jaime Hernandez's *Love and Rockets*, may find it difficult to know where to go to begin an expansive study of multicultural comics and cartoons. There are primarily five formats to consider—comic strips, editorial cartoons, magazine cartoons, comic books, and graphic novels. These formats can be categorized by genre. Comic books, for example, can be subdivided into superhero comics (some produced under mainstream imprints such as Marvel and DC, others that are independent), underground comix, romance comics, horror comics, etc. Much of the comics studies academic work to date focuses on manga or the superhero genre of comic books, so there is much research to be done in other formats and genres, such as underground comix focusing on multicultural themes or editorial cartoons by people of color. For the largely uninitiated, it quickly becomes apparent that you need to know what to look for in order to locate primary source material in these largely unexplored areas.

The reality of comics research is that most searches can and should begin outside the library. The Internet allows researchers to access the most expansive comics knowledge base—the fans. While not "vetted" by academic peer review, online fan sites, Wikipedia entries, and online chat rooms and message boards can provide an important starting point. Established comics sites such as Newsarama have an archive of useful articles and interviews, as well as message boards for research questions. Sites produced by individuals, such as Pioneering Artists of Color, provide brief biographies and introductions to cartoonists. People are also finding comics through online file sharing, but researchers should be attentive to copyright law when taking that path, as well as the challenge that might confront them when they need to cite material or reproduce an image for a journal or book. However, fan sites providing history and background are one of the first places researchers can go to discover the material available and determine what they might search for at a library. Because libraries often catalogue by name and title and not by subject or theme in the comics collections, acquiring the specific information on the titles you seek is an essential step prior to searching library catalogues.

Message boards on these sites can also be good resources for discovering where comics can be purchased. One of the difficulties in researching comics is the vastness of the medium, largely neglected by libraries, with many materials that are difficult or impossible to find. Online resources can provide researchers with a list of texts they may want to read, but accessing those texts could prove challenging. In some cases, researchers may want to consider whether or not the items can be purchased. Many local comic book stores have disposed of much of their backstock, but it is still possible to find back issues—particularly through online resources. In addition, comic book store owners—and customers in the store—often introduce researchers to material with which they may be unfamiliar.[2]

- -

The Labyrinth: Libraries and Comics Collections

The scholar of multicultural comics must tackle challenges in finding primary source material on several fronts that all comics scholars face. To begin with, comics material in general is not readily available at most academic research libraries. Until recently, these institutions rarely considered the material worth acquiring, preserving, and cataloguing. Historically, expending limited financial and space resources to purchase ephemeral popular culture materials produced as entertainment for children and the masses was not generally high on the priority list for most academic librarians. Newspaper comics fared better than comic books, since newspapers themselves, considered important primary source material, were a part of every research library's permanent collection. But even there, library policies have produced mixed results for comics researchers. Starting in the 1960s, libraries, facing space crises and fears of newsprint deterioration, turned to a new format originally developed for the military: microfilm. They discarded their bound volumes of newspapers in favor of microfilmed copies, which took up a fraction of the space and promised to last longer than the newsprint. Although this format could be copied and distributed more easily, unfortunately, for the comics scholar, microfilm is black-and-white. The beautiful color pages of the Sunday comics became impossible to locate. In addition, quality reproductions for study or illustration were difficult, if not impossible, to obtain from the microfilm versions. For multicultural comics scholars, the newspapers (such as black newspapers) containing cartoons they are researching can be even more difficult to find, and the poor reproduction quality of the images can make analyses particularly challenging. For example, a study of representation of the Asian phenotype in World War II–era comics would require that a researcher be able to clearly see the representation of Asian faces and reproduce them for readers of their analyses. Many newspapers are also included in electronic databases purchased by libraries, such as Proquest Historical Newspapers. Databases are much more convenient than microfilm, but as with microfilm, the quality of images is often very poor.

Fortunately, private collectors have long recognized the importance of comics and cartoon material. An active collecting community has preserved what libraries and archives did not. In the second half of the twentieth century, collecting popular culture exploded in popularity (see Russell Belk, *Collecting in a Consumer Society*, and Paul Martin, *Popular Collecting and the Everyday Self*). At the same time, popular culture gradually gained legitimacy as a subject of academic inquiry. Several pioneering collections dedicated to comics and cartoons were founded in the late 1960s and the 1970s, including the San Francisco Academy of Comic Art, the Ohio State University Cartoon Research Library, and Michigan State's Comic Art Collection.

In recent years, the popularity of manga and graphic novels among young adult readers has led public libraries to grow their circulating and leisure reading collections of these materials. Concurrently, the acceptance of comics and cartoons as a serious art form with aesthetic and literary merits has brought about a surge in scholarly interest and a corresponding effort by research libraries to acquire comics material. The private collections of historic comic books and other comics-related items built by fans and collectors are finding their way into special collections, while many university libraries have begun to build collections of contemporary comics and graphic novels.[3] Even museums and libraries that don't specialize in popular culture have begun to seek original comic art and the papers and manuscript collections of comics creators.

Librarians and archivists strive to make these collections discoverable and accessible, but it is not always easy for researchers to navigate the world of library catalogues, finding aids, indexes, and databases to find primary comics sources. Even within one library, there are likely to be multiple tools to search for materials held in the various collections. Given the high likelihood of varied places to search, a researcher's best strategy is to work with a friendly librarian in order to develop a search strategy.

While the challenges of searching for comics resources can be formidable, in general, most printed material such as comic books, cartoon reprint books, and comics history and criticism books are catalogued in the main library catalogue of the institution, whether they are part of the main circulating collection or are housed in special rare-book-type collections. These records are searchable by author, title, and keyword. The "keyword" approach offers unique challenges for scholars of multicultural comics. Does the catalogue use "African American" or "black"; "Native American" or "Indian"; "Hispanic," "Latino," or a division by more specific identities such as "Mexican" or "Chicano"? A good start-ing point might be to browse materials using the Library of Congress subject headings, but, unfortunately, the headings for cartoons and comics are not well developed or consistently applied. In the Library of Congress system, the main heading that encompasses *all* comics material is "Comic books, strips, etc." It can be appended to any topical heading, so, for example, in the Library of Con-gress catalogue entry, *Maus: A Survivor's Tale* by Art Spiegelman is assigned the subject headings "Holocaust survivors—United States—Biography—Comic books, strips, etc." and "Holocaust, Jewish (1939–1945)—Poland—Biogra-phy—Comic books, strips, etc.," among others. As this example shows, "Comic books, strips, etc." is often associated with a geographical designation and some-times with an ethnic group designation, such as Chinese Americans or African Americans. Also, there are authorized genre-specific headings such as "Horror comic books, strips, etc.," "Science fiction comic books, strips, etc.," and "West-ern comic books, strips, etc." "Cartoonists" is another Library of Congress head-ing that might be useful, although there is little consistency in the designations of multicultural sources. "African American cartoonists" is an authorized head-ing, but not, for example, "Hispanic American cartoonists," "Mexican American cartoonists," "Indian cartoonists," or "Asian American cartoonists." Although "multicultural," "multiculturalism," and "ethnicity" are used in many authorized subject headings (including "multiculturalism in art" and "multiculturalism in literature"), the terms do not appear to have been used much in conjunction with "Comic books, strips, etc."

The subject heading "Graphic novels" is misleading even without library framing—the term covers both fiction and nonfiction book-length narrative works in comics format. "Graphic novels" is a relatively new Library of Con-gress subject heading and is not used consistently. For example, in the Library of Congress catalogue, the book *American Born Chinese* (2006) by Gene Luen Yang has been given the "Graphic novels" heading, but Kyle Baker's *Nat Turner* (2008) has not.[4]

Researchers should be aware that some special collections catalogue their comic books in special finding aids or databases rather than in the main library catalogue. A finding aid is an inventory of an archival collection that usually contains a history of the collection and a description of its contents. It is used by special collections and archives to organize and describe non-book and -jour-nal materials, such as papers, manuscripts, art, and artifacts. Examples of comic book collections that use this approach are the Michael E. Uslan Collection of Comic Books & Graphic Novels at Indiana University's Lilly Library[5] and the Virginia Commonwealth University's Comic Book Collection, housed in its Special Collections and Archives.[6] There are special concerns for those researching representations of race and ethnicity in comics in this case as well. These finding aids may tell researchers what titles or issues the collections have, but do not necessarily indicate the subject matter. The absence of such markers yet again illustrates how important it is for researchers to become partners in either developing finding aids with librarians or providing information elsewhere, so that future scholars can benefit from their painstaking discovery of which texts are useful for multicultural research projects.

Besides published sources such as comic books, graphic novels, and reprint books, researchers may want to search for other types of primary sources, such as original cartoon or comics art, the papers or correspondence of cartoon or comics creators, historical newspapers or periodicals that include cartoons or comics, or other special material. The three largest collections of comics and cartoon materials can be found at the Library of Congress, Michigan State University's Comic Art Collection, and the Ohio State University's Cartoon Research Library.

The Library of Congress has amassed a collection of over 100,000 comic books through copyright deposit. During the 1990s, a major effort was made to catalogue them and make them available through the library's online catalogue (see David S. Serchay's "Comic Research Libraries"). In addition, the Prints and Photographs Division contains some wonderful special collections material of use to those studying multicultural comics. Original comics art can be found in the Cartoon Drawings Collection, the Swann Collection, and the unprocessed Art Wood Collection, including works by African American creators E. Simms Campbell, Oliver Harrington, Brumsic Brandon Jr., Barbara Brandon, Morrie Turner, and Sam Milai; Hispanic/Latino American creators Miguel Covarrubias, Gus Arriola, Tong Sarg, and Rubimor (aka Ruben Moreira); and Asian American creators Paul Fung and Choé (aka CAP; Hai Chi Nguyen). Another interesting example of multicultural comics material in the collection is the original art for the 9/11 comic book story *A Burning Hate*, featuring a confrontation between an African American boy and his friends and a Pakistani American boy and his sister. Some of these materials can be accessed through the Prints and Photographs Online Catalog: http://www.loc.gov/rr/print/catalog.html.[7]

The best source for individual comics issues is the Comic Art Collection at Michigan State University. Founded in 1970, the Comic Art Collection contains the largest catalogued collection of comic books. According to its collection development policy, the four major collecting areas are U.S. comic books, European comic books, U.S. comic strips in the form of scrapbooks and published reprint books, and the history and criticism of comics.[8] Vertical files of clippings and ephemera are maintained on such topics as "African Americans as portrayed in comics" and "Native American images in comics." Comic books, cartoon reprint books, and the most-used clipping files can be found by searching the MSU online catalogue system: http://prodi3.lib.msu.edu/search. Pioneer comics librarian Randall Scott has led the way in carefully cataloguing these materials, and, as a result, the MSU catalogue is the best one to use for searching or browsing comic books and graphic novels by subject or keyword. Also, for advanced researchers, the librarians at the Comic Art Collection have developed a Reading Room Index, which provides more in-depth information than can be found in the catalogue: http://www.lib.msu.edu/comics/rri/index. htm. This alphabetical index focuses on topics that users have previously asked for or that the library staff believes will be of particular interest to researchers.[9] This library thus serves as a perfect example of how researchers can help shape the archival search mechanisms for future scholars. Resources are listed under headings of particular interest to the multicultural comics researcher such as "African American Comic Artists," "African American Superheroes," "African American Women," "Hispanic Americans," "Asian Americans," "Multicultural," and "Multiculturalism."

While not focused on comprehensively collecting individual issues of comics, Ohio State University's Cartoon Research Library is the largest academic facility devoted to printed cartoon art in the world. Founded in 1977, the Library currently contains over 35,000 comic books and actively acquires graphic novels, cartoon reprint books, and comics history and criticism materials. These can be accessed through the main University Libraries catalogue: http://library.osu.edu/. The library also recently acquired the Jay Kennedy Collection of Underground Comics, which has yet to be processed and made available to researchers, but may contain interesting and hard-to-locate comics that deal with multicultural issues. The Cartoon Research Library's collections of comic strip and editorial cartoon material are a particular strength. The San Francisco Academy of Comic Art Collection contains millions of newspaper comic strip sections, tear sheets (newspaper pages), and clippings. Newspaper comic strips are crucial to the study of how people of color and people from diverse backgrounds were portrayed in the popular media and how that representation evolved throughout the twentieth century. This extraordinary collection was created by Bill Blackbeard from the bound volumes of newspapers that libraries around the country discarded in favor of microfilm in the second half of the twentieth century. It was transferred to Ohio State in 1998 and is organized largely by comic strip title in an online finding aid available at http://cartoons.osu.edu/finding_aids/sfaca/. The Cartoon Research Library's original cartoon art collection is the largest in the world at over 400,000 objects. Researchers can search for works by multicultural creators, as well as cartoons dealing with multicultural subject matter, in the Library's original art database (http://library.osu.edu/sites/cgaweb/db/). The Library also houses papers of cartoonists, including correspondence from noted African American cartoonists Sam Milai and E. Simms Campbell. Manuscript collections are accessible through the Library catalogue or through finding aids. Finally, the Library maintains several sets of clipping files, including biography clipping files of over 5,000 cartoonists and subject and topic files. Files on such topics as "African American Cartoonists," "Latino Cartoonists," and "Stereotyping in Cartoons and Comics" might be of particular interest.

Many other academic libraries contain smaller collections that could serve researchers exploring multicultural comics. For example, the Bancroft Library at the University of California at Berkeley recently acquired the papers of Gus Arriola. Arriola created the comic strip *Gordo*, which introduced Americans to Mexican culture and customs. The collection includes artwork, correspondence, personal papers, and promotional materials. The Browne Popular Culture Library at Bowling Green contains the Alternative and Underground Press Collection, which includes more than 250 radical, antiestablishment, and counterculture serial titles from 1950 to 1989. These titles are searchable in Bowling Green's library catalogue, but also available is a helpful research guide that indicates journals, magazines, newspapers, and other media that contain alternative/underground cartoons and comics (http://www.bgsu.edu/colleges/library/pcl/page38839.html).[10]

As has been noted, researchers should not rely exclusively on the main online library catalogues at these institutions, since many special collections and archives organize their materials through finding aids or indexes. Sometimes these tools are available digitally, but many are only available in paper form in the reading room of the collection. It is a good idea for researchers to contact the special collection to inquire about these tools and about collections that might be "hidden" or even unprocessed. If librarians know that there is interest in certain material, they will give it a higher priority for processing and for making available digitally through finding aids.

Another important resource for the multicultural comics scholar is the "ethnic" library. One of the purposes of constructing libraries with identity foci such as Black Studies libraries was to bring together texts around a specific ethnic group so that those doing interdisciplinary work could see what kind of materials would be available to them. Although they don't specialize in comics, they are likely to collect comics material by and about specific cartoonists that belong to the group represented by the library. Many ethnic libraries also house collections of newspapers or magazines published for their specific communities. Some of these titles contain comic strips or cartoons that have rarely been reprinted, although the presence of cartoon or comics material may not be indicated in the catalogue.

Doing research in these libraries can be challenging, but comics researchers have a much greater set of resources available to them than they had ten years ago. Many more people are interested in the topic, so librarians take the material more seriously, and a greater amount of information is online. In addition, the art for graphic storytelling is thriving in the twenty-first century, producing academic and mainstream interest. The success of texts such as Marjane Satrapi's *Persepolis* and its film adaptation demonstrated that people are interested in multicultural graphic storytelling. But while many interesting works exploring issues of race and ethnicity are now being produced, few have Satrapi's mainstream audiences. Comics can become difficult to find within one to two years of production, making it even more important that researchers, librarians, and curators be vigilant about preserving these texts.

Archiving Multicultural Comics—A Partnership between Scholars and Librarians

Given that multicultural comics are a subgenre within a medium that has long been considered "low-brow" and "trash" by many cultural arbiters in the United States (the history outside of the U.S. varies), the community of fans and collectors is essential to multicultural comics studies. While private collectors have long recognized the value of comics and cartoon material, these collections generally do not focus on race and ethnicity. Scholars researching multicultural comics can not only help the field by collecting these texts, but by informing others of the need for conservation and accurate and consistent cataloguing. An important source for comics studies is the creators themselves and their families or descendants. Although the creators may have an active interest in preserving their legacies, many may not realize that original drawings, diaries, sketchbooks, and other work products are valuable to researchers and libraries. Building relationships with producers and families can also be extremely important to people who hope to reproduce images in their scholarship. Scholars may find themselves unable to publish because they failed to obtain permission or because the cost of permission is too high.

And once published, these articles can provide an important introduction to general readers or other scholars in the field. Scholars of multicultural comics are thus essential participants in the building of archives. They can actively seek out collections. They can call attention to work that others should know. They can inform librarians about materials they should acquire as well as alert librarians to how this material should be catalogued. Given the inconsistent cataloguing of comics material, researchers may provide the most methodical framing of what is available to other researchers.

While comics have gained more cachet as valuable literary and artistic texts, many still scoff at the idea of entering into the subdued space of library archives, perusing comic books with white gloves. However, comics are an important record of not only a nationalist imagination but a counterculture imagination. What do the cartoons depicting abused slaves in the nineteenth century tell us about what images people thought would best sway the populace to the cause of slavery's abolition? How does racial stereotyping in WWII superhero comics teach us about nationalist fears and fantasies? What does the publication of twelve controversial images of Muhammad in cartoons in 2005—through which the Danish newspaper *Jyllands-Posten* inspired worldwide protest—tell us about readings of Islam in the early twenty-first century? One hundred years from now, these texts will preserve important information about race and nation, affect and identity. When researchers work to preserve these texts and write about them, they are not only safeguarding a record of artistic production, they are conserving history.

Resources

This resource list provides a starting point for the beginning researcher and suggests examples of the types of places and materials that might be useful. This is in no way intended to be a complete or exhaustive list of sources, and researchers should be aware that websites disappear or change.

WEBSITES

AFRICOMICS
http://www.africomics.com/index.html
This site focuses on African American comics and science fiction.

ASIAN AMERICAN COMICS
http://www.asianamericancomics.com/
This site focuses on not only Asian American creators but Asian American characters in comics.

ASIAN AMERICAN SEQUENTIAL ARTISTS RESOURCE GUIDE
http://www.jamesmarstudio.com/aasarg/home.html
This site lists and provides some images of work created by Asian American cartoonists along with links to a number of artists' websites.

COMIC BOOK DATABASE
http://www.comicbookdb.com/
The goals of this project are "to catalog every comic, graphic novel, manga, creator, character and anything else that could possibly relate to the field of comics" and "to make this wealth of information as useful as possible."

GRAND COMIC BOOK DATABASE
http://www.comics.org/
Aiming to list all comics, this useful database allows researchers to search for more than title and author. Search headings include penciller, inker, editor, publisher, and story title.

COLUMBIA UNIVERSITY'S GRAPHIC NOVELS PAGE
http://www.columbia.edu/cu/lweb/eguides/graphic_novels/index.html
This subject guide provides helpful information about researching comics in an academic library.

LIBRARY OF CONGRESS MEMORY PROJECT — "THE CHINESE IN CALIFORNIA, 1850–1925"
http://memory.loc.gov/ammem/award99/cubhtml/cichome.html
This resource contains primary source material, including cartoons, related to Chinese immigration to California.

NEWSARAMA
http://www.newsarama.com/
Newsarama is a corporately owned site focusing on comics- and cartoon-related material. The text also includes discussions and reviews of film, television, and games. Prominent artists and writers write for the site and are interviewed about their work.

PIONEERING CARTOONISTS OF COLOR
http://web.mac.com/tim_jackson/iWeb/Tim%20Jackson%20Cartoonist/Salute%20to%20Pioneering%20Cartoonists%20of%20Color.html
African American cartoonist Tim Jackson created this website to highlight the

work of black cartoonists publishing from the 1920s to 1960s. The site includes some brief bios and images.

ETHNIC LIBRARIES

Researchers may wish to consult the *Guide to Information Resources in Ethnic Museum, Library, and Archival Collections in the United States,* compiled by Lois J. Buttlar and Lubomyr R. Wynar (Westport, Conn.: Greenwood Press, 1996), for a more comprehensive list of ethnic collections. Keep in mind that not all of the collections listed in the *Guide* will contain material related to cartoons and comics.

CUBAN HERITAGE COLLECTION, UNIVERSITY OF MIAMI
http://www.library.miami.edu/chc/index.html
The Cuban Heritage Collection houses the Cuban Exiles Periodicals collection, which contains magazines, bulletins, newsletters, and newspapers that were published by and for Cuban exiles and Cuban Americans. Some titles that might contain cartoons and comics are *La Avispa, Chispa, Cubalegre, Loquillo, Zig-Zag Libre,* and *El Nuevo Zig-Zag.*[11] This collection is also available on microfilm from ProQuest.

UNIVERSITY OF CALIFORNIA AT BERKELEY, ETHNIC STUDIES LIBRARY
The UC Berkeley Ethnic Studies Library contains the Chicano Studies Collection, the Native American Studies Collection, the Asian American Studies Collection, and the Comparative Ethnic Studies Collection.

UNIVERSITY OF CALIFORNIA AT LA LIBRARIES
The UCLA Library system includes the Chicano Studies Research Center Library, the American Indian Studies Center Library, the Asian American Studies Center Library, and the Center for African American Studies Library. The American Indian Studies Center Library, for example, contains the *Kainai News,* which features the cartoons of Everett Soop, as well as other materials related to Native American cartoon creators.[12] The Chicano Studies Research Center Library contains printed material by Jaime and Gilbert Hernandez and Lalo Alcaraz, along with a variety of Chicano-related comic books.[13]

SEQUOYAH RESEARCH CENTER, UNIVERSITY OF ARKANSAS AT LITTLE ROCK

The Sequoyah Research Center contains the American Native Press Archives (http://anpa.ualr.edu/), which is the largest collection of Native newspapers and periodicals in the world.

NEW YORK PUBLIC LIBRARY, SCHOMBURG CENTER FOR RESEARCH IN BLACK CULTURE

http://www.nypl.org/research/sc/sc.html
Searching the Schomburg catalogue (http://catnyp.nypl.org/search~S5) for the subject heading "comic books, strips, etc." reveals a variety of materials related to comics. Also, the Prints and Photographs Division holds the Cartoons and Stereotypes Collection, which consists of caricatures and stereotyped images of African Americans from the 1830s to the 1960s. Several collections in the Manuscript, Archives and Rare Book Division also contain cartoons.[14]

MOORLAND SPINGARN RESEARCH CENTER, HOWARD UNIVERSITY IN WASHINGTON, D.C.

http://www.founders.howard.edu/moorland-spingarn/library.htm
The Moorland Spingarn Research Center contains the Black Press Archives and an extensive collection of black newspapers and historical records related to them, including the papers of cartoonist Clint Wilson Sr. of the *Los Angeles Sentinel*.

VIVIAN G. HARSH RESEARCH COLLECTION OF AFRO-AMERICAN HISTORY AND LITERATURE AT THE CARTER WOODSON REGIONAL LIBRARY, CHICAGO PUBLIC LIBRARY

The Harsh Research Collection contains the papers of two important cartoonists who worked for the black press, Greg Harris, whose work appeared in over fifty African American newspapers, and Chester Commodore, who cartooned for the *Chicago Defender* for over fifty years.

DATABASES AVAILABLE IN MULTIPLE LIBRARIES

CHICANO DATABASE

Produced by the Ethnic Studies Library, Berkeley, this database focuses on the Mexican American, Chicano, and broader Latino experience and provides access to over 2,470 journals and other materials, including Chicano-related articles in *The Comics Journal*.

PROQUEST HISTORICAL NEWSPAPERS—BLACK NEWSPAPERS
http://www.proquest.com/products_pq/descriptions/histnews-bn.shtml
Includes the *Chicago Defender*, the *Pittsburgh Courier*, and other African American press newspapers that are rich in cartoons and comics.

PROQUEST NEWSSTAND—BLACK NEWSPAPERS AND
U.S. HISPANIC NEWSPAPERS
http://www.proquest.com/products_pq/descriptions/newsstand_bn.shtml
http://www.proquest.com/products_pq/descriptions/ushispanicnews.shtml
These databases provide access to contemporary (1989–present) African American newspapers such as the *Chicago Defender* and *Los Angeles Sentinel* and U.S. Hispanic newspapers such as *El Diario/LA PRENSA* (New York City), *La Opinión* (Los Angeles), *Conexión* (San Antonio), and *Extra* (Chicago).

SECONDARY COMICS STUDIES SOURCES

BIBLIOGRAPHIES

Comics Scholarship Annotated Bibliographies
http://www.comicsresearch.org/
This online resource directed by Dr. Gene Kannenberg is an excellent place to begin comics research.

Comics Research Bibliography
http://www.rpi.edu/~bulloj/comxbib.html
This bibliography is maintained by Michael Rhode and John Bullough. As of the last update in 2007, it contained 23,900 entries searchable by keyword.

PERIODICALS

There has been a great deal of discussion recently within the community of comics scholars about the need for more peer-reviewed journals that specialize in comics studies. Currently, these are the most important periodicals, although many scholars choose to publish their research in journals in other related fields (e.g., English, History, Communications, Journalism).

International Journal of Comic Art
Founded and edited by Prof. John Lent, *IJOCA* is published twice yearly and has a strong international and multidisciplinary focus. Articles are listed on the website at http://www.ijoca.com/, but digital versions are not available.

WORKS CITED

Aaron, Jason, and R. M. Guéra. *Scalped: Indian Country*. Vol. 1. New York: Vertigo, 2007.

Abbott, H. Porter. *The Cambridge Introduction to Narrative*. Cambridge: Cambridge University Press, 2002.

Abel, Jessica. *La Perdida*. New York: Pantheon-Random, 2006.

Abel, Jessica, and Matt Madden. *Drawing Words & Writing Pictures: Making Comics from Manga to Graphic Novels*. New York and London: First Second, 2008.

Abel, Jessica, Gabe Soria, and Warren Pleece. *Life Sucks*. New York: First Second, 2008.

Abrams, M. H. *A Glossary of Literary Terms*. 7th ed. Fort Worth: Harcourt, 1999.

Acosta, Oscar Zeta. *The Revolt of the Cockroach People*. San Francisco: Straight Arrow Books, 1973.

Ahmed, Naseer, and Saurabh Singh. *Kashmir Pending*. New Delhi: Phantomville, 2007.

Alcaraz, Lalo. *La Cucaracha*. Kansas City, Mo.: Andrews McMeel, 2004.

Aldama, Frederick Luis. *Brown on Brown: Chicano/a Representations of Gender, Sexuality, and Ethnicity*. Austin: University of Texas Press, 2005.

———. "Jaime Hernandez." In *Spilling the Beans in Chicanolandia: Conversations with Writers and Artists*, pp. 119–128. Austin: University of Texas Press, 2006.

———. *Spilling the Beans in Chicanolandia: Conversations with Writers and Artists*. Austin: University of Texas Press, 2006.

———. *Your Brain on Latino Comics: From Gus Arriola to Los Bros Hernandez*. Austin: University of Texas Press, 2009.

Allatson, Paul. *Key Terms in Latino/a Cultural and Literary Studies*. Oxford, UK: Blackwell, 2007.

Althusser, Louis. "Ideology and Ideological State Apparatuses (Notes towards an Investigation)." In *The Norton Anthology of Theory and Criticism*, ed. Vincent Leitch, pp. 1483–1509. New York: Norton, 2001.

Anderson, Ho Che. *King: A Comics Biography of Martin Luther King, Jr.* Seattle: Fantagraphics, 2005.

Angel, Michael. *Preserving the Sacred: Historical Perspectives on the Ojibwa Midewiwin.* Winnipeg: University of Manitoba Press, 2002.

Anonymous. Friends of River Narmada. http://www.narmada.org.

Anonymous. Review of *La Perdida* by Jessica Abel. *Kirkus Reviews,* January 1, 2006, p. 3.

Anzaldúa, Gloria. *Borderlands/La Frontera: The New Mestiza.* San Francisco: Aunt Lute/Spinsters Ink, 1987.

Aparicio, Frances R., and Susana Chávez-Silverman, eds. *Tropicalizations: Transcultural Representations of Latinidad.* Hanover, N.H.: University Press of New England, 1997.

Arnold, Andrew D. "Lost in Mexico." Review of *La Perdida,* by Jessica Abel. *Time.com.* Time/Warner, March 8, 2006.

Baetens, Jan, and Philippe Marion. "Revealing Traces: A New Theory of Graphic Enunciation." In *The Language of Comics: Word and Image,* ed. Christina T. Gibbons and Robin Varnum, pp. 145–155. Jackson: University Press of Mississippi, 2001.

Banerjee, Sarnath. *The Barn Owl's Wondrous Capers.* New Delhi: Penguin India, 2007.

———. Interview with Himanshu Bhagat. *Tehelka.com,* February 3, 2007. http://www.tehelka.com/story_main26.asp?filename=hub020307This_Aint.asp (accessed July 4, 2008).

———. Interview with Samit Basu. *SamitBasu.com,* July 3, 2006. http://samitbasu.com/2006/07/03/sarnath-banerjee-interview (accessed July 22, 2008).

Barry, Lynda. *Cruddy: An Illustrated Novel.* New York: Scribner's, 2000.

———. *The! Greatest! of! Marlys!* Seattle: Sasquatch Press, 2000.

———. "It's me—Lynda Barry." Personal correspondence with Melinda de Jesús. December 2001.

———. "Lynda Barry." *The Lambiek Comiclopedia.* http://www.lambiek.net/artists/b/barry_lynda.htm (accessed September 24, 2009).

———. *One Hundred Demons.* Seattle: Sasquatch Press, 2002.

Basu, Samit. "Comics, Graphic Novels and Indian Speculative Fiction." Weblog entry. *Duck of Destiny,* July 3, 2006 (accessed July 22, 2008).

Belk, Russell W. *Collecting in a Consumer Society.* London: Routledge, 1995.

Benton-Banai, Edward. *The Mishomis Book: Voice of the Ojibway.* Hayward, Wisc.: Indian Country Communications, 1988.

Bijoy, C. R. "The Adivasis of India: A History of Discrimination, Conflict, and Resistance." *People's Union for Civil Liberties Bulletin,* February 2003. http://www.pucl.org/Topics/Dalit-tribal/2003/adivasi.htm (accessed June 27, 2008).

Boyer, Bob, Carol Podedworny, and Phillip Gevik. *Odjig: The Art of Daphne Odjig, 1960–2000.* Toronto: Key Porter Books, 2002.

Brennan, Timothy. "Cosmo-Theory." *South Atlantic Quarterly* 101, no. 3 (2002): 659–691.

Bright, Susie. "Introduction." In *Twisted Sisters 2: Drawing the Line,* ed. Diane Noomin, pp. 7–20. Northampton, Mass.: Kitchen Sink Press, 1995.

Brodie, Fawn M. *Thaddeus Stevens, Scourge of the South.* New York: Norton, 1959.

Brown, Jeffrey. *Black Superheroes, Milestone Comics, and Their Fans*. Jackson: University Press of Mississippi, 2001.

Bruce-Novoa, Juan. *Chicano Poetry*. Austin: University of Texas Press, 1982.

Bryant-Jones, Mildred. "The Political Program of Thaddeus Stevens, 1865." *Phylon* 2, no. 2 (1941): 147–154.

Busiek, Kurt. "Earth to Rita." *Trinity*, Issue 3. New York: DC Comics, 2008.

Busiek, Kurt, and Brent Eric Anderson. *Astro City: Family Album*. New York: DC Comics, 1999.

Busteed, H. E. "The Duel." In *Echoes from Old Calcutta*, pp. 109–119. Calcutta and Simla: Thacker, Spink & Co., 1908.

———. "Madame Grand." In *Echoes from Old Calcutta*, pp. 202–286. Calcutta and Simla: Thacker, Spink & Co., 1908.

Callahan, Bob. "Let It Bleed: An Introduction to the New Comics Anthology." In *The New Comics Anthology*, ed. Bob Callahan, pp. 6–14. New York: Collier, 1991.

Callahan, Kevin L. *The Jeffers Petroglyphs: Native American Rock Art on the Midwestern Plains*. Champlin, Minn.: Prairie Smoke Press, 2001.

Campomanes, Oscar. "The Empire's Forgetful and Forgotten Citizens: Unrepresentability and Unassimilability in Filipino-American Postcolonialities." *Hitting Critical Mass: A Journal of Asian American Cultural Criticism* 2, no. 2 (1995): 145–200.

Carey, Percy, and Ronald Wimberly. *Sentences: The Life of MF Grimm*. New York: Vertigo, 2007.

Carnegie Museum of Art. *Carnegie International 1999/2000* (catalogue). Pittsburgh: Carnegie Museum of Art, 2000.

Carrier, David. *The Aesthetics of Comics*. University Park, Pa.: Penn State University Press, 2000.

———. *Writing about Visual Art*. New York: Allworth Press, 2003.

Chandhoke, Neera. "Exploring the Right to Secession: The South Asian Context." *South Asia Research* 28, no. 1 (2008): 1–22.

Chaney, Michael A. "Drawing on History in Recent African American Graphic Novels." *MELUS* 32, no. 3 (Fall 2007): 175–200.

Cheng, Anne Anlin. *The Melancholy of Race*. New York: Oxford University Press, 2000.

Chetri, Satyajit. "Of Coffee and Cigarettes." Review of *Kari* by Amruta Patil. *Tehelka.com*, March 8, 2008. http://www.tehelka.com/story_main38.asp?filename=hub080308of_coffee.asp (accessed May 15, 2008).

Chopra, Deepak, and Saurav Mohapatra. *India Authentic TPB Vol. 1: The Book of Shiva*. New York: Virgin Comics, 2007.

Chute, Hilary, and Marianne DeKovan. "Introduction: Graphic Narrative." *MFS: Modern Fiction Studies* 52, no. 4 (Winter 2006): 767–782.

Cioffi, Frank L. "Disturbing Comics: The Disjunction of Word and Image in the Comics of Andrzej Mleczko, Ben Katchor, R. Crumb, and Art Spiegelman." In *The Language of Comics: Word and Image*, ed. Christina Gibbons and Robin Varnum, pp. 97–122. Jackson: University Press of Mississippi, 2001.

Clarke, Greg. "100 Notable Books of 2007." *New York Times*, December 2, 2007. http://www.nytimes.com/2007/12/02/books/review/notable-books-2007.html? (accessed September 24, 2009).

Crumb, Robert. *The Complete Crumb Comics Volume 7: Hot 'n' Heavy.* Seattle: Fantagraphics, 1991.

———. *The R. Crumb Coffee Table Art Book.* Edited by Pete Poplaski. Boston: Little, Brown and Company, 1997.

Cullen, Bradley, and Michael Pretes. "The Meaning of Marginality: Interpretations and Perceptions in Social Science." *Social Science Journal* 37, no. 2 (2000): 215–229.

Dabb, Andrew, and Seth Fisher. *Happydale: Devils in the Desert.* New York: Vertigo, 1999.

Dalrymple, Farel. *Pop Gun War.* Milwaukie, Ore.: Dark Horse, 2003.

Dávila, Arlene. *Latinos, Inc.* Berkeley and Los Angeles: University of California Press, 2001.

Davis, Rocío G. "Locating Family: Asian Canadian Historical Revisioning in Linda Ohama's *Obaachan's Garden* and Ann Marie Fleming's *The Magical Life of Long Tack Sam.*" *Journal of Canadian Studies: Revue d'études canadiennes* 42, no. 1 (Winter 2008): 1–22.

Davis, Stephen. "The Adventures of Antman." *Cornell Daily,* March 11, 2005.

Debord, Guy. *The Society of the Spectacle.* Translated by Donald Nicholson-Smith. New York: Zone Books, 1995.

DeFillipis, Nunzio, and Christina Weir. *Skinwalker.* Portland: Oni Press, 2003.

De Jesús, Melinda L. "Of Monsters and Mothers: Filipina American Identity and Maternal Legacies in Lynda J. Barry's *One Hundred Demons.*" *Meridians: Feminism, Race, Transnationalism* 5, no. 1 (2004): 1–26.

del Toro, Guillermo. *Cronos.* Mexico City: Fondo de Fomento Cinematográfico, 1993.

Dembicki, Matt. *Trickster Native American Tales: A Graphic Collection.* Golden, Colo.: Fulcrum Publishing, 2010.

de Varona, Esperanza B. *Cuban Exile Periodicals at the University of Miami Library: An Annotated Bibliography.* Madison: Secretariat, Seminar on the Acquisition of Latin American Library Materials, Memorial Library, University of Wisconsin–Madison, 1987.

Diawara, Manthia, ed. *Black American Cinema.* New York: Routledge, 1993.

Diaz, Elena Maria. *The Virgin, the King, and the Royal Slaves of El Cobre: Negotiating Freedom in Colonial Cuba, 1670–1780.* Stanford, Calif.: Stanford University Press, 2000.

Drucker, Johanna. "Graphic Devices: Narration and Navigation." *Narrative* 16, no. 2 (2008): 121–139.

Duara, Ajit. "Multi-tasking and Mixed Media." Review of *The Barn Owl's Wondrous Capers* by Sarnath Banerjee. *The Hindu,* March 4, 2007. http://www.hindu.com/lr/2007/03/04/stories/2007030400050100.htm (accessed June 5, 2008).

Dyson, Anne Haas. "Cultural Constellations and Childhood Identities: On Greek Gods, Cartoon Heroes, and the Social Lives of Schoolchildren." *Harvard Educational Review* 3 (1996): 471–495.

Eby, Clare. "Slouching toward Beastliness: Richard Wright's Anatomy of Thomas Dixon." *African American Review* 35, no. 3 (2001): 439–458.

Eisner, Will. *Comics and Sequential Art.* Tamarac, Fla.: Poorhouse Press, 1985.

——. *Graphic Storytelling and Visual Narrative.* Tamarac, Fla.: Poorhouse Press, 1996.

El Rassi, Toufic. *Arab in America.* San Francisco: Last Gasp, 2007.

Epstein, Daniel R. "Wilfred Santiago Talks *In My Darkest Hour.*" *Newsarama.com,* January 24, 2005. http://forum.newsarama.com/showthread.php?t=26002 (accessed May 21, 2008).

Erdrich, Louise. *The Birchbark House.* New York: HarperCollins, 1999.

——. *Books and Islands in Ojibwe Country.* Washington, D.C.: National Geographic Society, 2003.

——. *The Game of Silence.* New York: HarperCollins, 2005.

——. *The Porcupine Year.* New York: HarperCollins, 2008.

Espinosa, Frank. "Frank Espinosa." Interview. In *Your Brain on Latino Comics: From Gus Arriola to Los Bros Hernandez,* Frederick Luis Aldama, pp. 152–165. Austin: University of Texas Press, 2009.

——. *Rocketo: Journey to the Hidden Sea. Vol. 1.* Berkeley, Calif.: Image Comics, 2006.

Eysturoy, Annie O. *Daughters of Self-Creation: The Contemporary Chicana Novel.* Albuquerque: University of New Mexico Press, 1996.

Fellowship of Reconciliation. *Martin Luther King and the Montgomery Story.* New York: Capp Enterprises, 1957.

Fleming, Ann Marie. *The Magical Life of Long Tack Sam.* New York: Riverhead Books, 2007.

Frank, Barney. "In Praise of Partisanship." *The Gay and Lesbian Review* 11, no. 5 (September–October 2004): 10–13.

Fujikane, Candace. *"Reimagining Development and the Local in Lois-Ann Yamanaka's Saturday Night at the Pahala Theatre."* In *Women in Hawaii: Sites, Identities, and Voices, ed. Joyce Chinen, Kathleen O. Kane, and Ida N. Yoshinaga, pp. 41–61. Honolulu: University of Hawaii Press, 1997.*

Galang, M. Evelina. *Her Wild American Self.* Minneapolis: Coffeehouse Press, 1996.

Gamalinda, Eric. "Myth, Memory, Myopia: Or, I May Be Brown but I Hear America Singing." In *Flippin': Filipinos on America,* ed. Luis Francia and Eric Gamalinda, pp. 1–5. Philadelphia: Temple University Press, 1996.

Gardner, Jared. "Autobiography's Biography, 1972–2007." *Biography* 31, no. 1 (Winter 2008): 1–26.

——. "Reading out of the Gutter: Early Comics, Film, and the Serial Pleasures of Modernity." In *Repetitions,* ed. Michael Moon. Minneapolis: University of Minnesota Press, forthcoming.

Gewertz, Ken. "'Birth of a Nation'—The Remix: DJ Spooky Presents New View of Contentious Classic." *Harvard Gazette,* March 17, 2005.

Giffen, Keith, Cully Hamner, and John Rogers. *Blue Beetle: Shellshocked.* New York: DC Comics, 2006.

Glaser, Jennifer. "An Imaginary Ararat: Jewish Bodies and Jewish Homelands in Ben Katchor's *The Jew of New York.*" *MELUS* 32, no. 3 (Fall 2007): 153–173.

Goff, Cindy, Steven Premo, and Paul Fricke. *A Hero's Voice.* Onamia, Minn.: Mille Lacs Band of Ojibwe Indians, 1996.

Goldstein, Nancy. *Jackie Ormes: The First African American Woman Cartoonist.* Ann Arbor: University of Michigan Press, 2008.

Gregory, Roberta. "California Girl." In *Roadstrips: A Graphic Journey across America,* ed. Pete Friedrich, pp. 71–76. San Francisco: Chronicle Books, 2005.

——. *Life's a Bitch: The Complete Bitchy Bitch Stories Vol. 1.* Seattle: Fantagraphics Books, 2005.

——. *Naughty Bits #1.* Seattle: Fantagraphics, 1991.

Griffith, David W. *The Birth of a Nation.* Chatsworth, Calif.: Image Entertainment, 1992.

Groensteen, Thierry. *The System of Comics.* Translated by Bart Beaty and Nick Nguyen. Jackson: University Press of Mississippi, 2007.

Gustines, George Gene. "Straight (and Not) Out of the Comics." *New York Times,* May 28, 2006.

Guzmán, Isabel Molina. "Mediating *Frida:* Negotiating Discourses of Latino/a Authenticity in Global Media Representations of Ethnic Identity." *Critical Studies in Media Communications* 23, no. 3 (2006): 232–251.

Habell-Pallán, Michelle. *Loca Motion: The Travels of Chicana and Latina Popular Culture.* New York: New York University Press, 2005.

Harvey, Robert. *The Art of the Funnies.* Jackson: University Press of Mississippi, 1994.

Hatfield, Charles. *Alternative Comics: An Emerging Literature.* Jackson: University Press of Mississippi, 2005.

——. "Comic Art, Children's Literature, and the New Comics Studies." *The Lion and the Unicorn* 30, no. 3 (2006): 360–382.

——. "Graphic Intervention: Form and Argument in Contemporary Comics." Dissertation. University of Connecticut, 2000.

Hawley, John Stratton. "The Saints Subdued: Domestic Virtue and National Integration in Amar Chitra Katha." In *Media and the Transformation of Religion in South Asia,* ed. Lawrence A. Babb and Susan Wadley, pp. 107–134. Philadelphia: University of Pennsylvania Press, 1995.

Hayward, Jennifer. *Consuming Pleasures: Active Audiences and Serial Fictions from Dickens to Soap Opera.* Lexington: University Press of Kentucky, 1997.

Heer, Jeet, and Kent Worcester, eds. *Arguing Comics: Literary Masters on a Popular Medium.* Jackson: University Press of Mississippi, 2004.

Helfer, Andrew, and Randy DuBurke. *Malcolm X: A Graphic Biography.* New York: Hill and Wang, 2006.

Hempel, Amy. "Laugh Lines." *New York Times Book Review,* July 27, 1997. http://www.nytimes.com/books/97/07/27/reviews/hempel-chast.html.

Herman, Luc, and Bart Vervaeck. *Handbook of Narrative Analysis.* Lincoln: University of Nebraska Press, 2001.

Hernandez, Gilbert. "Palomar and Beyond: An Interview with Gilbert Hernandez." *MELUS* 32, no. 3 (Fall 2007): 221–246.

———. *Sloth*. New York: Vertigo, 2006.

Hernandez, Jaime. *The Girl from H.O.P.P.E.R.S.* Seattle: Fantagraphics, 2007.

———. *Maggie the Mechanic*. Seattle: Fantagraphics, 2007.

———. *Perla la Loca*. Seattle: Fantagraphics, 2007.

Hillsman, Don, and Ryan Monihan. *By Any Means Necessary: The Life and Times of Malcolm X—An Unauthorized Biography in Comic Book Form*. Tampa: Millennium Publications, 1993.

Holte, James. "Blade: A Return to Revulsion." *Journal of Dracula Studies* 3 (2001): 27–32.

hooks, bell. *Black Looks: Race and Representation*. Boston: South End Press, 1992.

Inge, M. Thomas. *Comics as Culture*. Jackson: University Press of Mississippi, 1990.

Inness, Sherrie A. *The Lesbian Menace: Ideology, Identity, and the Representation of Lesbian Life*. Amherst: University of Massachusetts Press, 1997.

Inzana, Ryan. *Johnny Jihad: A Graphic Novel*. New York: Nantier, Beall, Minoustchine Publishing Inc., 2003.

Jackson, Tim. "Pioneering Cartoonists of Color." http://web.mac.com/tim_jackson/iWeb/Tim%20Jackson%20Cartoonist/Salute%20to%20Pioneering%20Cartoonists%20of%20Color.html (accessed September 14, 2009).

Johns, Geoff, and David S. Goyer (story); Humberto Ramos and Sandra Hope (art). *9-11: The World's Finest Comic Book Artists and Writers Tell Stories to Remember #2*. New York: DC, 2002.

Johns, Geoff, and Grant Morrison. 52. Issues 1–52. New York: DC Comics, 2006–2007.

Johnson, Mat, and Warren Pleece. *Incognegro*. New York: Vertigo, 2008.

Johnson, R. Kikuo. *Night Fisher: A Comic Book Novella*. Seattle: Fantagraphics Books, 2005.

Johnston, Basil. *The Manitous: The Spiritual World of the Ojibway*. New York: HarperCollins, 1995.

Johnston, Lynn. "The Mtigwaki Series," appearing from August 2004 through February 2005 in *For Better or For Worse*, syndicated comic strip. United Press Syndicate.

Kading, Terry. "Drawn into 9/11, But Where Have All the Superheroes Gone?" In *Comics as Philosophy*, ed. Jeff McLaughlin, pp. 207–227. Jackson: University Press of Mississippi, 2005.

Kalesniko, Mark. *Alex*. Seattle: Fantagraphics Books, 2006.

———. *Mail Order Bride*. Seattle: Fantagraphics Books, 2001.

Kannenberg, Eugene. "The Comics of Chris Ware: Text, Image, and Visual Narrative Strategies." In *The Language of Comics: Word and Image*, ed. Christina Gibbons and Robin Varnum, pp. 174–198. Jackson: University Press of Mississippi, 2001.

———. "Form, Function, Fiction: Text and Image in the Comics Narratives of Winsor McCay, Art Spiegelman, and Chris Ware." Dissertation. University of Connecticut, 2002.

Karson, Max. "If It's War the Asians Want . . ." *Campus Press* [Boulder, Colo.], February 18, 2008.

Katchor, Ben. *The Jew of New York*. New York: Pantheon, 2000.

Kim, Derek Kirk. *Same Difference and Other Stories*. Gainesville, Fla.: Alternative Comics, 2003.

Kirkman, Robert. *Invincible*. Issues 2 and 6. Berkeley, Calif.: Image Comics, 2003.

Kitwana, Bakari. *The Hip Hop Generation*. New York: Basic Civitas Books, 2002.

Klein, Grady. *The Lost Colony Book 1: The Snodgrass Conspiracy*. New York: First Second, 2006.

Krensky, Stephen. *Comic Book Century: The History of American Comics*. Minneapolis: Twenty-First Century Books, 2008.

Lang, Robert, ed. *The Birth of a Nation: D. W. Griffith, Director*. Rutgers Films in Print Series. New Brunswick, N.J.: Rutgers University Press, 1994.

Lenik, Edward J. *Picture Rocks: American Indian Rock Art in the Northeast Woodlands*. Hanover, N.H.: University Press of New England, 2002.

Leschnitzer, Adolf. "The Wandering Jew: The Alienation of the Jewish Image in Christian Consciousness." In *The Wandering Jew: Essays in the Interpretation of a Christian Legend*, ed. Galit Hasan-Rokem and Alan Dundes, pp. 227–235. Bloomington: University of Indiana Press, 1986.

Lessig, Lawrence. *Remix: Making Art and Commerce Thrive in the Hybrid Economy*. New York: Penguin Press, 2008.

Lewis-Williams, David. *The Mind in the Cave: Consciousness and the Origins of Art*. London: Thames & Hudson, 2004.

Linmark, R. Zamora. *Rolling the R's*. New York: Kaya Press, 1995.

Macaulay, Thomas Babington. *Warren Hastings*. London: MacMillan and Co., 1922.

McCloud, Scott. *Understanding Comics: The Invisible Art*. New York: HarperPerennial, 1994; Northampton, Mass.: Kitchen Sink Press, 1993.

McCulloch, Derek, and Sheperd Hendrix. *Stagger Lee*. Berkeley, Calif.: Image Comics, 2006.

McGlothlin, Erin. "No Time Like the Present: Narrative and Time in Art Spiegelman's *Maus*." *Narrative* 11, no. 2 (2003): 177–198.

McGruder, Aaron, Reginald Hudlin, and Kyle Baker. *Birth of a Nation: A Comic Novel*. New York: Three Rivers Press, 2005.

McLeod-Shabogesic, Perry. *Baloney and Bannock*, featured cartoon in *Anishinaabek News* and *The North Bay Nugget*, 1995–present.

Marshall, Kerry James. *Every Beat of My Heart*. Wexner Center for the Arts, Columbus, Ohio. February 2–April 13, 2008.

———. "A Thousand Words." *Art Forum International* 38, no. 10 (Summer 2000): 149.

Marshall, Kerry James, Terrie Sultan, and Gary Sangster. *Kerry James Marshall: Telling Stories*. Cleveland: Cleveland Center for Contemporary Art, 1994.

Martin, April, and Kerry James Marshall, directors. *Behind the Scenes of Kerry James Marshall's Every Beat of My Heart*. DVD. Columbus, Ohio: Wexner Center for the Arts, 2008.

Martin, Paul. *Popular Collecting and the Everyday Self: The Reinvention of the Museum?* London: Leicester University Press, 1999.

Mehar, Rakesh. "Of True and False Histories." Review of *The Barn Owl's Wondrous Capers* by Sarnath Banerjee. *The Hindu (Metro Plus Bangalore)*, March 15, 2007. http://www.hinduonnet.com/thehindu/mp/2007/03/15/stories/2007031501320100.htm (accessed June 5, 2008).

Miles, David H. "The Picaro's Journey to the Confessional: The Changing Image of the Hero in the German *Bildungsroman*." PMLA 89, no. 5 (1974): 980–992.

Miller, Paul D. *DJ Spooky's Rebirth of a Nation*. Burbank, Calif.: Anchor Bay/Starz Media, 2008.

———. *Rhythm Science*. Cambridge, Mass.: Mediawork/MIT Press, 2004.

Milligan, Peter, and Mike Allred. *X-Force*, vol. 1, issues 116 and 117. New York: Marvel Comics, 2001.

Mitchell, Brandon, Nicholas Bradshaw, and Jean-Francois Beaulieu. *Sacred Circles*, No. 1 and No. 2. Listuguj, Quebec: Birch Bark Comics, 2003.

Mitchell, W. J. T. "Representation." In *Critical Terms for Literary Study*, ed. Frank Lentricchia and Thomas McLaughlin, pp. 11–22. Chicago: University of Chicago Press, 1995.

Mithen, Steven. *The Singing Neanderthals: The Origins of Music, Language, Mind, and Body*. Cambridge, Mass.: Harvard University Press, 2006.

Morrison, Grant, and Philip Bond. *Vimanarama*. New York: DC Comics, 2005.

Morrisseau, Norval. *Legends of My People: The Great Ojibway*. Edited by Selwyn Dewdney. Toronto: Ryerson Press, 1965.

———. *Return to the House of Invention*. Toronto: Key Porter Books, 2005.

Morrisseau, Norval, and Donald C. Robinson. *Norval Morrisseau: Travels to the House of Invention*. Toronto: Key Porter Books, 1997.

Nair, Vijay. "Unequal Music." Review of *Kashmir Pending* by Naseer Ahmed and Saurabh Singh. *The Hindu*, June 3, 2007. http://www.hindu.com/lr/2007/06/03/stories/2007060350310200.htm (accessed May 31, 2008).

Naraghi, Dara. *Lifelike*. San Diego: IDW Publishing, 2007.

National Commission on Asian American and Pacific Islander Research in Education. *Facts, Not Fiction: Setting the Record Straight*. New York: National Commission on Asian American and Pacific Islander Research in Education, 2008.

Navarro, Rafael. *Sonambulo: Sleep of the Just*. La Habra, Calif.: Ninth Circle Studios, 1996.

Noomin, Diane. Foreword. *Twisted Sisters: A Collection of Bad Girl Art*, ed. Diane Noomin. New York: Penguin, 1991.

———. Foreword. *Twisted Sisters 2: Drawing the Line*, ed. Diane Noomin. Northampton, Mass.: Kitchen Sink Press, 1995.

Norris, Frank. "Thoroughbred." *Overland Monthly* 25 (February 1895): 196–201.

Nyberg, Amy Kiste. *Seal of Approval: The History of the Comics Code*. Jackson: University Press of Mississippi, 1998.

Offenberger, Rik. "Who's That Bug? Hamner on Blue Beetle." *Newsarama.com*, undated. http://www.newsarama.com/dcnew/Beetle/hamner.htm (accessed April 29, 2007).

Oh, Sandra. "Sight Unseen: Adrian Tomine's *Optic Nerve* and the Politics of Recognition." *MELUS* 32, no. 3 (Fall 2007): 129–152.

Okubo, Miné. *Citizen 13660*. Seattle: University of Washington Press, 1983.

Palumbo, Donald. "Marvel's *Tomb of Dracula*: Case Study in a Scorned Medium." In *Scorned Literature: Essays on the History and Criticism of Popular Mass-Produced Fiction in America*, ed. Lydia Cushman Schurman and Deidre Johnson, pp. 51–68. Westport, Conn.: Greenwood Press, 2002.

Paparone, Lesley. "Art and Identity in Mark Kalesniko's *Mail Order Bride*." *MELUS* 32, no. 3 (Fall 2007): 201–219.

Parker, Robert Dale. *The Invention of Native American Literature*. Ithaca, N.Y., and London: Cornell University Press, 2003.

Patil, Amruta. *Kari*. New Delhi: Harper Collins India, 2008.

———. "Lost in Translation." Weblog entry. *Umbilical*, January 26, 2008. http://amruta-patil.blogspot.com/2008_01_01_archive.html (accessed July 20, 2008).

Pecora, Norma. "Superman/superboys/superman: The Comic Book Hero as a Socializing Agent." In *Men, Masculinity, and the Media*, ed. S. Craig, pp. 61–77. Thousand Oaks, Calif.: Sage, 1992.

Peterson, James. "Dead Prezence: Money and Mortal Themes in Hip Hop Culture." *Callaloo* 29, no. 3 (2006): 895–909.

Phelan, James. *Experiencing Fiction: Judgments, Progressions, and the Rhetorical Theory of Narrative*. Columbus: Ohio State University Press, 2007.

———. "Reading across Identity Borders: A Rhetorical Analysis of John Edgar Wideman's 'Doc's Story.'" In *Reading Sites*, ed. Elizabeth Flynn and Patrocinio Schweikart, pp. 39–59. New York: MLA Publications, 2004.

———. "Self-Help for Narratee and Narrative Audience: How 'I' and 'You' Read 'How.'" *Style* 28, no. 3 (1994): 350–365.

Pierce, Linda M. "Not Just My Closet: Exposing Familial, Cultural, and Imperial Skeletons." In *Pinay Power: Peminist Critical Theory: Theorizing the Filipina/American Experience*, ed. Melinda L. de Jesús, pp. 31–44. New York: Routledge, 2005.

Pilar, Jose A. Del, and Jocelynda Udasco. "Marginal Theory: The Lack of Construct Validity." *The Hispanic Journal of Behavioral Sciences* 26, no. 1 (2004): 3–15.

Pilcher, Tim. *Erotic Comics: A Graphic History from Tijuana Bibles to Underground Comix*. New York: Ilex Press Limited, 2008.

Porpora, Douglas V. "Personal Heroes, Religion, and Transcendental Metanarratives." *Sociological Forum* 2 (1996): 209–229.

Portillo, Jaime "Jimmy." *Gabriel*. Orlando, Fla.: Indyplanet, 2007.

Pritchett, Frances. "The World of Amar Chitra Katha." In *Media and the Transformation of Religion in South Asia*, ed. Lawrence A. Babb and Susan Wadley, pp. 76–106. Philadelphia: University of Pennsylvania Press, 1995.

Pustz, Matthew J. *Comic Book Culture: Fanboys and True Believers*. Jackson: University Press of Mississippi, 1999.

Reyes, Tom, and David Waldman. *Land of a Thousand Dances: Chicano Rock 'n' Roll from Southern California*. Albuquerque: University of New Mexico Press, 1998.

Rich, R. Ruby, and Lourdes Arguellos. "Homosexuality, Homophobia, and Revolution: Notes toward an Understanding of the Cuban Lesbian and Gay Male Experience, Part II." *Signs: Journal of Women in Culture and Society* 11, no. 1 (Autumn 1985): 120–136.

Robbins, Trina. *From Girls to Grrlz: A History of Women's Comics from Teens to Zines.* San Francisco: Chronicle Books, 1999.

———. Interview. Daniel Robert Epstein. UnderGroundOnline. http://www.ugo.com/ channels/freestyle/features/trinarobbins/.

Rodríguez, Juana María. *Queer Latinidad.* New York: New York University Press, 2003.

Root, Maria P. "Contemporary Mixed-Heritage Filipino Americans: Fighting Colonized Identities." In *Filipina Americans: Transformation and Identity,* ed. Maria P. Root, pp. 80–94. Thousand Oaks, Calif.: Sage, 1997.

Ross, Alex. *Heroes.* La Jolla, Calif.: WildStorm, 2007.

Ross, Steve. *Chesty Sanchez,* Issue 1. San Antonio: Antarctic Press, November 1995.

Royal, Derek Parker. "Drawing Attention or Slumming in the Gutters?: Representing the Ethnic Other in Jessica Abel's *La Perdida* and Mark Kalesniko's *Mail Order Bride.*" MELUS Conference, Columbus, Ohio, March 27–30, 2008.

———. "Introduction: Coloring America: Multi-Ethnic Engagements with Graphic Narrative." *MELUS* 32, no. 3 (Fall 2007): 7–22.

———. "Palomar and Beyond: An Interview with Gilbert Hernandez." *MELUS* 32, no. 3 (Fall 2007): 221–246.

Rushdie, Salman. "Kashmir, the Imperiled Paradise." *New York Times,* June 3, 1999; www .CndYorks.org. http://www.cndyorks.gn.apc.org/news/articles/asia/kashmir.htm (accessed May 16, 2009).

Ryan, Jennifer. "Black Female Authorship and the African American Graphic Novel: Historical Responsibility in *Icon: A Hero's Welcome.*" *Modern Fiction Studies* 52, no. 4 (Winter 2006): 175–200.

Sabin, Roger. *Comics, Comix and Graphic Novels: A History of Comic Art.* New York: Phaidon, 1996.

Saldívar, José David. "Postmodern Realism." In *The Columbia History of the American Novel,* ed. Emory Elliot, pp. 520–541. New York: Columbia University Press, 1991.

San Juan, Epifanio, Jr. "The Predicament of Filipinos in the United States: Where Are You From? When Are You Going Back?" In *The State of Asian America: Activism and Resistance in the 1990's,* ed. Karin Aguilar–San Juan, pp. 205–214. Boston: South End Press, 1994.

Santiago, Wilfred. *In My Darkest Hour.* Seattle: Fantagraphics, 2004.

Satrapi, Marjane. *Persepolis: The Story of a Childhood.* New York: Pantheon, 2003.

Schmidt, Peter. *Peace Party.* Culver City, Calif.: Blue Corn Comics, 1999.

Schwartz, Herbert T. *Windigo and Other Tales of the Ojibway.* Toronto: McClelland and Stewart, 1969.

Scott, Anna Beatrice. "Superpower vs. Supernatural: Black Superheroes and the Quest for Mutant Reality." *Journal of Visual Culture* 5, no. 3 (2006): 295–314.

Scott, Randall W. "A Practicing Comic-book Librarian Surveys His Collection and His Craft." *Serials Review* 24, no. 1 (Spring 1998): 52–53.

See, Maria Sarita Echavez. "Mourning the Blood That Spilled to Make This Stew and Laughing Loud, or Why I Hate My Cousin Pucha." In *Making More Waves*, ed. Elaine Kim, Lilia V. Villanueva, and Asian Women United of California, pp. 6–11. Boston: Beacon Press, 1996.

Sen, Orijit. *The River of Stories*. New Delhi: Kalpavriksh, 1994.

Serchay, David S. "Comic Research Libraries." *Serials Review* 24, no. 1 (Spring 1998): 37–38.

Shen, Dan. "Defense and Challenge: Reflections on the Relation between Story and Discourse." *Narrative* 10, no. 3 (2002): 222–243.

Sheyahshe, Michael A. *Native Americans in Comic Books: A Critical Study*. Jefferson, N.C.: McFarland Publishing Inc., 2008.

Shultz, Diana, ed. *AutobioGraphix*. Milwaukie, Ore.: Dark Horse Books, 2003.

Silva, Fred, ed. *Focus on* The Birth of a Nation. Englewood Cliffs, N.J.: Prentice-Hall, Inc., 1971.

Simmons, Danny, and Floyd Hughes. *'85*. New York: Atria Books, 2008.

Sinha, Manoj Kumar. "Minority Rights: A Case Study for India." *International Journal on Minority and Group Rights* 12 (2005): 355–374.

Solomon, Chad, and Christopher Meyer. *The Adventures of Rabbit and Bear Paws: The Sugar Bush*. Toronto: Little Spirit Bear Productions, 2006.

Spiegelman, Art. "Comix 101." Lecture. Porter College, University of California, Santa Cruz, April 1992.

———. "Commix: An Idiosyncratic Historical and Aesthetic Overview." *Print* 42, no. 6 (1988): 61–96.

———. *Maus*. New York: Pantheon, 1986.

Squier, Susan M. "So Long as They Grow Out of It: Comics, the Discourse of Developmental Normalcy, and Disability." *Journal of Medical Humanities* 29 (2008): 71–88.

Stavans, Ilan, and Roberto Weil. *Mr. Spic Goes to Washington*. Berkeley, Calif.: Soft Skull Press, 2008.

Steinberg, Erwin R., and Christian W. Hallstein. "*Ulysses*: An Anti-*Bildungsroman*." *Joyce Studies Annual* 11 (2000): 202–208.

Stokes, Melvyn. *D. W. Griffith's* The Birth of Nation: *A History of "The Most Controversial Motion Picture of All Time."* Oxford: Oxford University Press, 2007.

Sultan, Terrie. "This Is the Way We Live." In *Kerry James Marshall*, ed. Terrie Sultan and Arthur Jafa, pp. 11–23. New York: Harry N. Abrams, Inc., 2000.

Tamaki, Mariko, and Jillian Tamaki. *Skim*. Toronto: Groundwood Books/House of Anansi Press, 2008.

Tanner, Helen, ed. *Atlas of Great Lakes Indian History*. Norman: University of Oklahoma Press, 1987.

Taylor, Diana. *Disappearing Acts: Spectacles of Gender and Nationalism in Argentina's "Dirty War."* Durham, N.C.: Duke University Press, 1997.

Tensuan, Theresa. "Comic Visions and Revisions in the Work of Lynda Barry and Marjane Satrapi." *Modern Fiction Studies* 52, no. 4 (Winter 2006): 947–964.

Tingley, Scott. "Rabbit and Bear Paws: An Interview with Creator Chad Solomon." Weblog entry, *Comics in the Classroom*, October 15, 2006. http://comicsintheclassroom.net/002006_interview_rabbit_bearpaws.htm (accessed August 14, 2008).

Tomine, Adrian. "Hawaiian Getaway." In *Summer Blonde: Stories*. Montreal: Drawn & Quarterly, 2003.

——. *Shortcomings*. Montreal: Drawn & Quarterly, 2007.

Torres, Alissa, and Sungyoon Choi. *American Widow*. New York: Villard, 2008.

Trachtenberg, Stanley. "In the Egosphere: Philip Roth's Anti-*Bildungsroman*." *Papers on Language and Literature* 25, no. 3 (1989): 326–341.

Treuer, David. *Native American Fiction: A User's Manual*. St. Paul: Graywolf Press, 2006.

Tweed, Thomas. *Our Lady of the Exile: A Diasporic Religion at a Cuban Catholic Shrine in Miami*. New York: Oxford University Press, 1997.

Valentine, Rand. *Weshki-Bmaadzijig Ji-Noondmowaad "That the Young Might Hear": The Stories of Andrew Medler*. London: University of Western Ontario, 2000.

Vaughan, Brian K., and Niko Henrichon. *Pride of Baghdad*. New York: Vertigo, 2006.

Velez, Ivan, Jr. "Ivan Velez Jr." Interview. In *Your Brain on Latino Comics: From Gus Arriola to Los Bros Hernandez*, Frederick Luis Aldama, pp. 279–291. Austin: University of Texas Press, 2009.

——. *Tales of the Closet Vol. 1*. New York: Planet Bronx, 2005.

Versaci, Rocco. *This Book Contains Graphic Language: Comics as Literature*. New York: Continuum Publishing, 2007.

Villa, Raúl Homero. *Barrio-Logos: Space and Place in Urban Chicano Literature and Culture*. Austin: University of Texas Press, 2000.

Vygotsky, L. S. *Mind and Society: The Development of Higher Mental Processes*. Cambridge, Mass.: Harvard University Press, 1978.

Wallace, Michele Faith. "The Good Lynching and *The Birth of a Nation*: Discourses and Aesthetics of Jim Crow." *Cinema Journal* 43, no. 1 (Fall 2003): 85–104.

Walsh, Richard. *The Rhetoric of Fictionality: Narrative Theory and the Idea of Fiction*. Columbus: Ohio State University Press, 2007.

Ware, Chris. Interview. In *Dangerous Drawings: Interviews with Comix & Graphix Artists*, ed. Andrea Juno, pp. 32–53. New York: Juno Books, 1997.

Warren, Adam. *Empowered Volume 2*. Milwaukie, Ore.: Dark Horse Books, 2007.

Wertham, Fredric. *Seduction of the Innocent*. New York: Rinehart, 1954.

White, Richard. *The Middle Ground: Indians, Empires, and Republics in the Great Lakes Region, 1650–1815*. New York: Cambridge, 1991.

Whitlock, Gillian. "Autographics: The Seeing 'I' of the Comics." *Modern Fiction Studies* 52, no. 4 (Winter 2006): 965–979.

Wilson, G. Willow, and M. K. Perker. *Cairo: A Graphic Novel*. New York: Vertigo, 2007.

Winick, Judd. *Exiles*. Issue 11. New York: Marvel Comics, 2001.

Witgen, Michael. "The Rituals of Possession: Native Identity and the Invention of

Empire in Seventeenth-Century Western North America." *Ethnohistory* 54, no. 4 (2007): 639–668.

Wolk, Douglas. *Reading Comics: How Graphic Novels Work and What They Mean.* Cambridge, Mass.: Da Capo, 2007.

Yang, Gene Luen. *American Born Chinese.* New York: First Second, 2006.

Ybarra-Fausto, Tomás. "Interview with Tomás Ybarra-Fausto: The Chicano Movement in a Multicultural/Multinational Society." In *On Edge: The Crisis of Contemporary Latin American Culture,* ed. Jean Franco and Juan Flores, pp. 207–216. Minneapolis and London: University of Minnesota Press, 1992.

Zhou, Xiaojing. "Spatial Construction of the 'Enemy Race': Miné Okubo's Visual Strategies in *Citizen 13660.*" *MELUS* 32, no. 3 (Fall 2007): 51–73.

CONTRIBUTOR NOTES

FREDERICK LUIS ALDAMA is Arts and Humanities Distinguished Professor of English at the Ohio State University where he uses the tools of narratology and research in the cognitive- and neuro- sciences in his teaching and scholarship on Latino, Latin American, and Postcolonial literature, film, and comic books. He is the editor of five collections of essays and author of seven books, including most recently *A User's Guide to Postcolonial and Latino Borderland Fiction.*

MELINDA LUISA DE JESÚS is Chair of Diversity Studies, and Associate Professor of Diversity Studies and Critical Studies at the California College of the Arts in Oakland, California. She writes and teaches about youth and popular culture, feminist/gender studies, and comparative American ethnic studies. She edited *Pinay Power: Peminist Critical Theory* (Routledge 2005) and has published in numerous venues.

JARED GARDNER is a professor of English, film, and popular culture at Ohio State University. He is the author of *Master Plots: Race and the Founding of an American Literature* (1998), a contributing writer to *The Comics Journal*, and editor of the online comics review journal *guttergeek.*

PATRICK L. HAMILTON is an Assistant Professor of English at Misericordia University in Dallas, Pennsylvania, where he specializes in Chicano/a and U.S. multi-ethnic literature. His book *Of Space and Mind: Cognitive Mappings of Contemporary Chicano/a Fiction* is forthcoming from the University of Texas Press.

NICHOLAS HETRICK is a graduate student at Ohio State University. His work focuses on intersections among narrative studies, disability studies, and aesthetics across genres and media.

SUHAAN MEHTA is a graduate student in the English department at Ohio State University specializing in postcolonial literature and narrative theory. He has an MA in English from Mumbai University, India. Prior to joining the PhD program at Ohio State, he was a visiting lecturer in communications and literature at St. Xavier's College, Mumbai.

ELIZABETH NIXON is a graduate student in the English department at Ohio State University. She uses the tools of narrative theory, as well as research in the cognitive and neurobiological sciences, in approaching the analysis of postcolonial and Latino/a literature.

MARGARET NOORI received her PhD in English and linguistics from the University of Minnesota and teaches at the University of Michigan. She also holds an MFA in creative writing and is an active member of the Native American Journalists Association. Her work primarily focuses on the recovery and maintenance of Anishinaabe language and literature. For more information or to view current projects visit www.umich.edu/~ojibwe/, where she and her current students have created a space for language that is shared by academics and the native community.

JAMES BRAXTON PETERSON is an assistant professor of English at Bucknell University. His teaching interests include African American literature, the graphic novel (or comic books), and hip-hop culture. He is also the founder of Hip Hop Scholars, LLC, an association of hip-hop-generation scholars dedicated to researching and developing the cultural and educational potential of hip-hop, urban, and youth cultures. Peterson is a regular contributor to TheRoot.com, and he has appeared on Fox News, CBS, MSNBC, ABC News, ESPN, and various local television networks as an expert on hip-hop and popular culture.

LEONARD RIFAS teaches comic books and graphic novels at Seattle Central Community College. He welcomes correspondence at rifas@earthlink.net and requests for the catalogue of his educational comic book company, EduComics, at Box 45831, Seattle, Washington 98145-0831, USA.

JONATHAN RISNER is a graduate student in the Department of English and Comparative Literature at the University of North Carolina at Chapel Hill. His interests include Latina/o studies and Latin American popular culture.

JENNY E. ROBB holds master's degrees in history and museum studies from Syracuse University. She served as curator of the Cartoon Art Museum in San Francisco, California, for five years before joining the Ohio State University Billy Ireland Cartoon Library & Museum as assistant professor and associate curator. She recently cocurated the exhibitions "Political Cartoons and Caricatures from the Collection of Michael Alexander Kahn" at the Grolier Club in New York City and "To Be Continued: Comic Strip Storytelling" at Ohio State University.

DEREK PARKER ROYAL is chair and an associate professor of English at Western Illinois University, and the executive editor of *Philip Roth Studies*. His essays on American literature and comics have appeared in such journals as *Contemporary Literature*, MELUS, and the *International Journal of Comic Art*. His books include *Philip Roth: New Perspectives on an American Author* (Praeger, 2005) and *The Hernandez Brothers: Conversations* (UP of Mississippi, 2010), and he is currently at work on a manuscript concerning American ethnoracial representations in recent comics.

EVAN THOMAS is a graduate student in the English department at Ohio State University. His research seeks to expand the questions of narratology to comics and new media. His thesis addresses the issue of space, both as a technical device and as it relates to his hometown of Dayton, Ohio. Evan also writes and draws comics, including editorial cartoons for his student newspaper, *The Lantern*.

REBECCA WANZO is an associate professor at Ohio State University in the Departments of Women's Studies and English. Her research interests include African American literature and culture, graphic storytelling, U.S. genre fiction, critical race theory, feminist theory, and theories of affect. She is the author of *The Suffering Will Not Be Televised: African American Women and Sentimental Political Storytelling* (2009).

INDEX

Italic page numbers refer to illustrations.